THE ECONOMICS OF ACCOUNTANCY

JOHN B. CANNING

AYER COMPANY PUBLISHERS
LOWER MILL ROAD
NORTH STRATFORD NH 03590

Editorial Supervision: LUCILLE MAIORCA

Reprint Edition 1978 by Arno Press Inc.

Copyright © 1929 by The Ronald Press Company
Copyright renewed 1957 by John B. Canning

Reprinted by permission of The Ronald Press Company, Inc.

Reprinted from a copy in the American Institute
of Certified Public Accountants Library

DEVELOPMENT OF CONTEMPORARY ACCOUNTING THOUGHT
ISBN for complete set: 0-405-10891-5
See last pages of this volume for titles.

Manufactured in the United States of America

Library of Congress Cataloging in Publication Data

Canning, John Bennet
   The economics of accountancy.

   (The Development of contemporary accounting thought)
   Reprint of the ed. published by Ronald Press, New
York.
   Includes index.
   1. Accounting. 2. Economics. I. Title.
II. Series.
HF5625.C3 1978   657   77-16723
ISBN 0-405-10948-2

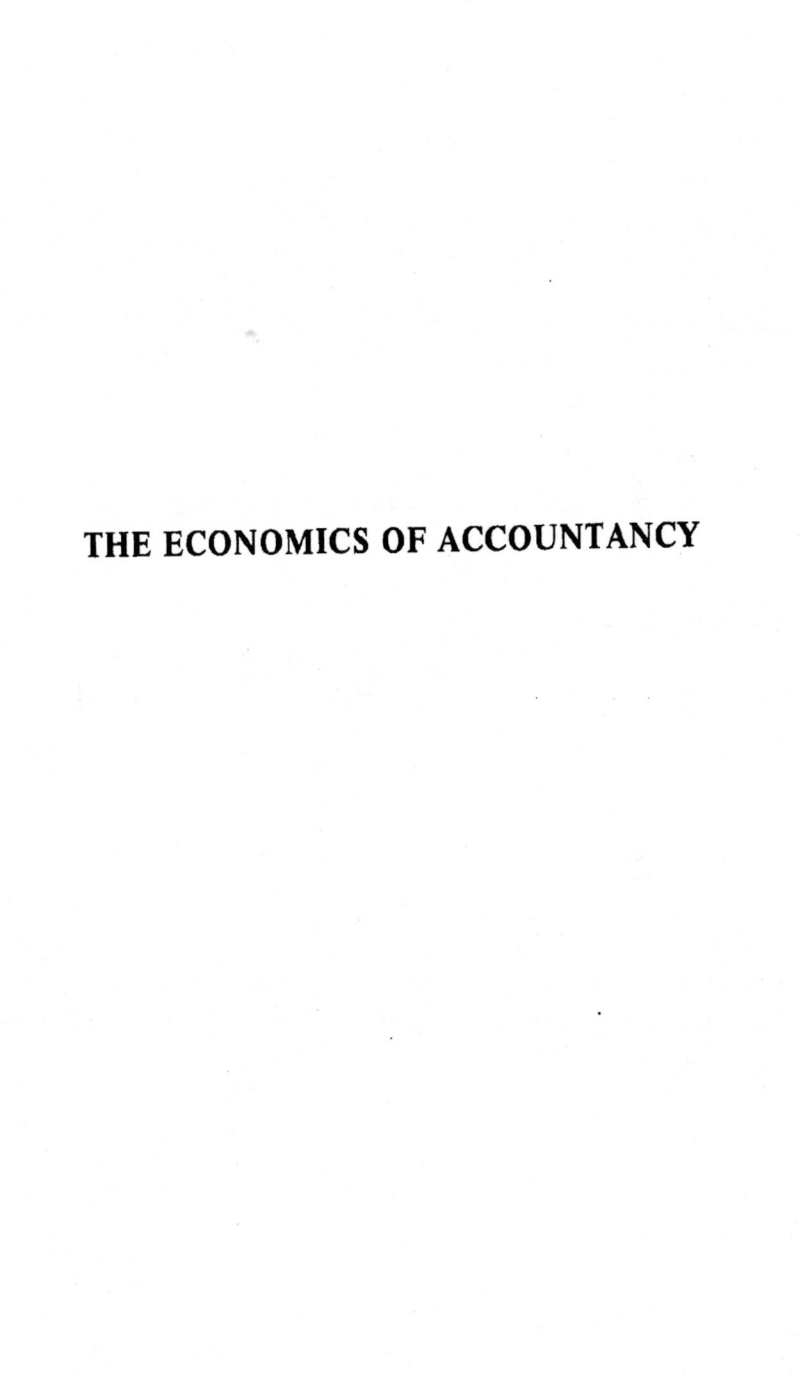

THE ECONOMICS OF ACCOUNTANCY

This is a volume in the Arno Press collection

THE DEVELOPMENT OF CONTEMPORARY ACCOUNTING THOUGHT

Advisory Editor
Richard P. Brief

Editorial Board
Gary John Previts
Basil S. Yamey
Stephen A. Zeff

See last pages of this volume for a complete list of titles.

THE ECONOMICS OF ACCOUNTANCY

A CRITICAL ANALYSIS OF ACCOUNTING THEORY

By

JOHN B. CANNING, PH**.D.**

ASSOCIATE PROFESSOR OF ECONOMICS, LELAND STANFORD
JUNIOR UNIVERSITY

THE RONALD PRESS COMPANY
NEW YORK

Copyright, 1929, by
THE RONALD PRESS COMPANY

All Rights Reserved

PREFACE

Some years ago, I undertook to build up at Leland Stanford Junior University a professional course of study suited to those who sought to become professional public accountants. Early in that task, the related problem of making the work of the professional accountant more fully intelligible to those in other branches of learning suggested itself. Both my previous training and interest in economics and the free, but somewhat indiscriminating, use of accountants' statistics that economists were then making led me to undertake a comprehensive study of accounting theory and practice from the point of view of the professional student of economics. This book reports a major part of the results of that study.

For reasons that must be obvious to the reader, the matter reported here relates to the theory and practice of professional public accountants. I make no pretense that the general statements made herein are applicable to the work of the private or resident staff accountants and bookkeepers of individual enterprises. To make a scientific study of this latter class of work is a task for a great field-research staff rather than for an individual.

A survey of the secondary literature of accounting soon made it plain to me that I must resort to source materials on all material points. The texts, of course, abound with statements that are both true and significant, but they also abound with statements about the intentions of accountants in adopting particular procedures. The writers do not agree about these intentions, nor are the systems of intentions declared notable for self-consistency. At best, intentions are a relatively unimportant matter; it is the statistical effects of a procedure that are significant. Intentions are private. Another man's intentions must remain largely a matter of conjecture. Statistical effects, on the other hand, are open to the world. This book attempts the task of pointing out the economic significance of certain of these statistical effects.

My chief reliance has been placed upon actual specimens of accountants' work whether published or privately circulated. Many thousands of these have been examined. Care has been taken to obtain statements prepared for a broad diversification of enterprise classes and industries. The minutest attention has been given to the language of the certificates attached to the statements. But, obviously, only a sample could be dealt with—no one can review all practice. I do not suppose that errors of omission have been wholly avoided nor that all observations have been accurately interpreted.

I owe a debt of gratitude to the text writers much greater than that implied in footnote citations. This is especially true of the writings of Cole, Hatfield, McKinsey, Montgomery, Paton, Stevenson, and Sprague. It is true in lesser degree only of a host of other authors of books and papers. I owe a still greater debt to former students. It is difficult for me to estimate, and wholly impossible for me to express, the gratitude I feel to them both for stimulus and for positive contributions to my ideas. To Professor Irving Fisher and to Doctor Royal Meeker I owe thanks for valuable critical notes and helpful comment on the manuscript of Chapter VIII. I need not declare my obligation to Professor Fisher for the influence of his writings upon my thought—that obligation appears throughout the whole book. My colleagues, Miss Margaret Milliken and Mr. Carl B. Robbins, have given me the benefit of critical readings and constructive comment on the entire manuscript. To my wife, most of all, I am indebted both for encouragement in the underlying study and for assistance in the writing of the book.

JOHN B. CANNING

Leland Stanford Junior University,
    September 10, 1929.

CONTENTS

PAGE

Chapter I

THE ACADEMIC STATUS OF ACCOUNTING 3

The recent appearance and rapid growth of instruction in accountancy in college and university curricula. The character of the early instruction staff and of the early instruction materials. The diversity of origins of accountancy and of economics. Certain mutual interests of economists and accountants. Certain difficulties experienced by accountants and by economists in utilizing one another's work. Statement of purpose of the study.

Chapter II

THE NATURE OF ASSETS 11

The fundamental equation of accounts. The accountants' definitions of assets. The mode of determining the definition adopted in this study. The attributes of assets. The definition of assets and of enterprise assets. Dissimilarities between "asset" and any major concept in economic theory.

Chapter III

ASSETS: DIFFICULTIES OF INTERPRETATION 24

(1) Misnamed items; (2) incompletely described or defined items; (3) the nature and confusing variety of "valuation account" balances; and (4) the nature and treatment of goodwill. The problems of attributive definition of statistical terms and the problems of measurement or valuation. Summary of Chapters II and III.

Chapter IV

LIABILITIES AND NET PROPRIETORSHIP 47

The fundamental "equation": a statement of identity rather than of mere quantitative equivalence. The position of assets, of

PAGE

liabilities and of "net" proprietorship within this statement of identity. The definition of proprietorship. The relation of proprietorship to the assets and to the holder of assets. The definition of liabilities. The definition of net proprietorship.

Chapter V

LIABILITIES AND NET PROPRIETORSHIP: DIFFICULTIES OF INTERPRETATION 59

(1) The subordinated debt; (2) incompletely labeled items; (3) misleading captions; and (4) valuation account balances. Meanings and modes of exhibiting capital stock. Meanings and modes of exhibiting surplus items.

Chapter VI

GROSS INCOME 89

Importance of the concept. Diversity of accountants' and economists' interests in gross income. Ultimate gross and net income. Time-distribution of income. Gross income of a period a mere summation of two qualitatively diverse income series, gross operating income and gross financial income. Gross operating income of a period defined. The attributes of gross operating income of a period. Gross financial income of a period defined. The attributes of gross financial income of a period. The two gross income series compared and contrasted.

Chapter VII

NET INCOME 125

The confusion of meanings of net income. The accountants' "net income" a mere difference between the gross income summation and a summation of negative items that have no perfectly general attribute peculiar to them. The subtrahend series considered. Avoidance of double counting. Non-uniformity of arrangement of income statements. Difficulties of interpretation of income statements.

Chapter VIII

THE MEASUREMENT OF INCOME: A COMPARISON AND CONTRAST OF THE ACCOUNTANTS' THEORY WITH AN ECONOMIST'S 143

Reasons for selecting Professor Irving Fisher's theory as the representative of economists' theories. Synopsis of Fisher's

CONTENTS

theory. Fisher's theory and the accountants' compared as to (1) scope of subject matter, (2) mode of analysis, and (3) point of view taken. The relative merits of Fisher's and the accountants' treatment of income.

CHAPTER IX

FINANCIAL POSITION 179

Vagueness of the concept in writings on accounting. Definition of financial position. Direct valuations of certain funds to be procured in operations or to be distributed according to the tenor of financial contracts. Indirect valuations. The hypotheses upon which indirect valuations rest. The diversity in meaning between "net capital value of an enterprise" and the "net proprietorship" item in the balance sheet.

CHAPTER X

THE ACCOUNTANTS' PROBLEM OF VALUATION 195

Differences between a theory of value and a theory of valuation. A valuation procedure does not imply acceptance of any particular theory of value. Valuation a branch of statistical theory. Certain propositions of statistical theory applied to valuation: (1) propositions about entire populations; (2) propositions about samples; (3) criteria of superiority of one valuation procedure over another.

CHAPTER XI

VALUATION PROCEDURE: DIRECT VALUATION 206

Conditions under which direct valuations are possible. Practical limits of direct valuation. Items usually directly valued. The problem of inventory valuation. The superiority of multiple valuations.

CHAPTER XII

INDIRECT VALUATION 229

The concept of capital value and of capital valuation. Certain propositions made by economists about capital values of items of wealth. Impossibility of finding a true capital value of certain "fixed tangible assets." The resort of accountants to "opportunity differentials." The accountant does not, properly speaking, value the serving agent at all. No necessary equality between value of assets and value of enterprise.

CONTENTS

PAGE

Chapter XIII

REVALUATION TECHNIQUE: SIMPLE MEASURES 248

Original book valuations. Conditions under which costs may be presumed to be prudent investment valuations. Outlay cost and replacement cost. The significant variables in indirect valuation. Statistical effect of revaluation errors upon net operating income and upon unit costs. A scheme of illustrative asset types. The properties of certain revaluation formulas: (1) straight line formula; (2) sinking fund formula; (3) fixed percentage on declining balance formula; (4) sum-of-the-year-digits formula; (5) the service-unit formula. The deficiencies of the simple formulas.

Chapter XIV

REVALUATION TECHNIQUE: ADJUSTED MEASURES . . . 284

The properties of certain modified formulas: (1) modified straight line formula; (2) modified sinking fund formula; (3) modified service-unit formula, two expressions; (4) the "unit cost" formula; (5) the equal profit ratios formula. Extent of the unsolved problems of the revaluation technique.

Chapter XV

SUMMARY AND FORECAST 310

Appendix A

REVALUATIONS AND SERVICE UNIT COSTS: A COMPARISON OF THE RESULTS YIELDED BY SEVERAL FORMULAS . . 337

Appendix B

CRITERIA OF SUPERIORITY: A METHOD OF TESTING THE RELATIVE MERITS OF TWO FORMULAS 353

THE ECONOMICS OF
ACCOUNTANCY

CHAPTER I

THE ACADEMIC STATUS OF ACCOUNTING

Accountancy is an infant in the academic family. Though the trade of keeping books is some centuries old, and though there has been a practicing profession of public accountants for some three-quarters of a century, the subject made only sporadic appearances in the curricula of American colleges and universities until two decades or so ago. But during this brief period few collegiate subjects have shown so great a gain in units of instruction offered, numbers of teaching staff, and numbers of students enrolled in courses of study.

It was not to be expected that the quality of instruction and writing should keep pace with the increasing quantity of work offered. The rapid rise of the study made it necessary to recruit the earlier teaching staff largely from those who had had no academic training in their subject. The earlier college texts, too, were largely manuals of procedure written rather for the bookkeeper and the ambitious junior clerk than for the college student. Nor can it be said that this beginning is a matter of the past; for the early patterns are all too plain in the annual product of those writing today. With the exception of a few notable books, the emphasis is still heavily upon procedure rather than upon systematic analysis; and even that which purports to be analysis of the problems of enterprise is often no more than a crude dismembering of enterprise operations. Forms of reports are discussed as though they were end-products rather than summaries of evidence upon which decisions of policy were to be based.

The Economists' Dependence upon Accountants

There seems to be a popular impression that accountancy is a branch of economics. Without materially enlarging the usually expressed scope of economics, this impression might be difficult to justify. Fortunately, little or nothing depends on the decision. What does matter and what is becoming increasingly plain is that economists are making a larger and larger use of the accountant's reports in their investigations. Economics, to be sure, has fostered accountancy from its academic advent, but the foster parent has been more influenced by the new relation than has the adopted child. The parent is far from understanding the child, and the latter is often bewildered by the interpretation placed upon its doings.

Let it be understood, though, that nothing said here is intended to belittle the progress made in accounting by its practitioners, particularly in the last quarter-century, in their attempt to build up a learned profession. Few groups of men in a common calling can show a better record of increasingly valuable public service. What is really intended to be said is that any public calling that has been changing so rapidly for the better can hardly be thought to have attained its majority. It will seldom be necessary, if at all, in the study that is to follow, to point to a serious shortcoming of the modern theory and practice of accounts that does not already show some signs of self-betterment.

When characteristic misreadings and misunderstandings of the accountant's work are charged to the economists, no lack of diligence will be implied. The form of the literature of accounts makes much of the real meaning of reports inaccessible to all except those who have had occasion to make a much more extended study of accounting than most economists can afford to make.

The Nature and Purpose of This Study.—It requires no little temerity to undertake a brief critical analysis of the principal concepts and operations of the accountant from the point of view of the economist. The state of flux of accounting itself and the great lack of uniformity, largely resulting from the rapid changes of practice, make it difficult to determine just what accountants do and do not do. Whatever measure of success is momentarily achieved in introducing one profession to the nature of the work of the other may, too, be quickly vitiated by the changes in theory and practice. Even in the course of preparing this study much of the earlier writing has had to be scrapped because it no longer seemed worth expressing in print. It is felt, however, that there is a sufficient body of practice nearly enough approaching uniformity and stability, and most certainly important enough to the economist (if only to prevent his misinterpretations of it), to warrant the attempt made here.

The analysis to be made requires the giving of much space to the economist's views of value and of valuation in enterprise relationships. To the extent that the two professions do work in a common field, each should be able to profit by the other's work. It is the aim of this study to make access to the result of the accountant's work more convenient and more certain, and to bring to the accountant's notice some of the work of the economists that seems applicable to the problems of theory and practice with which the accountants are dealing. If it can be shown, incidentally, that certain branches of thought of both professions are, and must remain, barren, all concerned should be the gainers. This study was undertaken in the conviction that the two professions are far from realizing their possibilities of mutual assistance. This conviction has been deepened as the study progressed.

No attempt will be made to examine the whole of accounting theory and practice, nor will economic theory, as an entirety, be considered. Only those fundamentals of accepted theory of accounts that are of major interest to the economist, and only those portions of economic theory that are believed to be most useful to the accountant, will be discussed. Differences of views between one school of economists and others, and differences to be found in the expression of accounting theory, interesting and important as they are, are not emphasized herein; the reconciliation of intra-professional schools is a large enough task to engage many. The present writer is interested in those zones in which the two professional fields have begun to coalesce.

Diverse Origins of Economics and Accountancy

Early Economics a Learned, Deductive Philosophy.— While no pretense will be made of finding the origin or of tracing the development of any concept, either of the economist or of the accountant, it may not be amiss in an analytical study to note briefly that differences of views and differences in terminology are to be expected from the different origins of the two literatures. The economists, from the time they began to show a group-consciousness, have always considered their subject to be a branch of social philosophy. They concerned themselves from the first with the phenomena of social problems and gave little thought, in their early work, to the problems of the individual. Like their learned parent they sought to develop, from a body of (more or less) self-evident propositions about human behavior, entire systems of thought, and to develop their systems largely by deductive methods.

The quasi-Euclidean mode cannot be counted a demerit in the early economists. The beginners had no such systematically harvested and stored fruits of investigation as are available to modern economists. And early economists, above all other academic groups, were influential in setting in motion and in staffing those information-gathering agencies that serve their present successors. Nevertheless, the pattern of the earlier writings has often been developed to a fault. All too often that which might properly have been treated as a hypothesis only has been unquestioningly assumed to have an existence in fact; and large portions of systems of theory have been based upon unsubstantial footings. Many instances are to be found, too, in which economists writing recently have continued to urge remedies for real problems when their conclusions rested upon reasoning about the behavior of imaginary individuals in an assumed market condition. And this they have done despite the fact that it has become possible to investigate the actual conduct of real persons in an existing market.

In the field of value, for example, certain propositions about the relations between cost and price hold true only when it is assumed that those in the market are possessed of certain information about costs that they not only do not have, but that they can never possibly get. Whatever else may be the utility of refinements upon such propositions, there can be no hope of using them either causally to explain past prices or to forecast future prices.

The lack of statistical information and statistical training and experience, too, may well have been responsible for many of the quasi-quantitative elements of economic theory. The notions of constant and variable costs and of production subject to conditions of constant, increasing, or decreasing cost are, as quantitative concepts, too coarse for practical analysis.[1]

---

[1] The often cited example of the telephone business as one subject to increasing costs may illustrate the point. If simultaneous observations are made both of large and of small telephone businesses with respect both to total enterprise cost for a specified period and to a mean number of local subscribers during the period, it may, indeed, be found that large costs per subscriber are associated with large companies and that small costs per subscriber are associated with small concerns. But such an analysis is insufficient to support the general proposition cited. Is the subscriber the most useful unit in terms of which to quote unit cost? The subscriber is certainly not a unit of product; nor is the service bought by subscribers approximately identical as between those served by large and by small companies. It would be no matter for surprise if, upon defining an appropriate unit of service, the telephone business turned out to be a striking example of decreasing cost. If costs per unit of service were plotted with the size of the company as the independent variable it would be still less surprising to find that the curve showed many marked changes of slope and many points of inflection. It may be true that no single operating enterprise has yet become large enough to show what the most economical size is.

Terminology of the Early Economists.—In the matter of terminology, it may well be supposed that the economists' wish to influence public affairs through making their works available to lay readers has led them to shun a systematic and peculiar terminology and to employ common words instead. Whether the immediate gains from the influence of economists upon the solution of specific problems have more than offset the hopeless confusion wrought by the multiple meanings assigned to such words as capital, income, cost, property, etc., may well be doubted. But one of the effects of this confusion has been practically to conceal from the accountants the most fruitful suggestions that the economists have to offer them.

Early Accountancy a Description of an Art.—Unlike the economists, who from their beginning have followed a learned profession, the early writers on accountancy were mostly without academic training. Their writings, at best, were merely descriptions of empirical practices of record keeping that had come to their notice or that they had devised for particular enterprises. Whether they were describing the long-known and employed double entry scheme or cruder practices, they made little showing of any systematic thought, though they were sticklers for unswerving adherence to the technical procedure shown. Like many another trade or occupational group, their dicta were amazingly positive and their argument as amazingly inconsequential.

With the increase in the scale of enterprise operations came a need for an expansion of the record-keeping schemes and for the organization of a greater wealth of detail in the records. Briefer methods, labor-saving devices, specialized forms, etc., were produced to keep pace with expanding enterprises; and descriptions of these found their way into writings. With the rise of a specialized group of auditors, experiences began to be exchanged in association meetings and in journals. Certain procedures began to be standardized and fixed. Practices that proved inconvenient or that visibly conduced to disaster were abandoned. But the work of the accountant and the writings on accounting, until very recently, proceeded by a sort of patchwork and tinkering. To be sure, the patching was often shrewdly planned and executed, but it was patchwork nevertheless in the sense that there was little going back to fundamentals for a fresh start. No "schools" of accountants are recognized. The introduction of so-called accrual accounting and of cost accounting (the latter very recently) are, in this field, the most notable single steps made since the invention of double entry bookkeeping.

Unlike the economists, the accountants have always had access to more facts (of a certain kind) than they knew what to do with. They were called upon to deal with that amazingly increasing mass of information about transactions, events, and changing relationships that is associated with the modern large-scale business enterprise. Moreover, that mass changed constantly in nature and content as the organization of enterprise changed. It is small matter for wonder that the accountant has never quite caught up. Business does not stand still to be analyzed, studied, and described.

Terminology of Early Accountants.—In the matter of terminology the accountants, as well as the economists, have stuck closely to the common language. They, too, speak of capital, income, cost, property, etc.; and with more meanings for each of them than the economists can show.[2] On the whole, the accountants show less awareness of the confusion of multiple meanings than do the economists. One finds a rule of valuation of inventories at "cost or market whichever is the lesser," asserted by writer after writer to be the prevailing

---

[2] Whether or not they have more meanings in *mind* than the writers in economics is a matter of guessing. It only happens that the statistical procedure followed in measuring a particular dimension like that of a "cost" often clearly *indentifies* the accountant's meaning of the term, whereas the economist, whose language is commonly in more general terms, is harder to pin down to the precise inclusions and exclusions implied by his words.

rule in good practice. Compare the definitions of "cost" and of "market," or the procedures whereby "cost" or "market," say of partly manufactured goods, are measured by these same writers, and at once it is found that instead of one prevailing rule, there is in reality a myriad of diverse rules. Examine the reasons assigned for the "rule" and note the procedure to be followed, and not only endless diversity appears, but also endless, though minor, inconsistency.

Need for Interpretation.—But the character of the public problems which concern the economist is often such that their solution cannot be sensibly attempted without a great deal of information that the accountant can give better than any other. And the interdependence of enterprises for their financial security and advantage is nowadays so great that the accountant who wishes to make the most valuable of reports to his client must turn to the economist, among others, for assistance. Neither profession will deny mutual usefulness, but it is very much to be doubted that either appreciates how very little it knows about the work of the other.

There is no need even to list the public problems with which economists are unable to deal intelligently without the accountant's help. Any student of public affairs could make a formidable schedule upon demand. Nor is there need to list the ways in which the economist may be of use to the accountant. Such a list would probably appear less striking, but would nevertheless be more fundamental.

CHAPTER II

THE NATURE OF ASSETS

The Fundamental Equation of Accounts

All economists are familiar with the expression, "assets less liabilities equals proprietorship." This, stated in one form or another, is what the accountants call the fundamental equation of accounts. But, for want of carefully formulated definitions of the terms of the equation, the economist, among others, frequently fails to grasp the whole of the meaning of the expression. Nor without more prolonged study of accounting practice than the economist can usually afford to make is it possible for him to obtain that grasp of its meaning that he needs for the proper interpretation of the accountant's reports.

It hardly needs to be said that the expression is verbally incomplete; for if "assets" are different from "liabilities" one cannot be subtracted from the other. A common measurement or the measurement of a common character, viz., a sum of the money valuations of each of the three terms is, of course, meant. But that hardly suffices. Is the expression one of equivalence or one of identity? That is, does one mean that the sum of the asset valuations *is equal to* the sum of the liability valuations plus the sum of the proprietorship valuations, or that the sum of the asset valuations *is* the sum of the other two quantities? It makes a very real and important difference which is meant. Is each of the sums representing the terms independently determinable, or must one (or more) of the sums be derived from a preceding sum (or sums)?

What is the nature of the items to be measured under the head of each term? Obviously the significance of any quantity found by whatever mode of measuring must be dependent upon the nature of the things measured. What is included within the term "assets"? Is the nature of assets such that the proper measures of the assets of each and every individual may be added together to find what might be called the measure of society's assets?

To say that only money valuations of the three terms is meant does not put one far on the way to interpreting an aggregate of the measures. It is obvious that some money valuations may be matters of fact. The money valuation of one's money assets can be got by counting in terms of the standard unit, but the money value of a yearling colt must be a matter of opinion; and any quantity assigned must be found by some rule (whether formulated or not) of valuation procedure. But if the rule of procedure followed in the valuation of one kind of asset is different from those followed in valuing other kinds, what meaning can be assigned to a sum of these valuations?

Meaning of the Term "Assets."—The true nature of the so-called equation may, perhaps, better be considered after the terms in it have been discussed. The present chapter will undertake only to give an exposition of the meaning of the first term, "assets." The nature of the measures of value that accountants apply to assets, though occasionally referred to for convenience, will not be systematically discussed until later. Having shown the expressed and implied meanings of those things which accountants systematically treat as assets, consideration will be given in Chapter III to the adequacy and convenience of the meanings. Perhaps the most difficult task of all will be to show the nature of those items often listed under the general caption of assets in the accountant's reports that are not generally considered by accountants to be assets at all.

Accountant's Definitions of the Term.—What does the accountant mean by the term "assets"? One who seeks an answer by searching the texts on accounting for formal definitions will first be surprised that many, perhaps most, of the writers offer none at all. Or he may find that what purports to be a definition confuses the nature of the thing with the measurement of it. He will not need to search far before he will find that the definitions given are confusingly diverse. If he tests an author's own use of the term, he will, in general, have no difficulty at all in finding things treated as assets that do not satisfy the definition given. Nor will he have difficulty in finding that many things literally within the formal definition fail to appear in the asset accounts and statements. The collecting of an extensive, not to say exhaustive, set of definitions does not repay the scissor-work.

Just why such a condition exists must remain a matter of conjecture. Possibly as good a guess as any is that the writers have either supposed that the readers knew the meaning of the term already, or else that all cases requiring a decision as to whether or not a thing is an asset are either easy to decide or else are trivial.

Whatever may be the cause of the deficiencies of the formal definitions, we have other resources; it is possible to read extensively to find the nature of those things treated as assets by the writers and by the practitioners. Here again the diversity appears—and in manifestations more difficult to detect— though, on the whole, probably in lesser extent and significance. What passes for reputable practice among public accountants is more nearly in accord as to just what may and what may not be included in assets than is the currently written theory. And it is more from observed practice than from the text writers that a meaning for this term is intended to be built up.[1] Ref-

[1] It is noted in advance that this method will be followed in connection with other fundamental terms. First, a set of attributes of the thing, or criteria whereby it may be identified, will be scheduled and illustrated. Discrimination between those characteristics which the logician calls accidents and those which he calls essential or distinguishing features will be attempted. And finally some constructive criticism of the practitioner's definition will be offered. Obviously nothing that appears here purports to be a final and authoritative statement of practice, since no one can review all practice; nor is any final word meant to be said on what ought, ideally, to be the meaning

erence will be made to the text writers only in those instances in which they, too, are describing practice.

The Attributes of an Asset

Services (Income) to Which There Is an Enforceable Right.—Neither the corporeal existence of a material object nor anything necessarily associated with that existence suffices to make the object an asset. Not all assets are even associated with specific objects in any immediate or proximate sense. What is essential is that there must be some anticipated, identifiable, separate (or separable) services (or income)[2] to be had by a proprietor as a matter of legal or equitable right, from some person or object, though not necessarily from an ascertainable person(s) or object(s). One speaks of a motor truck owned by a corporation and operated in its enterprise as an asset of the company. But neither the legal title in the object nor the existence of the object, nor the two together, constitutes the asset. That which is fundamental is that certain anticipated services of the truck will inure to the benefit of the corporation. Note that it is not the whole of the possible services of the truck, nor even all those services that could be rendered by it with maximum economy to society, but only those services which the company can *advantageously* obtain from it in the course of *its operation in their enterprise*.

The situs of legal title is not determining. Suppose the company to have procured the truck under a hire-purchase contract (not yet wholly performed by the company), in which it is specifically agreed that title shall remain in the vendor so

---

of the terms defined. Only that practical usage from which reputable usage departs by a minimum, a representative usage, is described. And only those changes in usage and practice that seem to be matters of real importance will be put forward.

[2] The term "income" is used in this, and in the three succeeding chapters, in the sense in which it is employed by Professor Irving Fisher in his "Nature of Capital and Income," i.e., interchangeably with "services" no matter what the form or nature of the particular service. "Income," so far as I am aware, has never been given so broad a meaning by any writer on **accounting**.

long as any of the severable portions of the contract remain unperformed by the vendee. So long as the vendee continues to perform according to the tenor of the agreement, no public accountant will hesitate to list the truck as an asset of the vendee nor to list the notes (or other form of promise to pay) as the vendor's asset.[3]

Both in the case of the vendee and of the vendor the privileged special service anticipated is the essence of the asset. It cannot be said of all assets that the source of the service is the asset. To distinguish between the source and the services from that source would be, for some items (indeed, for most), to split hairs, both practically and logically. But the source of the service to the holder of a negotiable note receivable, for example, may be either the person primarily liable, intermediate parties secondarily liable, or unascertained transferees, whether by full negotiation or by assignment "without recourse" and/or "without warranty," or it may be some person who "pays for honor." Obviously some source must be anticipated; but no particular or ascertained source, nor even an unconditional source is requisite. It is not the *source* that is the note holder's asset; nor is it the thing (or person) that *will prove to be* the source that is valued. It is the anticipated service, the payment of money at some future time, that is valued and that is fundamental to the existence of the asset.

"Assets" and "Sources of Service."—This fastening upon the service as the essential attribute rather than upon the source (whether ascertained or not) may seem to the economist to make "assets" an awkward or incomplete or unfruitful concept. This must be true particularly of those who are in accord with Professor Fisher's analysis of wealth, property, capital, and income. Indeed, for the economist in the whole of his general field it might not be a wholly satisfactory notion. For the

---

[3] The careful accountant will, of course, show in his statements and in his report what the full status of the parties is.

economist is interested in all sources from which scarce services may be had with advantage no matter to whom the benefits of the services run; and he is equally interested in all scarce services no matter from what sources the services proceed either immediately or ultimately. But the accountant's work lies within the domain of particular enterprises. What services proceed from a given source other than those that are to be availed of in the enterprise is not his concern. Income, not capital in the physical or material sense, is the chief concern of the accountant. He does not engage in making summations either of social capital or of social income, nor is it a part of his primary duty to supply statistics from which others may conveniently do so.

The danger of error in employing asset summations beyond their intended usefulness and of confusing "assets" with "sources of service" may be indicated by two illustrations. Take the case of the nurseryman who discovers among his experimental seedlings a variety of peach of superior shipping qualities that is otherwise as desirable, both to orchardists and to consumers, as any competing variety. The nurseryman, as is well known, cannot hope to appropriate more than a minute portion of the total new and better services that his seedling makes possible. Very quickly after he puts grafted stock or grafting stock upon the market his special advantage will be gone. The orchardists, too, who plant new stock of this kind or graft it upon aged trees will quickly lose much of their special advantage. Despite the very great social benefit to be had, no one's balance sheets will be greatly altered, nor will any aggregate of balance sheets incorporate explicitly or implicitly a measure of the total services proceeding either from this seedling as an ultimate source or from all the stock derived from it as intermediate sources. The services from sources are appropriable by the owners of the sources to only a very limited extent.

On the other hand, the services that can be appropriated by

a particular proprietor to his great personal advantage may add little or nothing to the aggregate of services available to society. The aggregate influence of gold mining upon enterprise balance sheets is not limited to those of the mining companies—all balance sheets respond to it to the extent that the purchasing power of money is depressed. Even if we could deflate all balance sheet valuations to a fixed purchasing power standard, a growth in the valuation of assets employed in gold mining would have a very different significance to society from the like growth in copper and iron mining. And this would be true even though we limited the comparisons to sources, i.e., physical agencies that are employed in all three types of mining. The accountant's interest is in services the beneficial interests in which can be appropriated in enterprises. The economist, in taking stock, is interested in sources capable of rendering services to persons in general, whether directly or indirectly.

"Redressable Rights" and "Expectancies."—In current accounting practice it is clear enough that the rights, to be sufficient for the asset relationship, must be legal and/or equitable and not mere "moral rights" or pure expectancies. If B has named A as his beneficiary in a life insurance contract, wherein B has specifically retained the right to substitute another for A without A's assent, A has no asset that accountants will recognize so long as B lives and does not cancel the reservation. No weight of moral duty of B to A is sufficient to replace a right redressable in court.

Moreover, the rights must be enforceable. If the rights persist after the remedy is withdrawn, the asset is gone. Instances of this kind are common. If X has been discharged in bankruptcy leaving his creditor Y with an unpaid deficiency, Y has no asset. But a discharge in bankruptcy does not destroy the debtor-creditor relation; it merely arrests the creditor's resort to judicial remedy; the debtor has become, during his pleasure, immune to suit. But if, after the discharge, X promises to pay Y, the latter can sue upon the old debt whether any new consideration moving to X can be shown or not.[4] Upon B's promise to pay the deficiency upon the old debt, an accountant would set up the asset again.

Executory Contracts Wholly Unperformed.—But not all enforceable rights to receive income are treated as assets by the accountants. If with the receipt of each increment of a service there is a concurrent and equivalent obligation to render an offsetting service, accountants omit the receivable income from the list of assets. Thus, if A has contracted for a year for the use of a building, rental to be paid in equal monthly payments on the last day of each month, no asset will ever appear on A's books unless he voluntarily pays in advance of a maturity.[5] And the only asset that will ever appear on B's books, with respect to this contract, will be the amount "earned," but not yet paid by A. If B has contracted to make goods and deliver them to A, and if no goods have been delivered and no payments made, there is no asset arising from this contract on the books of either A or B, nor is there any liability shown by either.

If the services to be received under contracts executory on both sides were always completely offset, both in time of exchange and in amount of value, by the services to be rendered, perhaps no inconvenience would be worked by the exclusion of such incomes from the category of assets. But little observation is required to show that this equality is often absent. B

---

[4] Brandenburg on Bankruptcy, 4th ed., Sec. 1538.
[5] Some accountants may take issue with the statement just made. They may say that a part of A's payments may be capitalized in the form of a rental cost of an inventory of manufactured goods on hand. But this inventory is a different asset; it depends, for its recognition, upon a wholly separate set of rights, and for its valuation, upon the benefits assured by those rights. No matter what the internal cost procedure of the books kept, a professional accountant would never set up a positive value for an inventory item if it will command no price. The building's past *service* is not capitalized. The cost of the building's service may be a term in the formula for *valuing* a different set of services, viz., those to be performed by the inventory.

may earlier have contracted to furnish goods to A in a period following A's balance sheet date at prices considerably below the current market. To exclude from A's assets such a resource as this is to make his balance sheet show a financial position less favorable than that which exists. On the other hand, the exclusion of all effect of this contract from B's balance sheet allows him to make an unduly favorable showing. The importance of contracts of this kind, a mode of valuing them, and a discussion of the desirability of giving effect to them in the balance sheet will be taken up in the chapters dealing with asset valuation.

Unequal Part Performance on Executory Contracts.—It may not be amiss here to distinguish the class of contracts just discussed from the class under which one party has performed in larger proportion than the other. Thus, if A has paid something on account for goods not yet transferred to him, accountants do not hesitate to show an asset of A. Or if B, having a lease on a building with ten years to run at $12,000 annual rental, should sell his rights under the lease to A for $10,000, A to pay the remaining rentals to the owner, the accountants recognize an asset of A.

"Assets" an Economic Concept.—The economist will be quick to note that the fundamental test for determining whether a thing is or is not an asset is economic rather than legal. No set of legal or equitable rights, however complete, is enough to bring an asset into existence. The desirable service, the income, is the primary element. The accountant *appears* to include or to exclude incomes according to whether there is a legal or equitable right to them. But the exclusion of those services not specially secured by redressable right is rather on the statistical ground of difficulty of valuation than on the ground that a legal right is inherently necessary. The accountant does not hesitate to set out in an audit report any specially favorable circumstance not amounting to enforceable rights to a prospective income (so long as it appears probable) that he finds in the course of an audit. But to include in the statements, e.g., the balance sheet, mere expectancies, would be to introduce items the value of which is highly speculative among items the value of which can be measured with much greater reliability. Instances may be found, to be sure, of mere expectancies the value of which can be more precisely determined than can that of some legally protected prospects of income. But these are rare; and probably it is better for all concerned that the accountant exclude them from his statements and so avoid that more serious difficulty of determining how remote an expectancy must be to be excluded entirely.

Not all services in prospect are admitted to the category of assets. Since a possible service, if it eventuates, will have the same effect in the enterprise as though it had been legally assured, we can say of any summation of assets that it is, at best, a summation of a sample and that it should be considered as an *index* to future services rather than as a measurement of the whole of such services. Supposing an equal likelihood of undervaluing or of overvaluing assets by any given amount, the summation of all future services should be greater than the summation of the assets. In general, of course, the sample measured, the assets, constitutes the very great preponderance of all prospective services. But we shall see when valuation of goodwill is taken up for discussion, that the omissions do have importance in some cases.

The Income Must Be Convertible into Money.—One may have an enforceable right to the services of a thing or of a person and have no asset. A money valuation is made necessary by the nature of the equation in which assets is one term. Services valuable in other than a monetary unit, but not in money, are therefore excluded. But a mere equivalence, expressed by the owner of a service, between the importance to him of (1) the service in question and of (2) the services of a sum of money in hand, is not enough. The service must either be itself a money income or it must have a money income consequence. It must be commutable or convertible into money. Thus, a life insurance policy paid for by A upon his own life is not an asset of A if the beneficial interest in the policy runs absolutely to B, even though B may be a donee beneficiary. The policy may procure a real service to A, that of providing for the security of B in the event of A's premature death. Moreover, that service to A not only can be, but actually has been, valued in money by A. But since no money income running to A can result from the contract, A has no asset.

It is often said, carelessly, that only things exchangeable for money are assets. If by this is meant "conceivably exchangeable" or "legally exchangeable," the qualification is obviously of little value in limiting the asset category. If, on the other hand, what is meant is "probably exchangeable" or "directly exchangeable," many items usually (and usefully) treated as assets would be left out. Thus many materials of manufacture are, at certain stages of process, of no value to anyone except those holding the entire assembly of operating assets of the enterprise. It is not the molten metal but the steel-making enterprise in operation, that can be exchanged. But there is much utility in treating the hot metal as an asset (convertible into money—though perhaps only through a long series of operations). Moreover, there are many probable and possible money incomes not supported by legal or equitable rights that are exchangeable for money, but they are not treated as assets by the accountant.

Sometimes it is said that to be an asset a thing must be "applicable to or subject to the *payments of debts.*" [6] If by this is meant "available to the owner for the satisfaction of his debts," it is but another way of saying "convertible into money." But if it means "available to the creditor," then the whole list of items exempted by statutes from execution is

---
[6] Kester, Accounting Theory and Practice, Vol. I, p. 14.

cut out.[7] No useful purpose would be served by this exclusion, although, of course, the careful accountant may call attention to the immunities.

Assets Defined

In general, then, the professional accountant's implied definition may be said to be: *"An asset is any future service in money or any future service convertible into money (except those services arising from contracts the two sides of which are proportionately unperformed) the beneficial interest in which is legally or equitably secured to some person or set of persons. Such a service is an asset only to that person or set of persons to whom it runs."*

No definition substantially in this form is found in the literature. The nearest foreshadowing of it is to be found in Sprague's "Philosophy of Accounts" (2d ed., p. 41), where he says of assets "they are a storage of service to be received."

If the matter in parenthesis were removed, the definition would be more useful to the economist, and probably to all concerned. Whether or not it is possible in practice to admit the excepted matter will be discussed later.

Personal Assets and Enterprise Assets.—The definition set out above relates to accounting as between persons. Usually the accountant has to do with the affairs of an enterprise rather than with the concerns of a person or of an association of persons. If A, a sole trader operating a retail hardware establishment, employs an accountant to make an audit, the latter, unless the contrary were expressed, would understand that it was the affairs of the business—not those of A in general—that were to be looked into. The balance sheet in the audit report would pay no attention to certain of A's assets; only

---

[7] "Availability to creditors" applied as a test would exclude from the balance sheet of a municipal corporation all public buildings, parks, etc. Resort to the test of "What do accountants treat as assets" shows plainly that this possible meaning of Kester's statement cannot be true.

those committed to the enterprise and those arising out of enterprise operations and not withdrawn by A would appear.

If A has more than one enterprise, or is a member of more than one business firm, accounts will be kept and reports made separately for the enterprises. Nor could a simple aggregate of all the assets shown on the balance sheets of his separate enterprises be taken as a schedule of A's enterprise assets. Suppose A does business under the name and style of the De Luxe Laundry and also as the Standby Garage, and that the garage has made a repair on one of the laundry trucks. The concurrent balance sheets would include this item as an account receivable in the garage's balance sheet and as an account payable in the laundry's statement. Only in the event that a consolidation of the reports of A's enterprises was asked for would all of A's enterprise assets appear in one schedule.[8] With respect to A, as a person, neither the asset nor the liability has a real existence.

The convenience and advantages of reporting by single enterprises are too obvious to require justification. On the other hand, one reading an enterprise statement should have the accountant's procedure in mind. It is quite possible that an enterprise balance sheet—or, for that part, a consolidated balance sheet of all the commonly-held enterprises—may show a large debt-free estate in the proprietor, who, as a person, may have debts far exceeding his assets. A sole trader's balance sheet may show debts exceeding the assets, and yet the trader, as a person, may be financially secure.

Since the established usage of accountants makes the term "assets," used without qualification, mean "the assets devoted to the enterprise under consideration" rather than the assets of the person whose enterprise it is, the term will hereinafter be employed in the accountants' sense unless the contrary is expressed.

---

[8] In what the accountant calls a consolidated balance sheet the foregoing paired asset and liability items would be eliminated.

CHAPTER III

ASSETS—DIFFICULTIES OF INTERPRETATION

The task of explaining the meaning of a term is not concluded by offering a definition. However good the definition may be, if the objects of defining are to enable the reader always to use the term correctly and to enable him to interpret the term properly when used by others, some care must be taken to resolve the chief difficulties of use. The writer foresees, possibly as clearly as any one, certain difficulties in employing the definition given in the preceding chapter.

Four principal classes of difficulty are anticipated. These are: (1) misnamed items; (2) incompletely described or defined items; (3) the nature and confusing variety of "valuation accounts"; and (4) the nature and treatment of goodwill.

Not uncommonly the accountant substitutes the name of a class or object of outlay for the class of service to be received. Thus one often sees in balance sheets items of "prepaid wages," "prepaid rent," etc. A *wage* cannot be an asset to the employer, nor a rent to a tenant. But the labor services and the services of the rented object still to be rendered are clearly assets within the meaning of the definition given in the preceding chapter; and supposedly, the services will be worth at least as much as they have cost.

Incompletely Defined Items

For the difficulties in reading the overcondensed balance sheet, there is no help. Nor can much help be given in the interpretation of items that occasionally carry too brief captions. There is one series of captions, however, in the use of which many otherwise excellent accountants are guilty of over-brevity.

Fund Accounts.—Every one is familiar with the items "Sinking fund," "Sinking fund in the hands of trustees," "Sinking fund cash," "Bond sinking fund," "Depreciation fund," "Replacement funds," etc. Accountants who stand well in their profession do not employ these terms unless there are real funds of assets segregated from those assets with which the enterprise is currently being carried on. But it is not always made clear whose asset the "fund" is; nor, even if it is the asset of the company publishing the balance sheet, is it always made clear what freedom the company has in the utilization of the asset.

Suppose that an issue of bonds has been made under the terms of which the debtor has engaged to pay into the hands of a trustee acting for the bondholders certain increments of money at specified times. The trustee may be under a duty not only to conserve the fund, but to improve it by investment and to pay over the amount accumulated to the creditors upon maturity of the debt. In such a case the company exhibiting the sinking fund may have neither a legal nor an equitable title to the fund. Legally the fund is the trustees', equitably it is the bondholders'. The debtor corporation can in no way enjoy the direct fruits of the fund. The amount of the fund merely evidences the extent to which the company has observed the conditions of a severable contract. The effect of the fund is rather to reduce the amount of an original debt than to swell the company's resources. It shows that some liability, shown usually at its nominal or par value, can be wholly discharged by future payments smaller (by the amount of the fund) than the gross valuation at which the balance sheet exhibits the debt. That is to say, the amount of such a fund merely measures the excess of the stated liability over the present adverse valuation of it to the debtor. The meaning of such a "sinking fund" in the balance sheet of a solvent corporation could be made much clearer by a fuller caption or, better still, by exhibiting it as a deduction from the originally stated value of the liability.

But not all "sinking funds" are of this type. Sometimes funds are voluntarily appropriated and invested to provide for the retirement of a debt. The contract creating the debt may impose no duty on the debtor to make instalment payments to a trustee. Nevertheless the debtor may appoint a trustee to hold and improve the fund and to pay the accumulated amount upon the trustor's order. Obviously such a fund has a greatly different significance from that of one of the kind previously discussed. Funds of this second kind are sometimes provided for the retirement of redeemable stock issues.

Intermediate between the "sinking funds" of the kinds described is a third type. The corporation may engage, future surplus sufficing and public law permitting, to redeem a preferred stock issue at holder's option (or upon company's call) at an agreed price at some future time or times. In the same agreement there may be a covenant requiring the company (again assuming no breach of public law to be necessary) to create a fund for stock redemption. That this is a different class of fund with a distinct significance is readily seen; for stockholders can never enforce such an agreement absolutely and at all events. But if, on the other hand, the company does prosper, and so long as it prospers, shareholders of the issue concerned can compel the reservation and segregation of such a fund.

Enterprises engaged in the extractive industries, such as mining, oil production, etc., sometimes show "depletion funds" in their balance sheets. These depletion funds, like the sinking funds discussed above, may be funds which the company, by contract, has engaged to maintain for the protection of creditors to whom the wasting asset has been pledged. Their amount may, therefore, represent the extent to which the diminishing value of a pledged, wasting asset has been made good by money or other assets pledged with a trustee. Such funds may or may not be found associated with concurrent contractual, sinking funds. Like the "sinking fund" too, these funds are sometimes voluntarily created funds wholly at the disposal of the company, or they may be created under agreements of stock retirement contingent as to their enforceability upon the financial status of the enterprise.

"Depreciation funds" and "replacement funds" may be employed to describe as widely different things as are described by "depletion funds." It may make a vast deal of difference whether the trustor may draw upon the fund at will or only when, and if, pledged assets subject to depreciation are replaced by others acceptable to the trustee in lieu of those cast aside. It may make a difference whether the trustor *must* make deposits corresponding in amount to depreciation or may do so at his own election.

Until accountants begin to describe these various funds more fully either on the balance sheet or in notes inseparable from it, or until they adopt a set of terms that, by established custom, separately designate the classes of fund, the reader of their statements should make independent inquiry about the status of the fund.

Valuation Accounts

The accountant often finds that a single valuation for a balance sheet item, whether an asset, liability, or element of proprietorship, gives too little information to be serviceable. Thus if an item merely exhibits

Machinery.................................. $150,000

no one, limited to the balance sheet for his information, would know whether the machines were all brand new, or were all nearly worn out, or were of some intermediate age-distribution. Such an amount of machinery, if it is all new, implies low cash requirements for replacements in the next few years. On the other hand, an item of old machinery, even though now worth $150,000, implies an early cash requirement for replacement; and how great a cash requirement could only be guessed at.

But if the item reads

Machinery	$165,000
Less reserve for depreciation	15,000
	$150,000

a great deal *more* is told.

The original cost, the probable cost of replacement, the amount of depreciation that has occurred, the present value, and the prospect of low cash requirements for replacements during the next few years are all told in a simple sum and difference. Accounts kept in the books and exhibited in the balance sheet in order to describe more adequately and to evaluate a major item are called "valuation accounts."

Certain valuation accounts, e.g., depreciation reserves, allowances for bad debts, etc., are nowadays so shown in the balance sheets of the best accountants as to make their nature and significance plain to any thoughtful reader. Unfortunately not all accountants have followed the leaders in this respect; nor have the leaders treated all valuation accounts systematically. Just why a systematic treatment is not found cannot be ascertained as a matter of fact. Perhaps the best conjecture is that in accounting as in many other arts, practice anticipates theory; and the earlier attempts to generalize—to formulate theory—fall short of the simplest and most significant statement. Such items, wholly separate in origin as reserves for depreciation, discount on bonds issued, prepaid taxes on real estate, "suspense" accounts, organization expenses, prepaid advertising, experimental expense on patents applied for, etc., may, when originated in practice, have commended themselves to their inventors in some particular set of conditions. Others, finding like conditions, may have adopted items under like captions. Through long usage each item has come to have a fairly definite, separate, technical meaning. But that the whole multitude of such items, as they appear in the balance sheet, *perform a common set of functions and no others* seems somehow to have escaped attention.

Valuation accounts may be set up either in connection with asset items, or with liability items, or with proprietary items. Any of these three classes of valuation accounts may contain accounts with either credit balances or debit balances. Thus, we may find in the same statement a reserve for depreciation upon a building and an item of prepaid insurance upon the same asset. The one evidences a measure of decline in value since the building was originally valued; the other expresses an increased value during the currency of the insurance policy by reason of relief from the risk of loss by the peril insured against. We find on a debtor's balance sheet with respect to one funded debt an item called "discount on bonds payable." With respect to another debt we may find "premium on bonds payable." The first evidences the amount by which the so-called par of the issue exceeds the present (adverse) worth of the bonds priced to cost the debtor the rate effective against him in the original issue. The other, the premium, expresses the excess of the present (adverse) worth over par if the issue is priced to cost that rate implicit in the original sale price of the bonds. A "suspense account" may in fact represent a loss incurred "not yet charged off to profit and loss."[1] A real

---

[1] The keeping upon the books and the showing upon the balance sheet for some years of an item like "Suspense account," or "Losses not yet charged to profit and loss," has often been condemned. The critics see only that the lost asset is gone and that the proprietary interest is reduced. No carrying forward of the loss will avert it or minimize it. But if the item is fully described there is not only no serious objection to it, but there may be valuable information conveyed by it. Take the case of a young corporation that has amassed a surplus of $250,000 from profitable operations. Assume a loss of $200,000 from a casualty not possible to avert and not coverable by insurance. Publish a balance sheet immediately afterward showing a proprietary interest equal only to the par of the capital stock plus $50,000. The balance sheet is "true," but it is far from expressing the "whole truth," for the fact that the concern has been, and has a prospect of continuing to be, a profit earner beyond its dividend rate is suppressed. This fact of the past is of much greater significance for the future than is the fact that a

diminution in the proprietary interest has already happened; the accountant is reluctant to extinguish a surplus that has been earned and that would exist but for the loss. A "reserve for contingencies" that, at its creation, effects a diminution of surplus, often means that the directors or the accountant wish, for the sake of conservatism to express a risk-free valuation of surplus. They may have in mind no particular possible liability, or no particular loss. The amount of such a reserve is purely arbitrary.

Function of Valuation Accounts.—Both because the function of these valuation accounts is often not understood, because accountants disagree about the real nature of specific valuation accounts, and because, so far as the writer knows, no one has hitherto shown either how extensive this class of items is or that, in the balance sheet, they perform a single common function, he thinks it preferable here to risk a charge of overemphasis and overfullness than to risk a failure of interpretation. No pretense is made, however, of treating all valuation account items specifically. Only a fairly full illustration of the commoner types will be discussed.

Organization Expense.—Consider the often-met item, "organization expense." Some accountants and writers on accounting assert that it is an asset; others treat it without comment as though it were an asset; still others rightly say

---

casual calamity has been experienced. If instead of showing the suspense item among the assets, it were shown as a deduction from the proprietary account thus:

Net Proprietorship:
    Capital Stock... $1,000,000
    Surplus from operations in excess of dividends....... $250,000
Less loss (date) by (cause)............................ 200,000   50,000
                                                                    $1,050,000

no one can profess himself deceived, and all are more fully informed. Of course, one can have no patience with vague or misleading representations. To leave grounds for misunderstanding of what has occurred is either stupid or shameful.

INTERPRETATION OF ASSETS

it is not an asset at all, but no one unconditionally denies the item a place in the balance sheet. To call such an item a "deferred charge" suggests merely an intent to treat it as an expense in some future period; to call it a "prepaid expense" merely raises the question of why it was incurred; the *nature* of the item is not implied by either general term. If, as is usually the case, the founders of the enterprise believed the form of organization adopted to be the best available in the circumstances (including the special costs of acquiring the form), the expenditure is originally justified.

As a result of the outlay certain assets have disappeared and their money value is gone, but the proprietary interest is not worth less by reason of the operation. Since no concurrent liability is affected, either the form of organization procured must itself be an asset, or the residual assets must be worth more to the proprietary interest under this form. That the former is not true is clear. A mere form renders no separate or separable services; it is not separately convertible into money; it possesses, in fact, none of the attributes of an asset. To call it an asset is to say that what are called assets have no attribute in common that is peculiar to assets. That the assets remaining after the outlay may be more valuable to those beneficially interested in the proprietorship is not difficult to show. A locomotive is capable of performing the same set of services for a sole trader, a partnership, or a corporation. But if only a corporation is capable of acquiring the funds needed to build, equip, and operate a specific railway system on an optimum scale, it is obvious that the services of the locomotive, as well as those of all other items, may be more valuable to a corporation than they could be to an individual or to a firm.

Since the enhancement in value of the assets is expected to be a continuing condition, it is statistically impossible, except by purely arbitrary division, to allocate any portion of the organization expense to the assets existing at any one time (as against those to be held in the future). The real meaning of the item, "organization expenses," is, therefore, "this amount was paid to procure the adopted form of organization in the expectation that the services or assets to be utilized under it would be worth more to the proprietary interest (by at least the amount of the outlay) than they would otherwise be worth." The discussion of revaluation of such valuation accounts must be deferred to a later chapter.

Items of "deferred charges" or "prepaid expenses," like "prepaid advertising," intended to enhance future sales whether of goods now held or of future goods, "developmental expenses," intended to hasten an increase in volume of business, and many others that come to the notice of the reader of balance sheets, will be found upon analysis to be essentially similar to organization expense.

So-Called "Prepaid Interest."—Another very different class of valuation accounts, including such items as "prepaid interest" and "discount on bonds payable," is very commonly misinterpreted. Here again is to be found the same confusion on the part of the accountants and the writers on accounting. Some of the most astute writers in the theory of accounts assert that they are assets;[2] others rightly deny this,[3] but most writers merely discuss the origin and subsequent treatment of the items without explicitly showing their true nature.

The term "prepaid interest" as usually employed by the accountant is a misnomer. To be sure, interest contracted to be paid *can* be paid before it is contractually due, but even such a prepayment has the effect of diminishing a liability—not of creating an asset. What is usually intended to be described by the term is the difference between the value of the net consid-

---

[2] See Cole, Fundamentals of Accounting, pp. 103-104, 380-381.
[3] Paton and Stevenson, Principles of Accounting, pp. 401-403, and Paton, Accounting Theory, pp. 415-423, show the true nature of issue discounts on contractual securities. In Modern Accounting, pp. 77, 118-120, and 186-188, Hatfield calls these discounts assets, but in his later book, Accounting, p. 230, he adopts Paton's views.

eration paid to the debtor and the "par" or "face value" of the debt created.

The true nature of the item can most clearly be shown, perhaps, by comparing two elements of practice. Let us suppose a debtor to have borrowed money on two notes issued simultaneously. Suppose the consideration to be $952.38 for each note. The first note promises to pay $1,000 one year from date; the second promises to pay $952.38 one year from date with interest at 5% to maturity. (Note that $1,000 will be payable at maturity in each case.) The performances contemplated by the parties on these notes are identical. The economic and financial effect of the two contracts are indistinguishable. If discharged according to their tenor, as the parties expect, the only difference between the notes is in the *mode of describing* the amount to be paid.[4] But accountants would treat these two notes differently. The first would be entered thus:

Cash..............................	$952.38	
Prepaid interest (or other title).......	47.62	
Notes payable...........................		$1,000.00

On a balance sheet drawn at the date of issue, the amounts of the two debit items would be included among the assets in the totals opposite their respective titles. The amount of the credit item, $1,000, would be included in the total of notes payable. The second note would be entered thus:

Cash..............................	$952.38	
Notes payable...........................		$952.38

---

[4] There are, to be sure, certain *possible* differences in legal effects of a breach of these two contracts. Thus, if both are dishonored for payment at maturity, the measure of damages on the first will include interest at the legal rate on $1,000, from date of maturity; the corresponding element of general damages on the other will be legal interest from the same date on $952.38, the "face" value of the note. An intervening bankruptcy of the debtor might conceivably give rise to other differences in discharge. No accountant and no writer on accounts, so far as the writer is aware, bases the difference in accounting procedure upon these differences in the effect of a breach.

Both of these amounts would be included in the totals opposite the respective titles in a balance sheet drawn at the date of issue.

Here are two notes issued simultaneously for equal consideration, that mature simultaneously and require identical amounts for their discharge. But both upon the books and in the balance sheet the one contract appears to have given rise to a liability greater than that of the other and likewise to have increased the total of assets by a greater amount. Of the "prepaid interest" item of $47.62, it can be said that there has been no pre*payment* of interest or of anything else. No loss has been incurred upon the one note that has not been incurred upon the other. No expense, financial or otherwise, has as yet been incurred upon either. Whatever future expense is incurred upon the one contract will be matched both in time and amount by the expense upon the other. There is no substantial difference between the two debts; there is only a difference in the procedure of recording and exhibiting them. At the date of original record the then existing present worth of the first note is expressed as a difference of two balances—that of the liability account (a credit balance) and that of the valuation account for "prepaid interest" (a debit balance). On the same date the then existing present worth of the second note is expressed in one figure—that of the liability account.

If the debtor's books are closed between the date of issue and the date of maturity—say six months after issue—an interesting adjustment is made with respect to the two notes. For the first the entry is,

    Interest expense.................... $23.81
      Prepaid interest.......................... $23.81

and for the second note,

    Interest expense.................... $23.81
      Accrued interest payable.................. $23.81

INTERPRETATION OF ASSETS

Note that the first instrument now has a greater liability value. It is expressed, as before, by a difference of balances, but the balance of the valuation account has become smaller. The second instrument, too, has a greater liability value—greater by the same amount. But the value of this liability is now expressed as the sum of two balances.[5] Algebraically, of course, both liability valuations are expressed by sums.

If at the same interim date a balance sheet is prepared in the conventional manner, the reader must search out three items, one among the assets and two among the liabilities, in order to determine the real status of the debtor on his notes payable. Seldom would more than one item and one valuation figure be necessary or convenient.[6] The simplest (and generally sufficient) exhibit would consist of the figure for present worth of current debt instruments set opposite the class of instrument. Even if the usual, somewhat cumbersome, procedure of recording such instruments is followed and if all the balances are to be shown in the balance sheet, they should be brought together in that exhibit. If, for example, a statement is to be made when the foregoing notes are three months old, the balance sheet item could be arranged as a group thus:

```
Notes payable, face value............ $1,952.38
Deduct issue discount....... $47.62
    Less accrued interest pay-
        able................  23.81    23.81
                              _____   _____  $1,928.57
```

This would accord with the best modern practice of grouping depreciation reserves with the assets against the original book valuations of which the reserve (valuation account) is set up.

---
[5] All accountants call "accrued interest payable" a liability. In the sense that it is a new or independent debt, this would not be true; in the sense that the value of the previously existing liability has increased with the lapse of time, it is true.

[6] A somewhat different case arises in exhibiting the status upon debt instruments upon which interim interest payments are to be made. (See page 36.)

Discount on Bonds Payable.—When long-term issues with many interim payments of "interest" are sold by the debtor at a net price less than par, that is, are capitalized at a rate higher than the so-called "nominal rate of interest,"[7] the accountant sets up a liability valued at par and debits the difference between the par value and the value of the net consideration [8] to "discount on bonds payable" or "discount and expense on bonds payable" or some other account title of like purport. Just as in the case of the "prepaid interest" on the notes payable in the previous illustration, the accountant adjusts the balance of the valuation account from time to time by diminishing its debit balance. If the balance sheet is drawn at an "interest" paying date, there are two components in the valuation of the liability, the par of the issue and the discount. But if the statement is prepared between "interest" paying dates, there are, ordinarily, three components—the third being the accrued "interest" at the rate of nominal interest. This last item is ordinarily placed in the current liability section. Probably the most informing and convenient arrangement of the three items would join the par and the unamortized discount in one group thus:

```
Bonds payable, par of issue.........$1,000,000
Less unamortized discount...........    5,000
                                     ─────────  $995,000
```

The accrued "interest," since it represents a cash requirement in the period following the balance sheet, should be shown, as it usually is, among the current liabilities. Ordinarily, however, the reader must seek out three scattered items. And even these three are often not separately shown; for the accrued

---

[7] This "nominal rate of interest" is not, in economic reality, a rate of interest at all. It is merely a percentage relation between one fixed amount, the par of the bond, and the rent of the bond annuity. Its only service is to provide a convenient description of the debtor's sequence of obligations.

[8] Expenses incidental to the preparation and issuance of bonds, such as legal fees, recording fees, costs of searching land titles, engraving, exchange listing costs, etc. are deducted from the gross selling price to determine the net consideration.

"interest" item may merge the amounts due both on bonds and on short-term debts; and the discount may be hidden in a total of "deferred charges" or of "prepaid expenses," or of "unadjusted debits."

Prepaid Taxes and Insurance.—A third class of valuation accounts, which includes such items as "prepaid taxes" and "prepaid insurance," asserts that the real asset items in connection with which the expenses have been incurred, are really more valuable than the amounts set opposite them indicate. It is a commonplace in valuation theory that the risks of loss incident to ownership tend to reduce the value of the thing exposed to risk. If a building burns, the loss, unless otherwise provided for, falls upon the owner. The building, freed of the risk of loss by fire, is worth more than if subject to that risk. If the owner conducts his affairs rationally and if the exemption from the risk is worth more to him than the cost of fire insurance, he will insure.[9]

Taxes that become a lien on specific property, while relatively seldom paid before the beginning of the tax period to which they apply, usually become delinquent if unpaid before the expiration of that period. Obviously the property freed of the lien is worth more than one subject to it. The customary terms of sale of realty show the clearest recognition of this principle. If payment of a tax is made before the expiration

---

[9] There is an apparent ground for calling an unexpired insurance contract an asset. By the usual terms of the fire insurance contract a short-rate premium rebate may be had upon a surrender of the contract; and by custom the insurer will assent to an assignment (in reality a novation) of the contract when the subject matter is sold, provided the moral risk of the new owner is acceptable to the insurer. In the case of a surrender the amount recouped is always less than the amount at which the "prepaid insurance" item is characteristically carried; and there is, of course, a concomitant decline in value of the subject matter whether that decline is recognized on the books or not. The common custom of bargainers for the sale of insured property to agree upon a purchase price and upon a *prorating* of the premium of the policy *to be assigned* is but a recognition of the fact that an insured property is worth more than one not insured. The custom of mortgagees and grantees under trust deeds of requiring insurance payable to them to be carried, is but another recognition of the principle.

of a tax period, clearly the subject matter, rendering services tax-free for the remainder of the period, is worth more by at least the amount of tax applicable to the remaining part of the period.

While it is possible to distribute to the several asset items the enhancement of value arising by reason of exemption from risk of fire loss, exemption from tax liability, etc., it would be endlessly tedious to do so. Moreover, the balance sheet that shows items of this kind separately, actually gives more useful information than could be given if the identity of the items were lost. The amount of such items so shown, in addition to asserting an enhanced valuation of the assets affected, indicates a diminution in the cash requirements for the period that follows immediately.

Goodwill

Accountants, writers on accounting, economists, engineers, and the courts, have all tried their hands at defining goodwill, at discussing its nature, and at proposing means of valuing it. The most striking characteristic of this immense amount of writing is the number and variety of disagreements reached. Perhaps the second most notable feature of the writings is the incompleteness of analysis in the output of single authors upon the subject. A formidable list of deservedly eminent writers could readily be made up in the product of each of which some unique contribution is made, but, unfortunately, each writer in turn seems not to have appreciated fully the work of his predecessors.

Most of those who have sought to analyze and to define goodwill have fallen into the error of seeking chiefly for ultimate or intermediate causes and for elementary components. There is endless discussion of reputation for integrity, of dependability of service, of brand names, of favorable location, of habits and tastes of customers, of personal relations in trade, etc. Each of these is capable of indefinitely complex

INTERPRETATION OF ASSETS

splitting up. But no *comprehensive* analysis of this character is possible, nor are the elements capable of statistical treatment. It is as if the physicist were to attempt to write the equations for the paths in space of each molecule of gas confined in a vessel. Life is not long enough to permit success. Elementary components of goodwill are interesting to speculate about but only the mass resultant, in any given enterprise, is capable of statistical generalization.

Much the best work that has come to hand is that of J. M. Yang. In the preface of his book, "Goodwill and Other Intangibles," he says:

> Much has been written on goodwill, and by eminent authorities, but, so far as the writer has been able to determine, the subject has not been adequately dealt with from the standpoint of accounting. This is noticeably true in the case of accounting textbooks, and even in the extended special works, such as those of Dicksee and Leake, most of the space is devoted to the legal characteristics of goodwill and the methods of its appraisal. In fact, it is fair to say that while the peculiarities of intangible assets have long been recognized by professional accountants and business men, not much advance has yet been made in the direction of a real understanding of the essential nature of intangibles . . .
>
> . . . it has been deemed necessary to discuss the various phases and interpretations of goodwill and related assets. In this discussion an attempt has been made, in particular, to show that the value of intangibles is essentially an expression of the superior earning power of the specific concern, and that on account of this fact there is inevitably a close and inseparable relationship among the intangibles as a group.

His book comes much closer to accomplishing the stated aim and to developing a comprehensive theory of the treatment appropriate to what he calls intangibles than any previous writing has done. Yang's debt to Paton, acknowledged handsomely in his preface, is great. Paton's book, "Accounting Theory," especially in the chapter on Goodwill and Going Value, affords the best brief discussion of goodwill, and, after Yang's fuller treatment, is much the best general discussion of the subject.

Both Yang and Paton, at several points in their writing, seem to have been on the verge of raising the question that is raised here, viz., is goodwill an asset at all? Thus Yang, in his discussion of the characteristics of intangibles (pages 8-19) considers one after another of the attributes generally supposed to attach to assets and finds them absent from the intangibles. Paton, in the chapter referred to says (page 310):

> The intangibles are the residuum, the balance of the legitimate values attaching to an enterprise as a totality, over the sum of the legitimate values of the various tangible properties taken individually. That is, the intangibles measure that part of a company's asset total which might be said to reside in the physical situation viewed as a whole, but which cannot be considered—except upon some highly arbitrary basis—to inhere in, or have a residence in, specific units of plant, equipment, etc. Or, to put it still differently, the amount by which the total of the values of the various physical properties within the enterprise, inventoried unit by unit, falls short of the legitimate asset total for the entire business, expresses the intangible asset value.

These two writers are in substantial agreement as to what items are intangibles. These items have a common set of attributes that, so far as the left-hand member of the balance sheet is concerned, are peculiar to them. This common set of attributes does not, at least in these writers' discussions, include any attribute common to all assets and peculiar to them. But neither writer seems to have asked the question, are these intangibles really assets at all? Neither these writers nor any others whose writings have come to my attention seem to have considered the question of the statistical homogeneity of the items that appear in the left-hand member of the balance sheet. When that question is considered rightly some light is thrown upon the nature of goodwill.

Certain Elements of Goodwill.—All will agree that future income constitutes the sole source of enterprise valuation. Certain sources of future services or income may be separately appraised with a degree of reliability sufficient to make separate valuation convenient and useful to all interested in an enterprise. Other sources, e.g., expectancies, persons with whom the management have executory contracts wholly unperformed on both sides, contingent services to which, if they eventuate, the concern has a claim, but which may never happen (or, if they do, may prove valueless) and so on, may be practically incapable of reliable valuation as individual items. Moreover, those items of income that the accountant does separately appraise—such as the incomes or services from particular sources, like land, machinery, trade debtors, etc.—cannot be accurately appraised. For not only is the future not wholly foreseen, but even if it were, the allocation of a total sales income among the material objects and persons whose services, as a totality, will have brought in this revenue cannot be made except upon a basis largely arbitrary. With the exception of money actually in the possession of a concern at a specified time, no valuation the accountant makes of a particular item can be more than an index of the present worth of its future earning power. The specific productivity theory of distribution is wholly incapable of statistical application in accounts.[10]

Take the case of an enterprise with a long operating history and consider what the accountant has actually done with respect to valuing its expected future incomes. Year after year certain separable items of future income have been omitted. No account has been taken of the possibility that certain services, say those of the general manager, may be worth much more than he has agreed to accept. No account in the asset valuations has been taken of a long succession of sales orders placed, but not filled at times of closing the books. Year after year certain items, like the services of land procured to the enterprise for a long term under a lease contract, the terms of

---

[10] The writer doubts that this theory of distribution, the influence of which is very far from being expunged from modern economic theory, ever did have any validity even as a conceptual basis of analysis.

which have turned out to be extremely favorable, are left out of an asset list. Year after year certain items that do appear in the asset schedule may appear at valuations far below their maximum worth to the concern. Land in a location more favorable than it appeared to be at the time it was bought or at the time the residual portion of a leasehold was taken over, may be carried at cost. Machinery, the valuations of which are based upon its cost in a market that was made for many purchasers, may be physically better adapted to the work required of it by this concern than to that required by other users of like equipment.

It is no matter for surprise that where many of the component elements of future income have been omitted from the asset valuations and where those component elements that have been included were predominantly undervalued, the concern should exhibit, year after year, a ratio of operating profit to book value of assets much above that which is found in other concerns in the same industry. Such a concern is said to have a valuable goodwill. If it changes hands, it will do so at a total consideration in excess of the difference between its book totals of assets and of liabilities. To the extent to which this goodwill is reliably appraised, all that can be said of it is that it results from, and amounts to, the sum of values of items of future incomes omitted from its asset schedule plus the sum of undervaluations of those future items (and series of items) of future income that are shown in its asset schedule, less the sum of corresponding overvaluations (if any) of those asset items that appear in the schedule.

Goodwill a Master Valuation Account.—Goodwill, when it appears in the balance sheet at all, is but a master valuation account—a catch-all into which is thrown both an unenumerated series of items that have the *economic*, though not necessarily the *legal*, properties of assets, and an undistributed list of undervaluations of those items listed as assets. It is the valuation account *par excellence*. It cannot under any circumstances be called an "asset," unless that term is confessedly meant to include at least two kinds of things which have no common attribute peculiar to them. But it can be shown to have a set of attributes common to those items here called valuation accounts; and that group of valuation accounts that are set out as adjuncts to such true asset accounts as are kept can be shown not only to have a common set of attributes, but a set that is *peculiar* to them.

Inferential support to the view expressed here is to be had from what accountants do with such items as goodwill, organization expenses, developmental expenses, etc., once these items find their way into the accounts. Characteristically, they write off these accounts in relatively brief periods. This they do despite the fact that the conditions that led to making the outlay may clearly be continuing conditions. When accountants preparing the balance sheet of the General Electric Company show therein an item of:

Patents, goodwill, and other intangibles......... $1.00

they do not mean that the company's huge outlays for such items have been mistakes, nor that the fruits of the operations in connection with which these outlays have been made are all gathered, nor that the company, if selling out as a unit, would sell at the difference between the sums of asset and of liability valuations. It will be found, on the other hand, that these same accountants have made the most searching inquiry to assure themselves that all those items belonging to the company and conforming to the definition of assets set out in this book are accounted for, item by item, in the books and are reflected in the balance sheet. That is to say, accountants incline strongly to exclude items that do not describe separable sets of services still to be had, and scrupulously endeavor to list all separable sets of future services that can be reliably valued. In other words, those things which are here called assets are always included, but mere deficiencies of the total valuation do not seriously concern them.

Those who are unconvinced of the soundness of the analysis made in these two chapters on assets, particularly as it deals with valuation accounts, are asked to defer final judgment upon that analysis until they have read the chapters on valuation. The analysis of the nature of things is a problem apart from the quantitative measurement of the same things, and must, in any sound statistical inquiry, or in any critical analysis of a statistical procedure, be dealt with first. But the two problems of analysis are not unrelated. On the contrary, the fullest significance of any proposal in the qualitative analysis cannot possibly be seen until the convenience (or lack of it) of that proposal in the quantitative work has been examined. Nor can any discussion of quantitative valuation be wholly lucid and significant unless and until the reasons for the qualitative or attributive classification have been disclosed.

Summary of Chapters II and III

An attempt has been made to discuss the realities of what accountants do in relation to defining assets. The nature of what the accountant lists as assets in the accounts and on the balance sheet has been sought by examining the attributes of the items thus treated rather than by reading what accountants and writers on accounting have said *about* the nature of assets. Much fruitful suggestion has been found in the writings, to be sure, both on this topic and upon those to be taken up, but the writer has endeavored neither to describe nor to approve nor to disapprove what accountants do until the things actually done and the probable statistical effect of what is done have been carefully considered.

That which the accountant systematically and completely treats as an asset can exist *as an asset* only in relation to some person or entity whose asset it is. In essence it is a future element or portion of income, a set of desirable future services that is valuable in money and may be realized upon in money either directly or through intermediate operations. The accountant excludes from his statistical treatment all such incomes as are not secured to their beneficiaries by some legal or equitable right. He excludes also incomes or services expected to accrue under contracts wholly executory and unperformed on both sides, and under the wholly unperformed portions of contracts, provided both sides are equally unperformed.

Not all the items listed under the caption of "assets" in a balance sheet are really assets. Some items are intended merely to show that an outlay has been made in the anticipation that, as a result, the true assets (present and/or future) will have a value to the going concern greater than the figures listed or to be listed for them. Some items express by the amounts set opposite them an overvaluation in one or more of the liability items. Others, again, express an overvaluation of the net proprietary interest in the enterprise; they merely account for certain diminutions in the value of the latter interest.

Quite aside from the mode of valuation or the reliability of the valuation of items appearing under the heading of assets in general statements, those who resort to the accountants' reports should keep ever in mind that not all items are of homogeneous character. They should be aware, too, that not all the available statistical information having to do with the financial condition of the concern under examination will be found in the conventional statements; for some items *having the probable effect* of assets are excluded.

Finally, the writer wishes to say that accountants of the best professional class are not wholly responsible for all that the writers on accounting have said about their work. Many an economist and statistician, in reading the accounting texts, must have been aware of a great mass of unsupported assertion, inconsequential argument, apparent statistical inconsistency, and lack of homogeneity and completeness. But any one who has the patience to find out for himself what accountants actually do and who will reflect upon what he finds, will discover that modern accounting practice is, on the whole, sounder than that which has been written about it. Apparently those who have really created accepted modern procedure have not been notably given to writing about it. In many an instance the writers would do well to consider the statistical effects of what the accountants do rather than to invent conjectural reasons for their procedure.

CHAPTER IV

LIABILITIES AND NET PROPRIETORSHIP

In the introductory paragraphs of Chapter II, the question was raised as to whether the equation of accounts is an expression of mere equivalence or one of identity. When the accountant says that assets equal liabilities plus net proprietorship, or, spelled out in full, that the sum of asset valuations is equal to the sum of the valuations of liabilities and of net proprietorship, does he mean that there are three classes of unlike things the valuations of which stand always in a certain equivalence relation? In a quantity of carbonic acid the number of oxygen atoms is equal to the number of hydrogen atoms plus the number of carbon atoms—is this the kind of relation meant by the accountant? Or are there, in essence, two things only? If so, are these two things: (1) assets, and (2) claims running against the assets; or are they: (1) the assets in their relations favorable to their proprietor, and (2) claims of others adverse to the proprietor of the enterprise in question?

Gross Proprietorship

A numerical value set down as a measure of *net* proprietorship suggests the contemplation of a possible larger, or more inclusive value. Many, indeed, have been puzzled to account for the qualifying word in that term. But accountants do not employ the term "gross proprietorship"; nor do they speak of "proprietorship," without qualifying the word, except to use it as a term interchangeable with "net proprietorship." One who searches the texts will find little to illuminate either the usage or the underlying ideas. It is certainly not enlightening to be told that if one subtracts the measure of one thing from the measure of a second, the resulting difference is the net measure of a third thing. If, on the other hand, one disregards what is said *about* net proprietorship and the mode of valuing it, and looks to what is done, and to the effects of what is done, in conventional practice, an approximate meaning of the terms of the second member of the equation can be expressed.

In the previous chapters it was said that an asset, as such, does not exist except in relation to some person (or persons) whose asset it is. Assets were there considered as services or elements of income. They are classified according to the kinds of sources from which the incomes proceed. In like manner the holder may be considered as the immediate personal recipient or beneficiary of the incomes or services. The term proprietor means merely a "holder of assets." To show the importance of the income expected from any existing controlled source, a money valuation is placed upon it. If for any set of assets, e.g., those dedicated by the proprietor to the uses of an enterprise, correct money valuations are found, the sum of these asset valuations is not only the measure of the services running from the designated items, but is also the measure of the benefits running to their recipient. That is to say, only one summation is involved, though that series is viewed in two ways. Taking assets as one member of the expression of equality, then, it can be seen that the other member is not found as a sum of two quantities but is, numerically, identical with the first, in origin, in method of measuring, and in amount. The only difference is the manner of regarding the amount.

Value of Assets and Value of Gross Proprietorship Identical.—That the difference in manner of regarding the items and their summation is not a mere conception is readily indicated. We have, on the one hand, the problem of the manipulation of assets, the problem of revenue-getting; assets (services that contribute to the procurement and making of salable commodities and services) must be brought together, altered, replaced. That is to say, we have the problem of management of operations. It is no accident that the cost accountant's and the engineer's analyses concern themselves chiefly with the accounts having debit balances. We have on the other hand the problems of manipulating the final, realized money income, the problem of distributing the fruits among the contributors in such a manner as to yield the proprietor a maximum final benefit. In our modern corporate enterprises in which the beneficial interest in the proprietorship is divided among many, in which these beneficially interested persons are largely not active in management, in which the several functions of managing operations are divided among many, this difference in the way of regarding the one series of valuations has taken on an importance both to individuals and to society that could never have been dreamed of by the inventor of the equation nor by those who employed his device for some hundreds of years after its invention. In fact the two great and almost all-inclusive problems of accounting are the accounts *of* operations and accounts *to* proprietors.

Much would be gained both in terminology and in ideas if this notion of identity were more widely expressed. Failure to see the identity, it is believed, lies at the root of much that is confusing in the treatment of liabilities, the third term of the equation. A liability in its most general sense implies a relation between persons. One who is obliged to do something adverse to his own interest and beneficial to another's has a liability to that other person. The classes of service comprised under the accountant's use of the term are all assets of the person to whom the services run. In formal accounts and statements, however, the term is used in a narrower sense. In the balance sheet of a sole trader, for example, the liabilities shown do not purport to be all of the liabilities of the person who is the sole trader; the liabilities shown are those only that have arisen in the course of financing and operating the business and that have not been discharged. Except where the more inclusive meaning is expressed or is plainly implied by the context (as in a "statement of affairs" of a natural person who is a bankrupt), the accountant restricts the use of the term liabilities to the designation of enterprise liabilities. That usage is followed hereafter in this book.

Distinction between Proprietorship and Liabilities

The fundamental equation in its most characteristic and most significant use, the enterprise balance sheet, exhibits the affairs of an enterprise in three qualitative ways. These are: (1) a set of services proceeding from designated items that the proprietor has either contributed to the enterprise (or that have been acquired in the course of enterprise operations) and that have not been withdrawn from enterprise use; (2) the interest of the proprietor as the recipient of the benefits of that set of services; and (3) the set of services that the proprietor has become bound to render to others as an incident to the running of his business.

Arithmetically there are but two quantities exhibited: (1) the money valuation (importance to the proprietor) of the ultimate benefits to be received from the services proceeding from the several items to the proprietor; and (2) the money valuation of the services which the proprietor has bound himself to render to other persons. Statistically the equation of accounts is epitomized in the difference between the volume of benefits expected to flow in (with reference to the proprietor) and the volume of adverse elements to flow out.

In the matter of valuation, liabilities do not differ from assets except in characteristic direction of flow.[1] Those writers who urge consideration of liabilities as negative assets express a view more fruitfully suggestive than do those who habitually

---

[1] Even this characteristic or *predominant* direction of flow is what the logician would call an accident rather than a distinguishing character. In the chapter on valuation of fixed assets the case of a true asset having a negative value at certain stages of its exploitation will be put forward.

associate liabilities and *net* proprietorship in their discussion.[2] But the problems of revenue-getting are so vastly different from those of procuring funds for it and from those of dividing the fruits of enterprise that no degree of similarity of quantitative aspects of the single items can ever make the groups of assets and the groups of liabilities homogeneous with respect to the accountant's principal inquiries.

The association in speech and writing of liabilities and of net proprietorship as though these two quantities were coordinate and had an independent existence, cannot but be misleading to those not fully informed. That they usually appear in the same member of the balance sheet as though they were coordinate is a mere statistical convention. Whether one sets down a minuend, subtracts a subtrahend, and expresses the difference as a footing or, alternatively, finds the difference, adds the subtrahend to it, and expresses the sum (the original minuend) as a footing, is wholly without substantive significance. Those who are in any substantial way interested in an enterprise, are interested in many relations between the total proprietorship and the total liabilities. The difference between the two, though significant, is only one of many significant relations in these two constantly changing quantities. The balance sheet equation may be statistically epitomized by the difference of the two amounts, but the whole of modern accounting is not so epitomized.

Liabilities and Net Proprietorship Not Homogeneous.— Then, too, we find writers who give a single name to the right-hand member of the balance sheet and treat the items in it as though they were not merely coordinate but homogeneous as well. The items are looked upon either as interests in or claims against the summation of the other member. As notable

---

[2] Notable writers who urge the similarity (except for difference of algebraic sign) of assets and liabilities include Sprague, Philosophy of Accounts, chapter on phases of liabilities, and Hatfield, Accounting, Chapter IX. Accountants, it is believed, would do well to reflect upon a procedure that Hatfield (and others cited by him) suggests in this connection.

instances of this practice Cole's "ownership claims" and Paton's "equities" may be cited.[3] But the unities found by these writers are quite different in character from those set forth above as between asset summation and proprietorship. The discussion of both these writers is full of useful suggestion—particularly to accountants. The only adverse criticism that can be made of their terms, as developed by them, is that they do not accurately describe what accountants do nor do they precisely accord with legal fact. Cole's "ownership claims" *against the assets,* and Paton's "equities" *in the assets,* they are careful to point out, do not, in the case of unsecured liabilities, attach to particular assets unless and until voluntary payment is made or execution is had under process of law. They indicate that items usually called liabilities run against the body of assets as an entirety. That this latter cannot be true in certain instances is readily shown. A debt may fall due against a municipal corporation at a time when no money appropriated for meeting it is on hand, when no levy has been made to obtain the funds, and when no unappropriated funds are at the disposal of the municipal officers. Even though the creditor obtains a judgment, there is nothing among the assets available to him for satisfaction. He must, by legal process, compel a levy to be made to meet the specific claim. His claim meanwhile stands in a balance sheet in which none of the assets is, in any real sense, a basis of his claim. If the municipal corporation is a state (in our special federal sense), he cannot even sue except by the state's permission.

In the case of the sole trader, the public extends him credit not upon his enterprise assets, in any peculiar sense, but, apart from a purely personal basis, upon the basis of his net estate, in his personal assets, i.e., both enterprise and non-enterprise assets. With some modifications, by reason of the rule of sepa-

---

[3] Cole, Fundamentals of Accounting, and Paton, Accounting Theory—citations indexed under the terms quoted.

rate funds, a similar case exists in respect to partnerships; and in the case of firm debts arising from torts (the obligations being joint and several), the whole body of non-execution-proof assets of any or all members of the firm as private persons is equally available with enterprise assets.

That which is generally true is that certain items in the right-hand member of the balance sheet are claims against the proprietor as a person, or group of persons. In the ordinary enterprise balance sheet these claims running against the proprietor are limited to those that have arisen as incidents to the conduct of the business. The first-hand, immediate claim to the fruits of enterprise is wholly and entirely in the proprietor. He need never, if he chooses, become a creditor at all in the conduct of his enterprise. If he does elect to do so, he may convert any asset he chooses, to the extent that he has not contracted to do the contrary, for the satisfaction of the debt. The source of the means of satisfaction is his own affair. Only when he refuses to pay at all, may creditors ever have recourse to any asset. When they do have recourse, it is not necessarily to the assets to be found in the balance sheet in which the claim appears; and in some cases the recourse is to a thing which no accountant treats as an asset at all. The bases of levies legally available to a municipal corporation—whether a state or a creature of the state's legislative powers—is never listed by accountants as an asset.

Other Terms for Net Proprietorship.—Other names for the groups in the second member of the balance sheet are often found. The term "net assets" is often found as an alternative to net proprietorship. The only objections to it as a term are that it carries no suggestion of the point of view implicit in proprietorship and that it suggests a deduction from, or diminution of, the asset summation. The deduction, in essence, is made from proprietorship—not from assets. The fact that the numerical valuation of assets is identical with that of proprietorship does not preclude logical ambiguity in the term "net assets."

"Capital" or "net capital" (used interchangeably) are often found. The objection to these is that they imply—in common business speech, in the writings of economists, and in the usage of many accountants—sources of revenues, incomes, and services to be rendered, rather than the interest of a particular proprietor in them.

Net worth is, perhaps, less objectionable than some of the other terms employed. There seems, to some persons at least, to be a suggestion in the term that somehow or other the figure found for it is a real or a true worth such as a fully informed, rational business man would accept either as a buyer or seller of the enterprise as an entirety, if he were acting in his own interests. The facts of business dealings testify that no such significance can be attached to it. The figure actually found can have, of course, no real meaning at all other than that given it by what is done (and what has been omitted) in the statistical procedure by which the figure is derived. The conditions under which the figure actually found is even a good *index* to a true worth will be considered in the chapters on valuation.

Net proprietorship, on the other hand, does not literally imply either: (1) an overstatement of assets (elsewhere in the statement); or (2) an identity with capital instruments; or (3) a positive opinion about the capitalized value of the enterprise; or (4) a coordinate footing of proprietor and creditor. It does imply that the set of operations in enterprise whereby some person (or persons) has become a holder of assets (a proprietor) may also have given rise to adverse items. It is this algebraic sum of interests of the proprietor that the term "net proprietorship" is intended to describe.

Finally some consideration of the term "liabilities," as applied to the entire right-hand member of the balance sheet, may be helpful. This is one of the oldest terms in use in writings in English on the subject. Whatever may have been the grounds for its early adoption, it can now be said that the term is seriously confusing and misleading. Some have sought to give meaning to it by the adoption of a figure of speech. The enterprise itself—as an entity separate and apart from the proprietor (or proprietors), the creditors, and those who have dealings of any kind with it—is personified. The accounts, it is said, constitute an accounting by this entity to all who have commercial and financial relations with it. Some writers even profess that, in the case of corporate enterprise, the entity may be more than a figure of speech. This they do by making the blunder of identifying the shareholders as the proprietor and making the corporation correspond to this entity. The shareholders, as such, are proprietors of their shares only—they have mere contracts with the corporation in which certain beneficial interests in the corporation's affairs are granted, for a consideration, to subscribers and their successors. Imaginary entities have their proper place in the conceptual world of analysis in pure mathematics, but never in the statistical analysis of realities. Figures of speech may be useful occasionally as a device in exposition, but to hang the whole exposition of a statistical analysis and synthesis upon a figure of speech is to run the risk of conveying a memory of the figure instead of an understanding of the reality.

Proprietorship, Liabilities, and Net Proprietorship Defined.—With respect to enterprise balance sheets, i.e., those in which the accountant concerns himself solely with the assets employed in a specified business, with the interest of the proprietor in these assets and with the obligations of the proprietor that have arisen as incidents to running the business, two terms affecting the second member of the equation can be qualitatively defined as follows:

Proprietorship consists of the entire beneficial interest of a holder of a set of assets in those assets. A liability is a service, valuable in money, which a proprietor is under an existing legal (or equitable) duty to render to a second person *(or set of persons)* and which is not unconditionally an agreed set-off to its full amount against specific services of equal or greater money value due from this second person to the proprietor.

Net proprietorship cannot be qualitatively defined except as a mere difference. It is the *difference found by subtracting the summation of the liabilities from the amount of the proprietorship.*

Liabilities under Unequally Performed Contracts.—Some further comment on the definition of liabilities is, perhaps, desirable. It will be recalled that certain separable items of income assured legally to the proprietor are not listed by accountants as assets. Thus, it was said that if A has contracted to make certain manufacturing machinery and deliver it to B for $1,000, and if A has done nothing toward the manufacture and B has paid nothing on account, neither A's nor B's books or statements show either an asset or a liability arising from this agreement. The amounts involved, as the accountant values them, are equal and are mutual set-offs. But when A delivers the machinery or a part of it as agreed, B has a liability to A (and A has an asset) until B pays. On the other hand, if C has given a note for $1,000, payable to D to order, and before the note has matured, D has bought goods from C on open account at an agreed price of $1,000, the obligations are not mutual set-offs. Legally, of course, if D still has the note, he can set it off against his debt for goods and C can set off the debt for goods against D, if the latter, as a principal, presents it for payment. But on their accounts, during the currency of the two debts, each would show both an asset and a liability. Notice that C's promise is not to pay D, but to pay "D or order." C cannot set off D's debt for goods against a holder in due course but against D only; and C's accountant could not know that D would not negotiate the note. D's bookkeeper, under instructions, might set off the note (if D was holding it) against the open book account debt. But a professional accountant, certifying D's balance sheet, would require D's account payable to be included and would include the note in notes receivable. The accountant cannot know whether or not D will negotiate the note and hence be required to pay in money the debt actually existing when the balance sheet is drawn. There is not an agreed unconditional set-off.

Signs are not wanting, however, to indicate that changes in practice may shortly become general that will give more inclusive meanings both to assets and to liabilities. Sporadic instances are found of balance sheets exhibiting such items among the assets as:

Purchase commitments not yet filled..	$10,000	
Less contingent loss at prices (date)...	2,000	$8,000

and among the liabilities a corresponding item of:

Purchase commitments...................	$10,000

That is to say, some accountants are beginning to list, as assets and as liabilities, the services to be had and the services to be performed under wholly unperformed contracts. This is especially true where, as above, a substantial loss on the order for future delivery seems probable at the date of the balance sheet. Montgomery, who is a compelling prophet in matters of practice, says:[4]

> It is not general practice to show future commitments (sales or purchases) in certified balance sheets and until it becomes fairly general, it cannot be good accounting practice to insist upon it, but *whenever the information is essential to the understanding of a true financial position,* it must be done.

As will be shown later, there are great possibilities of usefulness in an extension of this practice. The difficulties of proper extension, however, are very great.

---
[4] Montgomery, Auditing Theory and Practice, 4th ed., Vol. I, p. 307.

Limitations on Meaning of Net Proprietorship.—A word, too, is needed on the definition of net proprietorship given above. A numerical difference between two quantities can have a substantive meaning only when the two quantities are homogeneous. The valuations of both proprietorship and liabilities, it is true, are dollar valuations. But the valuation of proprietorship, being identical in amount with the summation of the assets, is determined by *unlike methods of measuring* as between one kind of asset and another (as we shall show in detail later); and the assets and liabilities are unlike one another in origin and in purpose. Moreover, as we have seen, not all those items having the economic essentials of assets are included in what are treated as assets. Mere differences in distribution of kinds of assets and as between those things which are included as assets and those that are not included, affect this difference between assets and liabilities. The mere *figure* for net proprietorship, therefore, far from being the tremendously significant valuation that many suppose it to be, has little definite or precise significance at all. Much more really useful information can be got from the several items that are commonly found in the net proprietorship section than can be got from their total.

CHAPTER V

LIABILITIES AND NET PROPRIETORSHIP: DIFFICULTIES OF INTERPRETATION

To make the definitions developed in the preceding chapter more useful it seems necessary, just as in the case of assets, to devote some space to their application in interpreting balance sheets.

Failure to note the true nature of proprietorship, it is believed, is largely responsible for the confusion some writers show in their attempts to distinguish clearly between certain liability items and elements of interest in the net estate of the proprietor. Especially is this true in the case of corporation balance sheets. Some who have achieved high standing, both as writers and as practitioners, admit the difficulty of making and applying this distinction. Thus Bell says:[1]

> Some accountants and writers on accountancy are greatly concerned over the distinction between liabilities and capital (net proprietorship) in relation to designations in balance sheets. It is, of course, necessary for an accountant to have a clear perception of the difference between these two classes of credit accounts, but in the author's opinion simplicity in financial statements, and in accounting terminology generally, is extremely desirable, especially when it can be attained without serious violence to principle; and for that reason he is not disposed to split hairs between "liabilities" and "capital" in the designation of the general class of accounts represented.

The most careful reading of Bell's book, though he discusses many items at length, affords the reader little help toward resolving this difficulty. Indeed, in certain instances he

---

[1] Bell and Powelson, Auditing, p. 261, and Chapters XIV and XV. (In the preface of this book it is indicated that Powelson's contribution is limited to the preparation of cases and questions.)

shows a willingness to stop somewhat before the "hair-splitting" stage is reached.[2]

Subordinated Debts

Montgomery, whose discussion is, perhaps, the best to be found on this subject, says:[3]

Exclusive of reserves [valuation accounts?], there are three classes of items on the credit or right-hand side of the balance sheet, viz., (1) liabilities, (2) capital (net proprietorship), and (3) items which are liabilities or capital, according to circumstances. . . . In the case of an issue of so-called debenture bonds, the maturity date is 1990: interest is payable only when declared by the directors and is not cumulative; by express language no claim can be made for principal or interest at any time when there is any obligation direct or contingent to others. The holders of the "bonds" are creditors only so far as the stockholders are concerned. The full amount shown to be due to the "bond" holders is at the risk of the business and ranks as capital so far as creditors and prospective creditors are concerned. These conditions illustrate the third class mentioned above.

With respect to subordinated debts,[4] Montgomery says:[5]

The purpose of the subordination of obligations is to protect creditors and to improve the financial showing of the concern affected. . . . When the fact of subordination is established, full effect must be given to it in the balance sheet, otherwise most and sometimes all of the intended effect will be lost. The inclusion of subordinated items in

---

[2] *Ibid.*, pp. 98-99, 292-293, 301, 304.
[3] Montgomery, Auditing Theory and Practice, 4th ed., Vol. I, pp. 261-262.
[4] A subordinated debt is a debt created by a contract wherein, by irrevocable agreement, the creditor agrees that his claim shall take a rank of priority lower than those of general creditors. The agreement may concede this priority to those who are creditors upon debts current at the date of agreement, or to these and to others who may become general creditors during a specified future time, or until a specified contingency occurs, or until specified conditions are fulfilled. There seems to be nothing in public law to prevent the creditor upon such a debt agreeing to become a claimant inferior in rank to preferred stockholders on capital account, or, for that matter, inferior to all claimants except the common stockholders with respect to dividends from surplus. The employment of such issues as means of financing in unexpected crises in which the stockholders must act both quickly and without notice to the public in order to save financial ruin, is little understood. Students of finance and financiers seem to have given little thought to this emergency device.
[5] *Loc. cit.*

accounts payable, even though an explanatory note appears, is not the proper form of statement; subordinated claims or debts should be separately stated next preceding capital items.

The commonest kind of subordinated debt occurs in partnership affairs when a partner lends money to the firm in order to provide additional firm funds either permanently or for the time being. Of this kind of transaction Montgomery says:[6]

... In the case of a general partnership [7] there can be no liability to any partner. So-called loans from the partners are not debts. ... In published balance sheets all the partners' accounts, *debit* and *credit*, should be merged in one, and set up as the net capital of the partnership.

In the case of so-called limited partnerships [8] the relationship of debtor and creditor between the partnership entity and individual partners may or may not exist, depending on the facts and the state laws. If the subordination is of a temporary character the limitation should be clearly shown.

The Definitions Applied.—Rightly viewed, the question is not is the item under consideration a liability or a capital (net proprietorship) item; the significant inquiry is rather is the item a liability or not a liability? Is the claim represented adverse to the interest of the proprietor? Observe that the latter question is not is the result of the transaction out of which the claim arose adverse to the interest of the proprietor, but is the claim itself adverse to his interest? When the suggestion test is made, the difficulties that have suggested themselves to the accountants and the writers on accountancy are much less puzzling.

---

[6] *Loc. cit.*
[7] A general partnership is one in which all members of the firm are jointly and unlimitedly liable for all debts incurred by the firm upon contracts of any kind, and jointly and severally liable upon all torts chargeable against the firm.
[8] A limited partnership is one organized in conformity to a statute that permits the limitation of liability of one or more (but not of all) partners to the amounts contributed by them. Such firms consist of one or more special partners having limited liability and one or more general partners having unlimited liabilities.

The application of the test in the "so-called debenture bonds" case quoted from Montgomery above makes these "bonds" clearly *not a liability.* The proprietor in question is presumably a corporation. By the terms of the issue no claim of any kind can be enforced against the proprietor "for principal or interest at any time when there is any obligation direct or indirect to others." That is to say, so long as there is any contract between the company and another person not wholly and completely performed on the company's part, and so long as any tort or criminal liability exists undischarged, no claim can be enforced. This clearly amounts to saying that so long as the corporate entity exists, or so long as the objects for which the corporation became a proprietor exist, no claim can be enforced under this contract. The payment of the interest and/or the principal is wholly within the discretion of the corporation so long as it operates an enterprise. To be sure the "bonds" have one of the attributes of a liability; they are, within their terms, legally or equitably enforceable; but the contingency upon which the remedy of the holder depends cannot occur until there is a winding up of the affairs of the company either voluntarily or by process of law other than action upon these instruments. Legally the "bonds" may be debts; but they lack the economic attribute of adverseness to the proprietor's interest.

The same test applied to any subordinated debt, once the full effect of the agreement is understood—and professional accountants take legal advice in such matters—will, it is believed, leave no room for doubt as to whether the debt is or is not a liability within the meaning of good accounting practice. Predominantly the treatment of subordinated debts actually found in accounting practice conforms to the definition given in this book. Indeed, the definition is framed to describe the best practice rather than to express the writer's notion of what ought, ideally, to be the definition.

Intra-Firm Debts.—The subordinated debt arising from a loan made by a partner to the firm may require some elucidation. Montgomery's statement quoted above that "in the case of the general partnership there can be no liability to any partner" is true with respect to the firm as a holder of assets. For the lending partner cannot enforce any rights by action at law against the firm so long as it continues to be a firm. The repayment, during the currency of the firm, is discretionary with the firm; and it is, therefore, not adverse to the firm's interest. But when Montgomery says in the next sentence "so-called loans from partners are not debts," he goes too far, farther, moreover, than is really necessary to the matter under discussion. As between the members of the firm as individuals, there is a debt to which due effect will be given in a winding up, or in an action against a member of the firm, as a private person, by his personal creditors. All liabilities in the accounting sense are debts in the legal sense, but the converse is not true.

Priority as a Distinction

The writings on accountancy are full of the notion that the distinction between liabilities and net proprietorship is in some way or other dependent on the relative legal priority of claims. To discriminate upon that basis would require a fixing upon some point along the scale between the claim for taxes due and that of the residual claimant (whoever he may be or upon whatever ground he claims) above which the claims are liabilities, and below which they are items of net proprietorship. Many have essayed that task, but none has suggested a mode of ascertaining that point that describes practice accurately. Let it not be understood that the writer disapproves of the attempt; for the notion of spacing of claims along the scale of priority often has much to commend it. The only objection urged here is that no one so far has proposed a realistic or *de facto* discrimination—one that is in substantial accord with practice.

Itemization of Net Proprietorship.—The fact that in the section of the balance sheet labeled "net proprietorship," or "capital," or "net worth," and so on, one usually finds several items the sum of the valuations of which is equal to the difference between the valuation of proprietorship and the sum of the liability valuations, is taken by many to mean that somehow or other this sum is found from the items. This, of course, is not the case. The items, if items are shown, are the result of analysis of the sum. Thus in a corporation's statement we may find:

Net proprietorship:		
Capital stock preferred............	$50,000	
Capital stock common............	50,000	
Surplus........................	25,000	
		$125,000

or we may find:

Capital stock preferred............	$50,000	
Capital stock common............	50,000	
Total capital stock................	$100,000	
Less deficit.....................	75,000	
		$25,000

The amounts shown for stock are but matters of legal history and represent, in their total, a minimum net estate of the corporation in its assets which may not legally be reduced by dividends to stockholders without the assent of the state. The surplus in the first case exhibits the amount by which the actual net estate exceeds this legal minimum dividend-paying limit; the deficit in the other, the amount by which the actual net estate falls short of this basis.

The surplus, it is often said, represents realized profits not distributed in dividends; the deficit, a loss. But we shall presently see that the determination of profit not distributed in dividends and of loss is really made by successive valuations of assets and of liabilities. To be sure, there is a concomitant analysis of the means whereby the changes in these two sums have come about.

Terminological Difficulties

Difficulties of Interpretation.—One whose work requires him to read many balance sheets must often read many that are faultily expressed. Much the same kind of difficulties are encountered in the right-hand member of the balance sheet as are found in the other. The chief faults include both faults of expression and faults of analysis. The incompletely labeled item, the misleading or vague caption, the presence of valuation account balances and misplaced items, all cause grief to the reader. There are, of course, faults of valuation in addition, but these will be discussed in later chapters.

For the too brief statement, either with respect to the adequacy of captions or the refinement of classification, there is no help. Financial journals often give a large amount of space to the publication of a multitude of balance sheets each so much telescoped together both in caption and in classification that almost no reliable opinion can be based upon them. Fewer and better balance sheets would be preferable.

Meanings of "Reserves."—That the work of the professional public accountant suffers from the poverty of technical vocabulary, is nowhere more patent to the careful reader than in the bewildering variety of "reserves" that he encounters in the balance sheet—particularly in its right-hand member. We may find "reserves for depreciation" of specified assets, "reserves for obsolescence," and "reserves for bad debts," that are but balances of valuation accounts and express, by their amounts, the overvaluation of the items of corresponding assets shown in the other member. "Reserves for inventory losses" may be a valuation account against an inventory overstated in the opposite branch, or may merely express a measure of fear of a further loss in a period of slow sales or of falling commodity prices. There are "reserves for replacement" which may or may not implicitly include both a valuation account for depreciation and a measure (in the same total) of an expectation of replacing at a higher cost. "Reserves for taxes" appear that are pure liabilities, although, of course, they may be mistakenly valued since taxes can seldom be accurately foreknown.

"Reserves for sinking funds" or for "depletion funds" occur—often without due explanation to show what really is being done or why. "Reserves for depreciation of goodwill" and of "organization expense" stand out as mere valuation accounts against opposed valuation accounts. Reserves for contingencies may mean expectations of loss that range from highly probable loss to remotely possible loss.

Where enterprises of established good reputation overwork the term reserve, one can usually determine by the context—particularly the items that enter into the same sub-total—whether the reserve is a valuation account only, a liability, an analytical element within the net proprietorship difference, or a recognition of a future contingent happening that may turn out well or badly. Where the reputation of the accountant is not known, the reader will do well to make broad allowances in his inferences, or make independent inquiry.

Fortunately, hope for relief seems reasonable. The efforts of The American Institute of Accountants, especially through their committee on terminology, and the writings of those who are both accountants and writers on accountancy, such as Finney, Jackson, McKinsey, and Montgomery, seem to be bearing fruit. In most balance sheets put out by the leading firms, nearly all the valuation accounts against assets and goodwill have disappeared from the right-hand member and are treated as deductions (on the face of the asset statement) from the items against which they are set up on the books. Few of the statements prepared by these leading firms omit a plain sub-totaling of current liabilities, of fixed liabilities, and of total liabilities. It is not too much to hope that others will soon follow this excellent example.

Despite recent improvements in practice, however, there are many items that are commonly misunderstood. As we have already seen,[a] discount on bonds, a valuation account, is characteristically not shown as a deduction from the par of the issue to show a present (adverse) worth; and certain other valuation accounts, such as accrued interest payable, are set up as though they were independent liabilities.

Working Capital Ratios.—Those to whom the ratio of current assets to current liabilities seems of importance are often mistaken in the amounts they insert into the ratios. If, for instance, a dividend has been declared by a resolution which directs a separate fund of assets to be created, such as a special dividend account with the bank that acts as fiscal agent, from which to pay this dividend, the status of this fund, once segregated, gives a special meaning to the item. For when such a fund is created the legal title may have passed to the banker and the equitable title to the shareholders. When this is true, the fund, though it may appear either as an unsegregated portion of cash or as a separate current asset, is not a true asset in the sense that its services are at the disposal of the concern. Nor will the shareholders be general creditors; rather they are absolute owners of the fund. Though this practice which fails to distinguish between that which is to be paid to shareholders from a fund that is theirs already and that which is to be paid to shareholders as creditors for a dividend declared (without a segregation of assets to discharge it), does not alter the difference between current assets and current liabilities, it does alter the ratio if only homogeneous assets and liabilities are to be taken as the ratio members.

---

[a] See pp. 36-37.

A similar mistake of interpretation is likely to be made at a time when readily convertible securities and bank balances are being amassed to meet an issue of funded debt. These funds may be exhibited as current assets and the issue itself as a fixed liability. But even if both are shown as current items (the issue being due within a year), both the special fund and a like portion of the debt should be subtracted from the totals before a ratio is taken if that ratio is to be employed as an index of the concern's current operating position.[10]

Net Proprietorship of a Corporation

While, on the whole, the practice of accountants in preparing balance sheets leaves least room for excusable mistake in construing the liability section, perhaps there is more failure in construing the remainder of the right-hand member than in all the rest of the balance sheet. For these mistakes the accountant is only partly responsible. Nowadays, when a great proportion of those whose balance sheets are matters of general interest and whose statements for publication are prepared by public accountants are corporations, the accountant's problems in this branch are difficult indeed. He must analyze a figure that is a mere difference; and he must do what can be

---

[10] Of late years much has been written about indexes of financial position and of operating position. Most of these indexes take the form of differences between designated summations or of ratios which one of these sums bears to the other. The present writer, far from regretting that attempts to generalize about certain of these ratios have been made, is hopeful that this kind of analysis will be pursued much further, if only to show how dissimilar in significance a given ratio may be for two enterprises in the same industry despite the large degree of uniformity in accounting that may prevail as between the concerns. The ratios commonly looked upon as significant are asked to support inferences that cannot validly be drawn from them. Though the accounts may be kept in substantially the same way, that way has seldom been determined with a view to giving a common meaning to like values of the ratios calculated. They are often comparable to birth rates, for example, that take no account of age, sex, marital condition, nationality, and religious adherence distributions of the populations to which they refer. No mere uniform method of counting births and of determining mean population can assure ratios of births that are numerically comparable without the widest logical reservations. Accounting ratios should be trusted both for their calculation and interpretation, only to "experts of good character."

done to give as much reasonably clear information as is possible in the circumstances. In the case of the corporation, too, the beneficial interest in the corporation's estate in its assets lies entirely in the hands of shareholders. The shareholders may be few or many, active as members of the board of directors or as officers or almost wholly inactive investors. The shares may be held year after year by the same persons or actively traded in on exchanges; they may seldom be employed as collateral or extensively so employed. There may be only one issue or many issues; and as between any two issues the rights, privileges, and immunities granted to holders may vary endlessly as to voting powers, rights to participate in surplus distributions, rights of conversion and transfer, rights of preference in dividends and of priority at redemption upon liquidation. The number and variety of special covenants that may appear in contracts of stock issue seem to be little understood even by writers on corporation finance, still less by writers on accounting, and not at all by the general run of educated people. The merging of all stocks into preferred stocks and common stocks, or into stocks having par value and stocks without par value is, in itself, evidence of how little of such matters is generally understood. The view that every issue is unique comes nearer being an informed and sensible view than does the one that lumps all stocks into two classes or that finds only two bases upon which to classify them.

Bases of Analysis.—But this is not the whole of the accountant's problem in accounting for shares. He must make a choice among many bases of analysis. He can analyze from the point of view of historical development of the stockholder interest. He can analyze on the basis of division of interest in surplus (or burden of deficit) as between one class of stock and another at the date of the balance sheet. He can organize his statement to show the character and amount of changes in shareholder interest since the last previous report or during a specified period. He can elect to exhibit only the amounts that result from conventional accounting, or he may give effect to revaluations on the basis of costs of replacement of tangible assets. He may elect to show only what is called "realized profits from operations" or he may attempt to account for goodwill or for earnings not yet realized. He may do any of these things, but he cannot do all of them—at any rate, not in the same balance sheet.

The enlightened public accountant (and there are many such), faced with this problem, does the best he can in the circumstances. These "circumstances" always include an estimate of the degree of familiarity with accounting reports possessed by those to whom the statement is to go. In general, those who have criticized accountants adversely for their treatment of this section of the statement, show, in the course of their writings, an inadequate grasp of the problem which usually faces the accountant.

No attempt is made here to consider all items that occasionally make their appearance in this section of balance sheets. Only those that are both of commonest occurrence and of greatest importance can be singled out. To write exhaustively on this subject alone would be to write a treatise—not a portion of a chapter.

Capital Stock.—Few terms used by every business man, investor, lawyer, economist and accountant are less understood.[11] The commoner meanings employed by the accountant include the following:

1. So-called "(Authorized) Capital Stock." This is an amount only—not a substantive thing. It is the maximum amount of the par (or stated) value of capital stock that a cor-

---

[11] To any one who doubts the existence of a multitude of meanings for this term it is recommended that he read the definitions of the term in our statutes, in decisions of courts of last resort, in law treatises on corporations, in texts in accounting and finance. A fair sample of the legal definitions can be got by reference to Fletcher, Cyclopedia of Corporations, items indexed under that title.

LIABILITIES AND NET PROPRIETORSHIP

poration *has been authorized to have*. It asserts nothing about the amount that it actually has except that it is not greater than a specified amount. The accountant rarely uses the term "capital stock" without qualifying word in this meaning.

2. "Capital Stock (Issued)." The par or stated value of those share certificates that have been originally issued to subscribers (not to transferees of those subscribers after first issue) and that have not later been returned to the company and canceled with the assent of the state of domicile. This term asserts nothing about the number and amount of other shares that have been subscribed for and not issued, nor about those that have been issued and are now in the hands of the company (true treasury stock), nor about whether or not the shares issued are wholly paid for. Most public accountants, but not all, employ the qualifying term "issued" where they wish to express this meaning.

3. "Capital Stock (Outstanding)." This is the amount of the par or stated value of share certificates that have been issued and are owned by stockholders. This does not include any share that has been acquired and kept by the company, whether acquired through forfeiture, gift, execution for debt, or purchase, and so on; for a corporation cannot be a stockholder in itself. Of course, it may include shares the certificates for which the corporation holds as a mere custodian or bailee. Nor does this term, in its full sense, include shares for which subscriptions have been accepted, but for which stock certificates have not been issued. It asserts nothing about the completeness of payment on subscription contracts. All too often accountants use the term capital stock without the qualifying term when some "issued" shares are not "outstanding," and/or when some shares have been subscribed for (and subscriptions accepted) but not "issued."

Definition of Capital Stock.—The commonest and best meaning for the term "capital stock," when used without qualifying words, may be expressed as follows: That minimum amount of net (or liability-free) estate of the corporation in its assets which the corporation cannot lawfully reduce by voluntary dividend or redemption distributions to its shareholders without the consent of the state of domicile.[12]

Measure of Capital Stock.—With respect to determining the amount of capital stock, in this latter sense, three classes of corporations may be distinguished and considered.

If a corporation has par value issues only, the amount is:

1. The sum of the par values of all shares to which subscriptions have been accepted under contracts enforceable:
    (a) At the instance of the company; or,
    (b) If the company is estopped, at the instance of the state on behalf of the company's unpaid creditors; plus
2. The sum of the par values of all shares issued, or legally resolved and announced to be issued, as stock dividends; plus

---

[12] This definition is said to be the commonest on the grounds: (1) that its terms actually include all that is included under the term in the overwhelming majority of those balance sheets, prepared by certified public accountants, that have come to the attention of the writer; and (2) that its terms exclude that which is, by a like overwhelming majority, excluded (or at least, not included) by the term in the same balance sheets. No suggestion is made that this definition is the one which a preponderance of certified public accountants actually have in mind. No one knows that. What has been attempted is merely to describe in a few words what characteristically results from the best practice.

To say that it is *the best* is only an expression of considered opinion. An amount conforming to the terms of the expression given above, it is believed, is of prime importance to directors, shareholders, creditors, prospective investors, and to the public dealing with the company in the case of almost all private corporations. The expression of it in a single figure, or in a determinate set of figures when there are several issues, in no way hinders the setting forth of any other information which it may be desirable to give. It is the amount of withholding upon consideration of which the state grants to contributors that special immunity, limited or restricted liability, in the event of failure of the enterprise, that is the shareholders' greatest safeguard and which, for that reason, has made the scope of enterprise operations extremely flexible. It is also the maximum amount upon which the creditor, in the absence of unusual statutory provisions for additional shareholder liability, can legally rely, unless, by contract with the corporation, he stipulates for a larger dividend-free estate during the currency of his debt.

LIABILITIES AND NET PROPRIETORSHIP

3. The amount, if any, subscribed to be paid in in excess of the par value of shares, provided, of course, that the statutes of the state forbid the later distribution of this excess as ordinary dividends; and less
4. The sum of the par values of shares that have, subsequent to acceptance of subscriptions, been redeemed and canceled with the assent of the state.

If all the issues of a corporation are without par values the amount is:

1. The amount of the stated or declared capital stock stipulated or implied by the company, within the limits allowed by the statutes and charter, attaching to shares to which subscriptions have been accepted under contracts enforceable:
    (a) At the instance of the corporation; or,
    (b) If the company is estopped, at the instance of the state on behalf of unpaid creditors of the company; plus
2. Any additions made from surplus legally made by the company, whether the number of shares is altered or not; less
3. The amount, assented to by the state, attaching to shares that have, subsequent to acceptance of subscriptions, been redeemed and canceled with the assent of the state; and less
4. Any reductions, without altering the number of shares, to which the state has assented.

If a corporation has both par issues and no-par issues the amount is:

1. The amount, determined as shown above, for its par issues; plus
2. The amount, determined as shown above, for its no-par issues.[13]

---

[13] No mode of determining the amount which accountants treat as capital stock or stated capital in the case of shares having no par value can be stated with full confidence. No-par shares are too new a phenomenon. It

Capital Stock and Subscribers' Liabilities.—Many attempts to express a mode of determining the amount of the capital stock of a corporation by reference to the liabilities of subscribers to capital stock have been made. No way of doing so simply and successfully has, as yet, come to the writer's attention. Certain numerical relations exist, to be sure, between the amount of the legal liability of a subscriber and the amount of capital stock added by his subscription, but not the whole of capital stock can be accounted for by subscriptions. The right to receive a 100% stock dividend involves neither a stockholder's subscribing for anything nor paying for anything. Such a distribution, however, does double the capital stock. Attempts to describe the measure of capital stock in terms of subscribers' liability are excellent examples of statistical measuring before the nature and significance of the thing to be measured are clearly defined.

Itemization of Capital Stock.—It is not uncommon to find the capital stock itemized. The commonest analysis is by separate issues. The purpose of such an itemizing is too obvious to require comment. Sometimes, however, one finds separate items of capital stock subscribed for and not wholly paid for, of capital stock subscribed and paid for, but for which certificates have not been issued, of capital stock for which certificates have been issued though something on account has still to be paid, and so on. But in the balance sheets in which these latter types of items are found, the accountant has also to account for the amount of assets in the form of unpaid subscription balances and/or for the status of the stock certificate books, i.e., he is accounting for the status of the

---

is too soon to expect uniform procedure to appear, both because the variety of the statutes on the subject is so great and because so little of the meaning of any of these statutes has been declared by courts of last resort. For

corporation in relation to the subscribers for shares or in relation to the holders of its shares.[14]

Surplus (or Deficit) Items.—One more class of items in the right-hand member of corporate balance sheets remains to be considered, viz., the surplus or deficit. In its most general sense surplus is merely the excess of a corporation's estate in its assets, the excess of its proprietorship as defined above, over the sum of its liabilities, its subordinated debts, if any, and its capital stock. A deficit merely measures the excess of the three latter items over the proprietorship. Obviously, there are many ways in which such an excess or deficiency may come about; and it is equally obvious that information of how an existing excess or deficiency came into being may be of prime value to balance sheet readers. The multitude of items, or classes of items into which surplus may be broken up represents chiefly the accountant's attempts to show how an existing surplus was created. Some of the items commonly found have a fairly uniform meaning; others, standing alone, do not.

A surplus or a deficit may exist from the very founding of a corporation. If the consideration paid in by the first subscribers has a value greater than the amount of capital stock, that is to say, if the initial subscriptions are "at a premium," the corporation finds itself with a ready-made surplus. The amount of such a surplus is usually carried forward from year to year under some such title as "paid in surplus," "contributed surplus," or "premium on stock." Excepting in banking corporations, this initial surplus is relatively rare in the case of corporations organized to begin a wholly new enterprise, but

---

[14] It may be worth noting in passing that what the holder of a share has, is not, either in economic or in legal fact, a share in capital stock at all—at any rate not a share in that which is the corporation's capital stock. What the shareholder really has is an undivided beneficial interest in the estate of the corporation in its assets. It is a beneficial interest in the proprietorship. The total amount of all the beneficial interests of shareholders not only may be, but usually is, different from that of capital stock. This is true as well with regard to what is shown on the books and statements as it is with respect to investors' valuations expressed in the stock markets.

is relatively common in recent financing of corporations to take over existing enterprises, or to unite a number of existing enterprises. Not all items of "paid in surplus," "premium on stock," etc., mean that the item was created in the beginning. If additional shares are to be issued by a corporation after its enterprise has proved to be a profitable one, or after a large surplus has been accumulated, they may be issued at prices in excess of par or stated value. The amount of this excess, together with any profit on shares of treasury stock sold, is usually credited to the same account with initial surplus, if any.

A "discount on stock," on the other hand, represents the amount of the deficiency of the consideration received below the par or stated value of the shares issued. Often this "deficiency" is not a deficiency at all in the full legal sense. It sometimes happens that in case of need for the protection of creditors, a corresponding amount could be compelled to be paid in either by the subscribers, or by their transferees, or by the directors who, without proper authority issued the shares at a discount. But a financially embarrassed corporation may issue its shares at a discount without the subscribers' incurring a liability to pay more than the agreed price.[15] This presupposes, of course, that there is no statutory prohibition and that the directors have acted in good faith, i.e., for the good of the entire community in interest. Usually a "discount on stock" item disappears from the books and statements as soon as earnings of a corresponding amount are accumulated.

"Surplus from appreciation" makes many appearances of late years. The amount of this item in some cases represents a true appreciation, that is, an increase in value of assets now held over their value when they were acquired. Increase in land values is the commonest source of true appreciation. In many cases, however, no appreciation has occurred at all. What has happened is usually that buildings, machinery, and so on,

---

[15] Handley v. Stutz, 139 U.S. 417. This case has greatly perturbed the law writers.

are really worth more than the previously recorded book valuations. To the extent that this previous book valuation is smaller than it should be because of excessive depreciation charges, accountants do not hesitate to credit earned surplus for the overcharge. But to the extent to which the previous book value is smaller than conversion value because of increasing costs of replacing such items with new ones of their kind, accountants, if they set up an increase in book value at all, usually credit it to an account called "surplus from appreciation."

"Capital surplus" is commonly seen nowadays. It has no uniform meaning. Sometimes it includes elements of such diverse character as premiums on stock issued, profits on dealings in the company's own stock, appreciation in the value of assets, increase in the book value of fixed assets representing an increase of replacement cost less depreciation over original cost less depreciation, profits from the sale of fixed assets, or it may really mean only the excess of total surplus over surplus resulting from ordinary operations less dividends paid. If an item of surplus under this caption is found, it will usually, but not necessarily, represent an amount of surplus which the directors have no present intention of reducing by dividend payments.

"Appropriated surplus," like "capital surplus," may indicate an amount of surplus not intended by the directors to be reduced by dividend payments in the near future. Unlike the latter item, it usually contains elements earned in ordinary operations. It may also contain any of the elements, except "surplus by appreciation," that are sometimes found in "capital surplus." This "appropriated surplus" is often found in statements that incorporate a "free surplus" also. "Free surplus," when associated with "appropriated surplus," usually means an element of present surplus not intended to be retained, i.e., that is expected to be extinguished in the next regular dividend distribution. Sometimes, but not always, an excess of liquid assets over current requirements, aside from dividends, has been accumulated, though not segregated, in anticipation of a future dividend declaration.

Surplus "Reserves."—"Reserves for plant expansion" (or extension) and the like not only declare an intention not to distribute the surplus but also declare contemplated changes in operating scope and policy. But an intention to "expand out of earnings," or to "plow in profits," is not always, or even usually, declared through items of this kind.

As might have been anticipated from the discussion of sinking funds, depreciation funds, and depletion funds in Chapter III, "reserves for sinking funds," "reserves for depletion funds," etc., are difficult, and in many instances impossible to interpret without going beyond the face of the balance sheet for information. Some bond issue indentures not only require that the debtor pay periodical amounts into the hands of trustees but also that a "reserve of surplus earnings" be created in some stipulated amount or amounts. This "reserve from surplus earnings," or profits, when closely analyzed, is usually found to mean that, in addition to the providing of a segregated fund in the hands of trustees, there must be a stipulated withholding of dividends, during the term of the loan, greater than is required by statute.

In the extractive industries like mining, for example, the deposit under exploitation may be impossible to value reliably. This may be due to a lack of knowledge of its physical extent, of the composition of the unexposed portions, of the conditions of extraction that will be encountered, as well as of the conditions of the market for the refined product. Under such conditions the mineral deposit does not, independently, constitute a good special security for a debt that is large in proportion to the most probable value of the deposit. But this security may be improved, and better rates made available to the debtor, if, in addition to giving a lien upon the deposit, the debtor will agree both to make periodical payments into a fund in the hands of trustees and also to withhold payments of dividends to the extent of some stipulated schedule. A series of prosperous early years followed by later adversity will not leave the creditor upon the secured debt wholly dependent upon the pledged property for the excess of the debt over the fund accumulated. The provision for this increasing difference between assets and liabilities during prosperous years, too, improves the general credit of the corporation; unsecured creditors, as well as the secured creditors, are provided with a greater margin of safety during the currency of the indenture. The two covenants may be better than either standing alone regardless of the amounts involved. To fix upon too large a deposit with trustees may deprive the concern of funds needed for the expansion of the scope of operations; the debtor may be crippled without necessarily bettering the position of any existing creditor. To rely upon a reserve covenant alone may be simultaneously to lose the better marketability of a secured debt and to compel the management, selected with respect to their skill in mining, to take upon themselves the role of general investors.

The writers on accounting, of course, all say that a "reserve for sinking fund" of this kind is an element of surplus, but they do not commonly show the full financial significance of the "reserve" thus provided. Nor do they commonly show that the "reserve" and the "fund" bear no relation to one another, numerically or otherwise, except as provided for in separable covenants in the indenture. It is more accurate financially to speak of a sinking fund *and* of a reserve (or portion) of surplus contracted to be maintained (and/or accumulated) free of dividend reductions. The fact that the fund of assets and the withholding of dividends are provided for in the same contract is a legal accident only. Economically the "fund" and the "reserve" are quite separate things. It is unfortunate, to say the least, that the fund and the reserve should have come to be terminologically associated.

This confusion of the relation of the fund and of the

reserve would not be so mischievous if all "sinking funds" were of like kind, e.g., deposits made, under contract, with a trustee for the benefit of specified creditors, and if all "reserves" were of a like kind, say, withholdings of dividends provided for by contract. But just as we saw in Chapter III that items under the caption "bond sinking fund" may be of materially different character, so, too, do we find that "sinking fund reserves" or "bond sinking fund reserves" are not all of like kind. Sometimes there is no contractual obligation to withhold at all. The reservation may merely record the nonpayment of maximum dividends and/or the intention not to pay maximum dividends, that is, it may merely show the existence of a surplus. The withholding may be made with a view to retiring a debt without refunding and without diminishing the book value of assets below the amount shown immediately after the debt was incurred. But since there may be an intention only, it is clear that either the present management or their successors in office may alter the adopted policy. A contractually prescribed reserve has for the time being most of the effects of a like increase in capital stock. A voluntary reservation has no such effect.

The significance of balance sheets to creditors and prospective creditors could be materially improved if distinctive terms for the several kinds of funds and for the several kinds of reserves could be agreed upon and uniformly employed. Pending this enrichment of nomenclature, an accountant who wishes to be precise can be so only by a fuller description, either on the face of his statement, which is preferable, or in footnotes not detachable from the statement.

"Reserve for replacements" may or may not contain an element of allowance for depreciation of the assets for the replacement of which a reservation is made. The best practice, in the sense that it is more clearly informing, excludes the allowance for depreciation. If an asset has really declined in going concern value since its acquisition and if the balance of the asset account has not, itself, been correspondingly reduced, then *somewhere* in the balance sheet the accountant will have introduced a valuation account. Preferably the amount of this should be separately stated, but unfortunately, this is not always done. If it has become highly probable that a building must be replaced with one of like kind, but at a higher initial cost, instances have been found by the writer in which the "reserve for replacement" account is intended to accumulate to the estimated cost of rebuilding. The increments to this account, therefore, are, on the average, greater than the increments to an account that is intended to grow only to the magnitude of actual cost less scrap value. To set out this larger balance *in place of* the smaller is to mingle what is usually a valuation account with what is usually an element of surplus.

For the sake of uniformity the accountant who wishes to reflect in his balance sheet the measure of withholding necessary to provide for the excess of rebuilding cost over actual cost should show separately the usual allowance for depreciation and the element of surplus withheld to finance the increase of future over past cost. The one item is an element of surplus; the other is a mere valuation account. The writer has found no instance in which a certified public accountant, after having determined an allowance for depreciation that seemed proper to him, has set up a reserve for replacement *smaller* than his estimate of accrued depreciation on the ground that replacement can be made at a cost less than original cost. That is to say, a "reserve for replacement" may sometimes contain an undisclosed element of surplus, but, apparently, professional practice never permits the substitution of a smaller rebuilding reserve for a larger depreciation reserve.

"**Reserves for Contingencies.**"—"Reserves for contingencies" standing alone is always an unsatisfactory term to the reader who has to rely on the balance sheet. The writer has found items with this or similarly vague titles, included among liabilities, among elements of surplus, and in sections headed "reserves," that were not on their face clearly liabilities, clearly surplus, or clearly valuation accounts. Not even the section in which the item appears is conclusive. "Reserve for contingencies," appearing among the liabilities, has been found upon investigation to merge in one figure:

1. A possible loss upon a disputed account receivable.
2. A possibility of a customer's recovery in damages for defective goods sold and paid for.
3. An allowance for loss on notes and bills negotiated by endorsement—not the estimate of the liability, but of the loss resulting therefrom.
4. The balance of excessive provisions made in earlier years, despite the fact that the "contingencies" with respect to those years had become extremely improbable.

This last is an exceptional case, to be sure. In the great majority of cases when this entry appears among the liabilities, it will be found to express the accountant's estimate of:

1. True liabilities, admitted to exist, the maximum amounts of which could only be estimated.
2. True liabilities that in all probability will never have to be paid, as is often the case in subscribers' liability on stock issued, but not wholly paid for, in corporations that show every indication of success.
3. Claims that can be pressed only upon a future factual contingency more or less likely not to happen.
4. Claims asserted by creditors but not yet proved by them to the auditor's satisfaction nor admitted by the debtor.

Since all these listed matters are matters of legitimate doubt, the meaning of the total is clear; it is the accountant's estimate of the maximum amount of doubtful items which may become due by reason of operations, transactions, or other events that have occurred before the balance sheet date. If many independent items enter into the total, the chance that the whole sum may become due is, of course, the product of the chances of the several items. Carefully employed in this way, and accurately and fully described, this item is a truly valuable item of information.

If this practice is followed, "surplus" as a separate figure is generally an understated figure, but the range and limiting values of surplus are clearly exhibited. That is to say, the accountant's figure for surplus (items) is one that he does not expect to have to reduce by reason either of liabilities arising out of past operations or of overvaluations of assets held on the balance sheet date. On the other hand, he does expect *some* increase to be made; and the maximum limit of this increase is the sum of "reserve for contingencies" plus any present undervaluations of assets. "Reserve for contingencies" that the event proves to be in excess of actually maturing claims is credited back to surplus. Undervaluations of assets inevitably find their way into surplus, either by explicit entry or by decreased future charges for depreciation and other expense.

"Reserve for contingencies" among the valuation accounts, if a separate section is given over to them, is relatively rare. No uniformity in its makeup appears in the instances of it that have come to the writer's attention. Perhaps it is only a chance occurrence, but it is true nevertheless, that the balance sheets that do place the item thus commonly bear implications of an unwillingness on some one's part to permit the statement to give a clear picture.

When the item appears in the capital or net proprietorship section of corporations that have enjoyed a long history of prosperity, it may almost always be considered either as an amount of surplus which the directors intend not to diminish by distributions, or as an amount which they will diminish by dividend payments only in the event of a temporary period of reduced profits, or of losses, and even then only after prosperous conditions have returned. But when it appears in the surplus section in the statements of new corporations or of corporations that have had a stormy career, the best guess is that the surplus is overstated. Of course, this may not be the case, but the reader should look beyond the balance sheet.

With respect to "deficits" exhibited as such in the balance sheet, the writer can say that no case has been investigated in which a deficit, when expressed by a certified public accountant, was not real. Unfortunately the converse cannot be stated, nor can it be said that the deficits that do appear tend, on the whole, to be as great as the really existing deficits. As will be more fully discussed later, the commonest case of overstatement of surplus and of understatement of deficit arises out of excessive valuation of assets taken over in exchange for stock issued, particularly in new corporations.

By and large, it can be said here, in anticipation of the discussion of valuation to follow, that large surpluses, particularly of old successful corporations, are understated and that small surpluses and deficits, particularly of new corporations, declare a state of affairs better than that which exists. A somewhat crude but illuminating corroboration of this can readily be made by the reader. If he will merely make parallel arrays of the successive book values of stocks selected at random and of the market prices on corresponding dates, giving due weight, of course, to the dividend-paying record, he will be able readily to see the two extremes emerge. Another easy but not very reliable test is that reflected by the income taxes paid as compared with the sum of dividends declared and increases in surplus, after adjusting for stock dividends, new issues, etc.

"Book Value" of Shares.—Quite apart from what is, and what is not surplus or elements of surplus, and quite apart from the diverse origins of surplus, is the question of beneficial interest in whatever surplus exists. Balance sheets, for some reason or for various reasons, seldom show how the interest in an existing surplus is divided among the several stock issues. Some issues by specific contract can never participate in the gains of the issuing corporation beyond the fixed rate of preference dividends. Surplus beyond an amount necessary to assure the meeting of the dividend requirements is a matter of indifference to holders of such shares. To the extent that events prove the real existence of a surplus, the entire beneficial interest in surplus, no dividend arrearages existing on preferred stock, is in the holders of the junior issues. But not all preferred stocks are of this kind; and the variety of modes of participating in surplus distributions is great, indeed.

About the only attempt to show a division of interest, as between issues, in an existing surplus which one occasionally sees, is an expression of the amount of dividend arrearages (passed dividends) on preferred stock. If a corporation has, let us say, an issue of $100,000 of 7% non-participating cumulative preferred stock, $100,000 of common stock, both issues being divided into $100 par shares, and a surplus of $100,000, and if for any reason no dividends have been declared on the preferred shares for three years, the beneficial interest in the proprietorship is divided between the shares as follows:

Preferred shares:		
Ultimate redemption claim (usually par)......................	$100,000	
Interest in present surplus by reason of passed dividends...........	21,000	
		$121,000
Common shares:		
Ultimate redemption claim (usually par)......................	$100,000	
Surplus attaching.................	79,000	179,000
Total interest in net proprietorship.............		$300,000

That is to say, the "book value" of the preferred is $121 per share, and that of common shares is $179.

But if the preferred shares participate share and share alike with common shares after each has been paid 7% per year, these book values would usually be very different. If the common shares have had total dividends per share equal to those paid on the preferred, the "book values" per share of the two issues would be equal; for the existing surplus is greater than 7% per year on the two issues for the years in which no dividends have been made. If the shares participate, but not equally after 7% to each, still another set of figures would result.

This problem of "book value" of shares seems not to have attracted much attention either on the part of accountants or of writers on accounting. Beyond a footnote on preferred dividend arrearages or a segregated item of surplus shown in an internal column, little help can be got from the balance sheet toward segregating the interests in surplus. Both stockholders, prospective stockholders and those who lend on stock as collateral security, would undoubtedly benefit by such an analysis. But, as was noted earlier, only one basis of analysis is, in general, possible on the face of the balance sheet.[16]

If analysis is made of the same amount on two separate bases, there must either be a series of items not incorporated into the total, or a supplementary exhibit must be prepared, or different balance sheets must be made for different sets of users. What is said of "book value" analysis above should not be taken as an adverse criticism of the prevailing mode of analysis; it is merely to point out that at least one alternative analysis not often made would be useful *in addition* to the one usually made.

Special Purpose Balance Sheets.—Just why the public accountants have, in the main, fought shy of organizing bal-

---

[16] If the primary analysis is on the basis of source, e.g., initial surplus, surplus subsequently contributed by stockholders (premiums on later issues), surplus by appreciation, and surplus from operations, in excess of all dividends declared, it would be a purely arbitrary as well as a confusing procedure to subdivide any or all of the foregoing items into "interest attaching to preferred stock," "interest attaching to common stock," "dividend arrearages," etc.

ance sheets freely with respect to their clients' principal need for information, and have tended, on the whole, to prepare "all-purpose" balance sheets, is impossible to determine. Certainly it cannot be because they do not possess the ingenuity necessary to bettering the usual form of analysis with respect to any one class of interested persons; nor is it because they lack appreciation of the differences in needs for information as between one class of interested persons and another. "Balance sheets after giving effect to proposed financing," "*proforma* balance sheets," "the Federal Reserve Board" forms of balance sheet, which have become familiar to all, are evidence enough both of ingenuity and of awareness of the special needs of particular groups. Perhaps as good a guess as any is that suggested by Montgomery [17] when he says:

> There is much truth in the claim (of the advocates of special purpose balance sheets) that more balance sheets are prepared for the use and assistance of clients who are not interested primarily in seeking credit than are prepared for credit purposes, but as long as the auditor has no practicable method of restricting the ultimate use of the balance sheet which he submits, he is *forced to assume that in every case the balance sheet may be submitted to credit grantors.*[18]

Careful inspection of many balance sheets that have appeared within the last decade prompts the inference that public accountants have had the banker's need for information more prominently in mind than any other's, or that, alternatively, the short-term credit grantors have been able more effectively to express their displeasure over balance sheets in which their requirements are not given precedence than have other groups. The writers on auditing within the same period show a considerable degree of preoccupation with the creditor's reception of their statements.

The day may come when public accountants will elect to serve notice in the headings of their balance sheets that one

---
[17] Auditing Theory and Practice, 4th ed., Vol. I, p. 433.
[18] Italics are author's.

who employs the statement for any purpose other than that for which it is stated to have been made does so at his own risk. Or the public who resort to balance sheets for information may come to appreciate the fact that the all-purpose balance sheet must not be too specially interpreted.

That readers who are statistically untrained are likely to make wrong inferences from a special-purpose statistical exhibit is the common observation of all statisticians—not of accountants only. Accountants, like other statistical workers, must make a choice. Either they must define and limit the objects of their statements and let all who employ the statements beyond the limits take the consequences, or they may try to make their statements as nearly fool-proof as possible. If they elect the first course, they can be sure of much criticism from those who, disregarding the warnings, burn their fingers. This criticism is likely to take that effective form of withdrawal of business. If they elect the other, they incur the charge of being superficial and formal. But certainly it is illusory to hope that any all-purpose balance sheet can ever be well suited to each legitimate class of use; statistical compromises are never successful statistically.

CHAPTER VI

GROSS INCOME

In the four chapters next preceding this one, an attempt has been made to lay before the reader a comprehensive qualitative analysis of the terms which enter into the so-called fundamental equation of accounts. The nature of the interrelations among the terms has been enquired into to ascertain whether we are dealing with an expression of mere equivalence or with one of identity. But an understanding of the mere nature of assets, of liabilities, and of proprietorship, and a comprehension of the interrelations among these terms, is not a sufficient condition to an interpretation of accountants' statements. Not to know the nature of the things measured limits, to be sure, the serviceability of any set of quantitative measures, no matter how familiar one may be with the method of measuring employed. On the other hand, to rest content with a knowledge of the nature of the items without a knowledge of how the measuring is actually done, is to run the risk of serious fallacies and confusions in drawing inferences from the numerical valuations.

But to proceed directly to the discussion of the accountant's valuation procedure without at least an introductory discussion of his treatment of income and of expense would be to invite failure of full comprehension both of the significance of the things measured and of the meaning of the many numerical interrelationships among the measures themselves. Every one who is really familiar with accounting procedure knows it is difficult to draw valid and reliable inferences from accountants' statements even when one's problems are those with which the accountant is dealing directly. But it is much more difficult to avoid errors of inference in employing data drawn from accountants' statements in the study of problems that are not the problems uppermost in the mind of the accountant when he determines his procedure.

The Income Concept

Irving Fisher writes:[1]

> I believe that the concept of income is, without exception, the most vital central concept in economic science and that on fully grasping its nature and interrelations with other concepts largely depends the full fruition both of economic theory and of its application to taxation and statistics.

Unless, indeed, he means to include accounting theory within economic theory and to include accounting procedure within the statistical applications of economic theory, he should certainly have added accountancy to the list of fields of learning within which clear notions of income consistently and intelligently adhered to, are essential to progress and success. Whether the writers on accounting theory have on the whole done better or worse in their analysis of the income problem than the economist, the statistician, and the students of taxation, is hard, indeed, to show. But the practices which are commonly employed in accounting, at least to the extent that public accountants accept them, constitute an analysis of a portion of the problem of income that compares most favorably with the analysis of income made by other professions.

Nevertheless, the writer believes that the accountant's procedure in dealing with income is, in some respects, the least satisfactory part of his procedure. And while the procedure, accurately described in general terms is, comparatively, a respectable procedure, it is felt that a considered analysis of the problems of enterprise income is more likely to become the foundation of improvements in accounting practice than is any other kind of study.

---
[1] *American Economic Review*, Vol. XIV, p. 64.

The Economist's and the Accountant's Income Problems.

—It is of the utmost logical importance that economists who refer to the work of accountants for measures of income should clearly see the differences between the general economic problem of income and the accountant's problem of income. The income problems of the two professions are very unlike both with respect to what is included and to what is excluded; the primary objects of their analyses are different; the relative importance properly attached by each of the professions to what appear to be elements common to their problems is different.

The economist is concerned with the incomes of persons, of groups of persons, of society in general. The accountant is concerned with income as it emerges in enterprise relations; he undertakes to show to whom the beneficial interest in income runs, but he is not concerned with the use to which the beneficiary turns his income. The ultimate concern of the economist is with the subjective appreciation of income; objective valuations of income are to him indexes of that appreciation. The accountant is not, as an accountant, concerned with subjective appreciations at all; his care is devoted to determining a proper dollar measure. Nor has the accountant anything to do with the problem of distribution. To be sure, he endeavors to express correctly the amounts paid to each person and the reasons for the payment; but whether a particular payment is an element of what the economist calls rent, or interest, or wages, or profits, is a proper matter of indifference to him. He has concluded when he correctly describes the class of enterprise operation or transaction that has given rise to the payment. The great preponderance of enterprise income, nowadays, inures in the first instance to corporations. The accounting for income of corporations differs in no essential way, so far as accountants are concerned, from accounting for the incomes of enterprises in which the proprietor is a natural person or persons. The economist, on the other hand, is not ultimately concerned with the incomes of corporations at all; he is interested in the matter of what natural persons benefit by these incomes (and who is injured by them), as well as in the question of when the benefits become available to natural persons.

With social income, as the economist conceives it, the accountant has nothing to do. Whether the income arising out of enterprise affairs is associated wholly with a concomitant beneficial service rendered to society or is totally divorced from such a service, is not for him to inquire into. Whether a profit is a wholly speculative one gained at the expense of another, losing speculator, or is a profit arising from the sale of goods that allow a large consumer's surplus to all purchasers, is no concern of the accountant.

The accountant pays little attention to what the economists call "real income" and "final objective income," in contradistinction to money income. Indeed, in what accountants explicitly refer to as income or expense, they pay no attention to changes in purchasing power at all; their income is dollar income. The amount of this dollar income, as will readily be seen, is not unaffected by changes in the purchasing power of money, but as we shall see, the influence is due to the methods of valuation employed and not to a conscious attempt to set up a "purchasing-power accountancy."

Confusing Terminology.—Differences between the problems of the two professions cannot be shown, however, to account for all the differences in the meaning of the terms employed in discussing income, nor can the differences in problems account for all the differences in modes of measuring income. One finds the terms "gross income," "gross receipts," "gross earnings," "gross revenues." Any two or more of these terms are likely to be found in use as synonyms. On the other hand, attempts are made to show distinctions, but there is no agreement as to the distinctions to be observed. In some attempts to differentiate, one term will be said to include all that is included in the other, and something in addition. In other attempts, each term will be said to include something not included in the other. The like confusion exists in the terms that refer to net income. "Net income," "net profits," "surplus for the year," "net earnings," "net gains," "net revenues," are all commonly found. No given difference between any two of them can be said to prevail. Intermediate between the gross and the net amounts are to be found a host of items all without generally observed meanings. "Net operating revenue," "net income from operations," "net income before depreciation," "net income before interest and taxes," and so on, appear in the statements of all manner of enterprises.

A diligent search of the literature of accounting discloses an astonishing lack of discussion of the nature of income. One could hardly expect that the profession which, above all others, is most constantly engaged in the statistical treatment of income should have found almost nothing at all to say about the nature of the thing they measure so carefully. Nor could one have expected that the academic writers on accounting, many of whom are economists and statisticians as well as students of accounting, should have paid so little attention to this lack of definition and should, apparently, have made little effort to supply the wanting proposition. But the failure to define is plain; and even those semblances of definition that one finds break down when put to the test; for they do not fit, even approximately, what the accountants do. Just why this state of the writings exists can be a matter of conjecture only. Do accountants suppose the nature of income to be so plain and obvious that a definition of it is not needed, even by beginners and by the public who read their statements? Do they, on the contrary, suppose that no generally serviceable definition is possible? Or have they never considered the difference between the nature of a thing and the measurement of the amount of it? Probably none of these extreme guesses is anywhere near the mark.

But when one attempts to read what is written on the measurement of income both by the practitioners and the academic students, one essays a task indeed! From the introduction of the rules for debit and credit in the most elementary texts, to the conclusion of the most comprehensive manuals, handbooks, and treatises on theory, the problem of measuring income continually crops up. Not only are long sections of the books expressly devoted to it, but also the interrelations between the amount of income and the other numerical values that go into the reports come in for incidental discussion at all points.

Income of a Specified Period.—Nearly all of this discussion of determining the amount of income, however, is limited to the measuring of the income that is attributable to, or is to be assigned to, a particular time-period that is *past*. The preoccupation of the accountant is with the question of what is the amount of the income of a particular year or series of years in the past—not with income as a continuing, flowing thing extending indefinitely into the future. Simple, contractual incomes of specific increments afford the chief exception. There is very little space given to the consideration of the ultimate statistical effects that must result from the succession of periodic measures and subsequent numerical adjustments of those measures.

"Ultimate Total Income" Defined

When one goes beyond what is said about determining annual incomes and considers the inevitable, ultimate effect of the procedures employed, it becomes possible to phrase a general definition of income that does qualitatively fit that which the accountant will ultimately have treated as income.[2] This

---

[2] In Chapters II to V inclusive, the term "income" was employed as a synonym for services (of whatever nature). As noted (page 14), this is in accord with certain economists' usage but not in accord with the accountant's meaning. Hereinafter, where the context does not show plainly the sense in which the term is used, it will not be used without some qualifying word.

can be done both with respect to what may be, for the moment, called ultimate total income and ultimate net income; and qualitative descriptions may also be given to many useful partial summations intermediate between these two.

Ultimate total income is the final fruition in money both of the enterprise assets and of those other services not listed as assets that prove, nevertheless, to have the economic attributes of assets.[3] It is a *final conversion* into money receivings of all those services of whatever nature and from whatever sources that have been devoted to, and employed in, the affairs of the enterprise. Note that it is not *money* but the *conversion* into money through exchange or otherwise. The *amount* of the conversion is numerically equal to the *amount* of the money so acquired, just as the amount of a sale is equal to the money obtained, or to be obtained, as a result of the sale. The money is an asset; and so long as it continues to be held for use in the enterprise, it derives its importance from anticipated future services for which it can be exchanged. Its valuation, in the economic sense, is derived from its anticipated enterprise services. The money and the income, the *incoming of money*, are as clearly distinguishable as are the growing of trees and the trees that have grown.

No pretense is made that this term, ultimate total income, or any other corresponding to it is in use among accountants, but a quantity does inevitably come into existence, the valued items of which have the common qualitative nature attributed to this term above. It is, in a sense, only a concept implied in what the accountant does. The concept has a number of conveniences. The most important of these is that it describes a real thing, real not only in the sense that it inevitably results from what accountants do, but also in the sense that it describes an actual state of affairs. It is a matter of fact.

Being a real fact that marks, in a way, the terminus of the accountant's work in income, it is a useful landmark upon

---
[3] See Chapter III.

which to set a course in observing what the accountant does on the way to this goal.

Ultimate Total Income Illustrated.—An examination of a few familiar instances of this final total income may serve to show its significance as well as to show how difficult it is to determine partial or intermediate incomes. Suppose by the terms of a will $1,000 have been paid into the hands of a trustee to be invested and accumulated for the benefit of a child one year old. The fund is to be realized in money and given to the child upon his attaining the age of majority. Here we have all the necessary elements of a separate enterprise. Suppose that among the first investments is a tax-free, non-interest-bearing note with ten years to run, bought at $613.91. At its maturity the debtor pays to the trustee $1,000. With respect to the entire period from the time money is paid for the note, to its surrender for money, there has been an earning of money. The amount of that earning is the amount of money brought in as a result of the operation, the difference between what was paid and what is received, or $386.09. This, again with respect to this operation only, is the final total income. Suppose now that with $200 of the original trust money two shares of a 7% preferred stock in Company A are bought, one is held throughout the twenty-year period and is sold for $110. During the period the twenty dividends of $7 each on this held share were paid to the trustee. Clearly an earning has occurred here also. From the beginning money status to the terminal money status the amount of bringing in, as distinguished from what was there at the beginning, is $150, i.e., is equal to the number of dollars *brought in*. But suppose that the other share of stock in A were held for one year and sold for $110. Immediately the trustee bought a share of stock in B for $110. This he held for one year, received a $7 dividend upon it, sold it for $115, and again bought a second share of Company A's preferred stock at $115 which he held until the end of the trust period. At this time he sold it for $110. Here we have three separate money-to-money operations, the final total incomes of which are $17, $12, and $121, respectively.

Without specifying the nature of the investments of the rest of the original fund or of the interim dividend and other receipts, suppose that the total turned over to the beneficiary at his majority was $1,790.85. The amount of final total income with respect to the enterprise is $790.85, the difference from money-beginning to money-conclusion. All of these are absurdly simple, the reader may feel. But if one pays no attention to the necessary ultimate results, the significance of what the accountant would report at one-year intervals might easily be lost.

"Ultimate" and "Annual" Income.—Consider what the accountant would find as the annual income for the shares of A stock. Consider first the share held for the full twenty years. For the first nineteen periods the incomes shown would be $7 in each period. In the 20th period the amount would be $17. For the other share the first year's income would be $17. During the second year, no share of A being held, no income appears. During the next seventeen periods, assuming that "market" does not fall below $115, incomes of $7 each will appear; and in the final period an income of $2 only will show. For in this last period a "loss," a difference between buying and selling prices, will be permitted to diminish the year's income. Note particularly that at the beginning of the third year the trustee is no better off than he would have been if he had held the two shares throughout the two-year period. But the accountant will have shown more income for those two years than he would have shown had the two shares been held continuously. The accountant will not in general consider as income the increment in market value until the shares are sold.

Consider next the "non-interest-bearing note." If no reason for doubting the final payment in full should arise in the ten-year period of this note, an annual increment of income [4] calculated at the "yield" rate (in this case *at the rate of* 5% per year compounding annually—although there is, of course, no compound interest paid or agreed to be paid) will be credited to income. The amounts of the successive increments will therefore be amounts ascending at a common ratio of 1.05. The note account or an adjunct accumulation (valuation) account will be periodically debited, and will be given effect in the balance sheet.

The extremely simple character of the enterprise discussed above, together with the extremely simple kind of operations entered into, makes the income problem with respect to single operations easy. But the moment expenses not incurred wholly with respect to and because of a specified operation are encountered, a different problem is met. In the ordinary mercantile or manufacturing enterprise it is wholly impossible, except by purely arbitrary methods, to disengage the elementary operations, complete from cash to cash, from one another. Expenses are incurred that cannot be allocated to particular sale contracts except by methods of which one can say nothing more favorable than that the arithmetical calculations may be correct. The only final total incomes we can find that we can say are facts are those determined as between the dates upon which a proprietor begins and quits an enterprise or between the dates of founding an enterprise and of its final winding up.

Obviously, no one contemplates running one of our great modern enterprises without *some* income reports at relatively brief intervals. It is equally obvious to all who have considered the actual conditions that face the accountant that no annual measure of income, not even gross receipts of money, can be looked upon as a matter of fact. And what is set out as a

---

[4] Some accountants, in the "disposition of income," will credit a "deferred income" or other such balance sheet item rather than an undifferentiated surplus or other proprietary account, but this is no longer common so far as an "accumulated discount" becomes a component in the net adjustment of the net proprietary accounts.

measure of net income can never be supposed to be a fact in any sense at all except that it is the figure that results when the accountant has finished applying the procedure which he adopts.

The ultimate or final income, with respect to a proprietor's *whole tenure* in an enterprise, which the accountant's completed procedure finds is in entire accord, both in nature and measure, with what Professor Fisher calls "realized money income."[5] This is true both as to the gross and the net amounts. But neither the gross annual income nor the net annual income found by the accountant bears more than a rough correspondence, either in nature or amount, to any concept or measure of annual income that economists speak of in their writings.[6]

Gross Income of a Period.—No brief qualitative definition of gross income can be accurate in the sense that it conforms to the practice of public accountants; for practice is not uniform. However, the lack of uniformity is not great enough to make an attempt at a "best fit" definition useless. But fair approximation to accuracy is not enough; for if the proposition can be employed only by those who need no definition as a guide, the labor of phrasing the statement is wasted. To be convenient a definition must enable the person employing it to determine whether any elementary item under observation is, or is not, a component of gross income. Furthermore, when this person finds an item of gross income or a summation of gross income he needs to know the real meaning of the proposition, not merely to remember the "form of words," if he is to make reliable inferences about its importance.

---

[5] See his "Nature of Capital and Income," citations indexed under "realized income" and "money income."

[6] There are, to be sure, a good many definitions to be found that could be stretched to cover what accountants do, but they are either so vague as to be useless as guides, or else the writers of them show in the accompanying text that what they really have in mind to include is very different from that which the accounts treat as income. Some economists have imputed to accountants measures that the latter do not adopt. Fisher's "standard income" is an example. This will be discussed more fully in Chapters VIII, XIII, and XIV on valuation.

In a book of this kind the definition of gross income is of critical importance. But the writer has been unable to find anywhere in the literature either a simple definition, or a simple set of propositions amounting to a definition, that satisfactorily meets the tests just proposed. Nor has he ever been able to phrase a definition of his own that, tested upon good students, seemed to be a sufficiently apt one on the score of convenience. Here, where the writer can have no means of correcting a wrong impression, it seems needful to buttress the major propositions employed with many partial restatements and many comments upon their meaning. While the writer feels that the propositions to be made are at least as good as any in the literature, he would be the last to wish for their adoption apart from what is said about their meaning and apart from what is to be implied from the whole section on valuation.

The gross income of a specified period is a mere summation. It is a measure only. *It is the summation of the amount of gross operating income plus the amount of gross financial income.* It is a summation only, both because the nature of the two classes of income have nothing in common that is peculiar to gross income, and because the *methods of measuring* (not the *unit of measure*) of the two kinds of income are different.

That there are two kinds of gross income distinctly to be recognized and separated is made evident in many ways. Separate summations of classes of items corresponding to the two foregoing kinds of gross income are commonly found in the accountant's statements. Whenever there is any gross income other than gross operating income one seldom sees, in the absence of governmental regulation, a formal total of gross income in the accountant's statements. When segregations are made into more than two items not formally added into a single total it will, nowadays, almost never be found that financial items have been merged in any undifferentiated sub-total with operating items unless the amount of the financial items is too small to deserve a separate listing.

It is plain both from the writings on accounting and from what is said by accountants in their reports that they have regard for a summation of the two classes of gross income, whether they express that summation in a single figure or not. An examination of things treated as operating income shows that these do have qualitative aspects in common that are peculiar to them. This is true also of the items of what are here called financial income. The natures of these classes will now be discussed in detail.

Gross Operating Income of a Period

When professional accountants speak of the gross operating income of a period they mean the *fruition in money (or the equivalent of money), effected within the period, of all those elementary services which are the components of enterprise operations.*

The Fruition in Money.—Note that it is the *fruition* in money—not the money-fruit—that is gross income. When a grocer makes a cash sale, the money he receives is an asset—not income. It is the *bringing in* that is income, it is this *last conversion* in a long chain of events, i.e., of establishing a place of business, of equipping the salesrooms, of acquiring stock in trade, of preparing the wares for exhibit and delivery, and so on, that constitutes gross income. Many objects and persons within the establishment will have rendered non-monetary though valuable services to the grocer that are necessary antecedents to this final service of the object sold. It is this final service only, this service of bringing in money, that counts as income. To the extent that these antecedent services are applicable to future sales, future bringings-in of money, the grocer has assets—not income. In a "cash" business the income cycle and the operation cycle are co-terminous. The cycle begins with money passing from the proprietor; it ends with the receipt of money that cannot be recovered by the person paying it.

The Equivalent of Money.—In many connections this term means only "money's worth," but in the accounting literature on income it has a much more restricted meaning. In the latter connection it almost always means "an ascertained or unconditionally ascertainable obligation to pay money within the customary trade-credit period provided that period does not exceed one year." Moreover the receipt of this money, when paid in, must be a receipt that constitutes a fruition—not a mere change-making. In accounting for most mercantile and manufacturing concerns that sell on short-term credit, the receipt of the unconditional promise to pay money is treated as income in just the same way as the receipt of money is treated in "cash" businesses. The date of the sale, rather than the date of collection, determines the period in which the income will be counted.

Effected Within the Period.—To give an accurate and comprehensive expression to what the accountant considers to have been "effected within the period" is difficult. Paton, whose detailed discussion of this problem is the best in the literature says, in part:[7]

> ... there are many important considerations of law and business expediency to be recognized in the computation of gross income. The ascertainment of the revenue figure is a problem in itself, ... Indeed, the development of methods by which the amount of gross earnings may be determined on a rational basis is one of the most serious tasks facing the accountant.
> For the accountant the problem of assigning income credits to a particular period simmers down to the question, what is the proper criterion of revenue? What is the satisfactory test or evidence of

---
[7] Acounting Theory, pp. 443-444. The student is particularly advised to read his Chapter XIX, "Criteria of Revenue." It will be noted that although he distinguishes between net income (or net profits) and net revenue (elsewhere in his book) he employs "gross revenue" as a term interchangeable with "gross income."

revenue? When is revenue realized? Or, putting the matter more specifically in terms of the accounts, what shall be the signal or occasion for credit entries in the revenue account?

Most commonly the fruition will be considered to have occurred when that stage of a particular kind of operation has been reached at which all the following conditions are fulfilled: (1) the future receipt of money within one year has become highly probable; (2) the amount to be received can be estimated with a high degree of reliability; (3) the expenses incurred or to be incurred in the cycle can be estimated with a high degree of accuracy. The first two conditions relate particularly to gross income itself. There must be little room to doubt that the receipt will occur within a year and no substantial amount to be received must be subject to doubt. The third condition is made necessary because doubt as to the amount of net income and as to the successive partial summations lying between net and gross must be reduced to a conservative minimum.

It is not asserted that acountants *consciously* consider the three classes of conditions set out in the preceding paragraphs. Perhaps many do; and there is evidence in many reports that all these have been considered. On the other hand, the writer has not found a formal expression of these conditions anywhere. They are expressed here merely as approximately descriptive of what actually results in prevailing practice.

It can be said with assurance that recent practice is tending toward finding the critical stage earlier and earlier in the cycle of operations. This does *not* mean that accountants are becoming more willing to take chances in their estimates. There is, rather, less valid ground for doubting the reliability of income measures in the statements of recent years. Accountants have learned more about estimating income; they have more and better statistical records with which to work. Moreover, business operations themselves have become more stable materials with which to work. One of the clearest indications of the latter condition is the decline of the ratio of inventories to total assets that one can readily see in published statements.

There are many stages in the cycle of operations that have been made to serve as the critical stage at which income emerges. In many enterprises that stage is cash receipts; in most great enterprises it is the stage at which the sale occurs (or at which the service has been rendered for which a future ascertained payment separately becomes due); in some instances it is the completion of the goods which are contracted to be sold even though delivery has not been made or tendered; in a few instances the completion of the goods ready for sale even though no sale is made or contracted to be made, is the critical point.

Conservatism, Timeliness, and Reliability.—There are many comparisons and contrasts of these stages in the literature. Far too much of this discussion is given over to the relative "conservatism" of the optional stages. But that overworked term "conservatism" is too often a means of calling hard names and is too little used in any objective, statistical sense. It is quite possible that the receipts of money, in one instance, should be less conservative statistically than sales not yet paid for in another. Where "cash" sales of non-standardized goods are made under guaranties of quality or of performance, the amount of fruition in money that *will ultimately prove to have resulted* from the operation cycle may leave more room for reasonable doubt than there is in the case of credit sales of other kinds of goods. "Sales allowances" and costs of making good on guaranties in the early history of the automobile tire industry bulk large in comparison with the bad debt losses of manufacturers of expensive jewelry. The fluctuations of bad debt losses to which physicians are subject are much greater than the fluctuations of losses by repudiation of orders and bad debt losses together for manufacturers of structural steel. Finally, it would be difficult, indeed, to find an estimate of a final, gross fruition in money more "conservative" statistically than the amount of gold recovered by a gold-mining company even if that gold has not been sold or contracted to be sold. "Conservatism," especially when it merely means "highly probable understatement," is not meritorious. Nor is "conservatism" in any sense more important than convenience. With respect to gross income there are two great tests of convenience: reliability of the estimate, and earliness of the expression of the estimate. A "most probable" estimate, with indicated probable limits of estimating error, is more convenient than a mere estimate of probable minimum. Obviously, the earlier one can predict or estimate the ultimate *effect* of what has been done with a given degree of reliability, the more confidently all concerned may make plans for the future.

It is historically a fact that each new step of the accountants toward recognizing gross income at an earlier stage has evoked a storm of criticism from those who like to regard themselves as more "conservative." But in the discussion thus provoked too little attention has been given to what the reader of the statement may safely or "conservatively" *do* as a result of the condition shown. Attention has been directed upon the "conservatism" of the statements with respect to what will *ultimately prove to have been* the gross income attributable to the past period. A special extreme case will illustrate this.

Suppose a concern all of whose gross income is operating income except that implicit in sales prices which imply a three-month credit period without explicit interest. Assume that all sales are made on 90 days credit and that no cash discounts are offered. Let the books be closed and statements made up four times per year. Consider, now, two schemes of accounting:

First scheme: No gross income is shown either on the books or in the statements until collections are made. The gross income of the three-month period is measured by cash collections only. On the successive balance sheets the inventories of goods on hand *and the goods sold but not paid for*, are shown at cost.

Second scheme: Gross income is shown on the books when a sale is made. The gross income of the period is the summation of sales effected. It is not affected by cash collections at all, although, of course, the net income may be. On the successive balance sheets, accounts receivable are shown at the whole contractual amount less an expressed allowance for bad debt losses.

It is obvious that to the extent of bad debts encountered the latter is a less "conservative" estimate of the amount that will ultimately *prove to have been* the actual gross income resulting from business completed up to the stage at which gross income is first recognized. But of what use would an exact figure for an ultimately proved income be to the management or to the banker of whom a loan is requested? Does the correctness of the last gross income figure, if it represents collections, throw much light on the actual cash resources to be available during the next three months?

If, on the other hand, the second scheme is followed, the amount of gross income of one period becomes the maximum amount of ordinary cash receipts for the next period. The error in estimate of cash resources to become available is limited to error in the estimate of bad or slow debts. Ordinary cash resources for the next period will be the sum of cash on hand, accounts receivable less bad debts, and borrowings made. Cash requirements can usually be more reliably estimated than cash receipts. Both the management and the banker have, in the last period's gross income figure, a value nearly equal to the next period's receipts. Lagged one period, cash receipts and gross income will be highly correlated. Unless the error in the estimate is very great indeed, the management and the banker can "conservatively" plan their forward-looking policies much more conveniently and safely than if they were merely told the amount of money collected during the last three months as a result of sales made more than three months earlier.

Some, but not all, of this predicting value would be lost if the statements were made annually instead of four times per year. For the sales volume, represented by accounts receivable, for the last three months can be compared with the like figure a year earlier. If the amount of cash to come in in the first quarter compares favorably with that of the previous first quarter, there is not merely an evidence of what is likely to happen as a result of sales already made. For the existence of that larger volume of sales in the last three months, as compared with the volume for the corresponding three months a year earlier, is favorable to the inference that a greater volume of sales will continue into the period now opening.

Again, if we cut the credit period to thirty days, something more of the predicting values is lost, but it is not cut to a third of the preceding one. For short-term credits in any particular business can be made to show a smaller fluctuation of bad debt loss. Increased amounts of accounts receivable as compared to the item in the previous balance sheet, since they report the results of a shorter period, argue more strongly for a continuation of large sales into the next month than would a three-month exhibit of sales.

Accuracy with respect to the results of what was done a long time ago does not, unfortunately, carry with it a basis for determining what may conservatively be embarked upon in the future. What may conservatively be done is the all-important matter—not what may conservatively be said to have occurred under conditions no longer present.

If instances are to be found in which the goods on hand are contracted to be sold to vendees in good credit standing and if the vendees can be expected, without expensive compulsion, to perform their contracts, it seems plain to the writer that the accountants' statements would be more convenient if they recognized completion of the goods as the critical stage rather than completed sale. They should show in their statements, of course, what the stage of recognizing income is.

The two tests of convenience, reliability and timeliness, are, of course, opposed to one another. In any given set of circumstances the further back into the operating cycle one goes, the more difficult it becomes to make reliable estimates of that future, final gross income that will prove ultimately to be a fact. Just how far timeliness should be sacrificed to reliability is necessarily a matter to be left to that elusive and intangible thing called judgment. The tendency of modern professional accounting seems to the writer, though obviously he cannot prove it, to be following a middle course. With the improving stability of business itself and with the improving technique of information-gathering services the accountants seem to have managed both an increasing reliability and an earliness of estimate. A higher relative evaluation of earliness of report, the writer believes, would be generally advantageous.

The Elementary Services.—By the expression "elementary services which are the components of enterprise operations" is meant something closely analogous to the economist's form, place, and time utilities. These latter are really utilities only in the sense that they represent an elementary analysis of desirable combinations of service. All of the combinations of services that enter into enterprise operations are mentally resolvable into these economic elements. Accountants, however, do not make this analysis, nor is there any occasion for them to do so. A building may give rise simultaneously to two or more of these utilities. Its structural strength may be a necessary adjunct to moving parts of machines engaged in performing a form utility. At the same time the building is a storage place for holding stock-in-trade until a more favorable time of sale. The combined services of the building in their entirety are the unit services with which the accountant, particularly the cost accountant, deals.

Fruition.—In an earlier paragraph [8] the phrase "fruition in money" was considered primarily with respect to a *money* fruition. That is to say, only those fruitions that *take the form of receipts of money* or the equivalent of money are there asserted to be elements or items of gross income. But not all receipts of money constitute fruitions. Fruition implies an antecedent development, a conversion of one or more kinds, a maturing of something. Some receipts of money imply none of these events. A sole trader brings money funds from his non-enterprise holdings to the founding of his enterprise; he may later add to his contribution, share subscribers may pay in their subscription money to a corporation; creditors may become such by advancing money, and so on. In all these cases and many others there are enterprise receipts of money, but no enterprise development, no conversion, no maturing is antecedent to them: there is no fruition; and no accountant treats them as gross income. Such receipts are antecedent to operations. They neither mark the close nor the prospective results of the close of operations, nor do they mark a closing stage of any mutually completed part of any transaction.

The Gross Financial Income of a Period

The gross financial income of a period consists of the hire earnings, effected within the period, arising from grants of monied funds made by one person (or persons) to another (or others).

Hire Earnings.—The sense in which this term is used here has nothing necessarily to do with either the anticipated or the actual earnings of the granted funds in the hands of the grantee. Whether the actual funds granted are usefully and profitably employed or have been dissipated by mistake or intention is not necessarily of moment to the grantor's accountant. He is concerned with the *earnings arising from the*

---
[8] See page 101.

grant—not with the earnings of the fund. Ordinarily not even the identity of the fund is ascertainable. The ability of the grantee to pay from any and all future funds, and the amount that, under the terms of the grant, is expected to be paid are the material matters to the accountant. Only so much of the amount expected to be paid as represents an earning for the holder of the grantor's rights within the present period becomes gross financial income; that amount of future receipt which represents the amount granted never becomes gross income.[9]

It makes no difference who the original grantor may have been. One who is a successor in interest to an original grantor is treated by the accountant exactly as though he had been the original grantor. The amount of the earnings on 100 shares of United States Steel common now held by corporation Z is entirely independent of the number of times these shares may have changed hands before Z became the holder. The amount of the cost of the shares to Z becomes the statistical point of origin from which measurements of gross financial income are made during Z's continued possession.

Arising from Grants.—"Grants" is used in a common, general sense—not in a narrow or technical one. One who subscribes for a share of stock agrees to grant its subscription price to the corporation for the entire period that the share shall be part of its capital stock. One who takes a share by assignment from a subscriber or other previous holder is not a grantor, but his rights are those of a successor to a grantor; he enjoys the earnings arising under the grant during his tenure of the original grantor's rights. "Grants" is intended to include all loans of money and all extensions of money credit even for deferred payments for goods or services sold, if the difference between selling price and the amount to be paid in

---

[9] Note the difference from gross operating income. The whole sale—not the difference between cost or outlay and sales—is gross income in the operating accounts; in the financial accounts only the difference between the earlier and the later funds, the premium on present over future funds, becomes income.

the future is expressed or clearly implied in the bargain.[10] What we call financial enterprises consist of those whose principal gross income arises from transactions in which the enterprise becomes a grantor or succeeds to the position of a grantor.

Monied Funds.—"Monied funds" is intended to include something more than funds of money. The grant of any funds whatever as *so many dollars worth* is a grant of monied funds within the intended meaning. A subscriber may agree to surrender his plant, equipment, and stock-in-trade *at an adopted money valuation* in exchange for stock in a corporation. Whether that valuation is good or bad, whether it is in excess of the par or stated value of the shares or not, it is this *valuation adopted by the grantor* that marks the point of origin from which the grantor's financial income will be determined. "Monied funds," as used here, does not include any funds of which the grantee becomes a mere bailee even though he is to be a bailee for the whole future service life of the thing. Thus rents of objects, royalties upon patented articles the uses of which are permitted to another, do not become financial income. That of which the use is granted must become the *grantee's own fund* at a money valuation.

Effected Within the Period.—The criteria whereby it is determined whether or not a given earning has been "effected within a period" are various. Two general cases can be put: (1) the transaction that becomes a "closed transaction" within the period; and (2) the transaction that continues after the closing date. The first case is simple. All of the excess of receipts during the period over the value of the asset item at

---

[10] When goods are sold under price quotations that express or imply short-term commercial credits, the accountant does not ordinarily segregate the small financial from the larger operating gross income. But if there is an expressed interest rate during this waiting period, he does make the separation. If there are "cash discount" terms, many accountants—and an increasing proportion of accountants—treat the neglected "cash discount" on sales as an item of financial income. The segregation of financial from operating income is coming more and more to be observed.

the beginning of the period (or at the date of acquiring the asset, whichever is earlier) is gross income in the period. The discussion in the remainder of this section is devoted to those transactions that continue beyond the period.

Of this latter class three sub-classes are recognized: (1) ascertained debts of other persons to the grantor or his successor; (2) shares of corporate stock held; and (3) other transactions continuing beyond the period.

The unlimited variety of forms of ascertained debts makes it impossible here to undertake any exhaustive description of the operations performed by the accountant in determining the amount of gross income from all types of debt security. The effect of these many methods of calculating gross income can be shown briefly and with substantial accuracy. From the price paid and from the time schedule of the increments to be received, no matter whether these are called interest or not, an "effective rate" or "rate of yield" is calculated. Whether this rate is an annual rate, as is usually the case for short-term paper, or is a rate regarded as periodically compounding, as is usual for long-term debts, the security is revalued "to yield" this rate [11] at the close of each succeeding period. If the beginning and closing valuations are equal, the amount received measures the gross income. If the closing value is the greater, the gross income amounts to the sum of the receipts and of the increase in value. If the closing value is the smaller, some accountants show the total receipt as gross income and, later, deduct the decline in value in determining net income. Others show as gross income only the difference between receipts and decline in value, but the latter practice is less common. Revaluations of interest-bearing securities on any other basis than

---

[11] Often this revaluation, with respect to a particular issue, may be scattered among several accounts and several items in the balance sheet. Thus, a 5% bond bought to yield 6% may be shown at cost on successive balance sheets of the same holder, but an "accrued interest receivable" item may value the earning at 5% on par from the last interest-paying date and the residual revaluation at the yield rate may be implicit in a "discount on bonds receivable" valuation account.

"accumulation (or amortization) at original yield rate" will, of course, affect net income and the balance of surplus, but they need not affect gross income at all.[12]

It should be noted that the calculated yield rate—no matter what its time-form, i.e., simple annual, annually compounding, semi-annually compounding, etc.—is made to apply to all units of prospective receipt. In revaluing a bond bought at a discount, this rate is applicable to all future increments, whether these are called interest payments, instalments, or principal. The rate is applicable from the date of the revaluation to the anticipated date of the receipt. But the moment a receipt occurs, the rate ceases to run with respect to the amount received. Figuratively, one can say that the transaction ends with respect to any increment at the date of its receipt. The new use to which the money received is put determines the amount and kind of gross income later to be recorded with respect to that invested asset.

Except in the case of holding corporations, the gross income from stocks held is usually measured either by the amount of dividend receipts or by the amount of dividends declared during the period. The former method is invariably followed if the accounts are kept on a "cash basis." If the accounts are kept on an accrual basis, either method may be followed, but the second predominates. It is seldom that book revaluations of stocks held are allowed to affect gross income; the effect is seen in net income only. Even if the revaluation figure is the higher, the amount of the increase will usually be shown in an "unrealized surplus" or "deferred income" item in the balance sheet, and will not be reflected in the profit and loss statement unless a "surplus analysis" section is added to the usual form of statement.

---

[12] But if a bond has been bought at a discount and, within the period, circumstances have cast sufficient doubt upon its safety to make its "accumulated" value a too high carrying value, the gross income recorded may be either the amounts of nominal interest receipt or interest receipt less a book value decline.

Holding Company Earnings.—If a holding company has all, or nearly all, of the stock of a subsidiary, the gross income of the parent with respect to that investment is, in the best practice, the sum of dividends declared by the subsidiary plus the increase in book value [13] of the shares held by the parent company. If, as is usually the case, the books of the holding company and its subsidiaries are closed simultaneously the amount of the gross income to the holding company is the amount of net profit of the subsidiary that attaches to the proportionate share interest held. It cannot be said, however, that there is even an approximation to uniformity in the treatment of gross income in holding company statements or in consolidated statements. One who wishes to see the extent of the difference in practice can find those differences reflected in the recent treatises on consolidated statements.

This case of adopting the issuer's net income per share as the holder's measure of gross income (earning) per share is interesting for the light it can throw upon the essential unity and likeness of all gross financial income. Here the holder, by virtue of its voting power, has had, in general, a practical power to realize money dividends, had it chosen to do so. The failure to bring about dividend payments clearly expresses a preference for increased investment in the corporation that earned the profits as against any alternative investments that could have been made from cash dividends. The increased interest per share has been looked upon not as a mere equivalent of money dividends but as superior to a like amount of ready money. The exhibit of the earnings not realized in money is, if anything, a more rather than a less conservative measure of gross earning than an exhibit of dividends paid.

From the fact that the small holder could not have com-

---

[13] The book value meant here is the book value in the accounts of the issuing subsidiary. If, for example, the book value of S's stock on its balance sheet is $150 per share at the beginning of a period and $160 at the close of a period, and if, during that period it has declared dividends of $10 per share, the gross income to H, the holding company, is $20 per share on its holdings.

pelled dividends to be paid, it cannot be argued that he would have done so had he been able. His continued holding of a non-dividend-paying stock in a profit-earning company despite the fact that he can readily convert his investment to get a steady dividend payer, should be sufficient evidence of the reality of the earning to warrant the accountant in treating book net income of the issuer as gross financial income (earnings) of the small holder as well as of the large holder. Accountants do not do so, however. On the other hand, it has been their practice for only a few years to show share net income of the issuer as gross income of the holding company. It would be no matter for surprise if the practice were to be extended to apply to all large holders and even to all holders, whether of large or small interests. Especially in the case of stocks, the book value of which lies constantly below market value, and of stocks which advance more rapidly in market than in book value, there could be no valid criticism made of the accountant who took up the issuer's exhibited net profits per share as the holder's financial gross income. If an accountant did so, since this is a departure from custom, he would have to show plainly in his statements that he had treated income in this manner. If detailed annual audits of all corporations were made by accountants appointed by the shareholders who are not active in management, this view would be greatly strengthened.

The question may be raised whether or not increased book value of a share on the issuer's books can ever become a generally satisfactory measure of gross financial income or earnings to the holder. Probably it cannot. In many instances changes in market value might be better, but this latter measure is so open to abuse and to error that it, too, will be unsatisfactory. All that the present author means to assert here is his belief that, in many present instances, the enhanced book value of stock on the issuer's books is a better, more convenient and timely measure than are dividend receipts. Furthermore an important extension of this useful measure could be made conservatively if more corporation accounts were audited by accountants responsible chiefly to shareholders.

Gross Financial Income and Gross Operating Income Compared

The dissimilarities of the two forms of gross income are plain. The service for which operating income is a reward is a service rendered at or near the *close* of the cycle of operation; financial income results from a service rendered (grant of monied funds) at the beginning of a transaction. Operating income reports the results of productive agencies at work in enterprise; financial income reports the results of a bargain. In the operating cycle (from money outflow to money inflow) there may be indefinitely many intermediate conversions from one form of service to another; in the financial transaction there is no service intervening. The sole point that they necessarily have in common is that the recipient has anticipated a procession of dollars toward his cash drawer. The accountant, while he expresses the measure of both processions in dollars, does not make like measurements upon the two processions. Dollar for dollar, the two measures do not purport to have a like significance. The accountant's preoccupation is not with gross income but, as we shall see, with net income. Whether, dollar for dollar, net income can have a common significance despite changing proportions in the two forms of gross income, we shall see at a later stage in the examination.

On an earlier page [14] it was said that no brief definition or brief set of propositions about the nature of gross annual income could be quite accurate; for practice is not uniform by any test yet suggested or that the writer has been able to devise. But deviations from the qualitative descriptions given here are of little quantitative importance. The kinds of in-

---

[14] See page 99.

stances of deviation are many—so many in kind, but so trivial in the importance of any one kind, that it would be foreign to the central aim of this book to give space to them.

Confusion in the employment of the main propositions about gross income given here is, however, inevitable unless the reader is constantly careful to discriminate between the nature of gross income and the measure of gross income. The chief care of this chapter is to show the nature of gross income. To the extent that measures of gross income have been discussed at all, it has been done to show evidence of qualitative differences recognized in accounting procedure. It is recognized, of course, that differences in method of measuring are a tricky kind of evidence from which to infer recognition of qualitative differences. It has been suggested that the gross income resulting from the sale of fixed assets not originally intended to be sold is measured in a way different from that applied to sales of the usual product. Let us take the case of a machine expected to operate for ten years that, at the end of five years, has become inadequate to the concern's needs. Let us say its cost was $1,000, that a reserve for depreciation to the date of its sale in the amount of $500 has been accumulated, and that the machine was sold for $510 in excess of costs of removing it. To set up the entry:

Cash..............................	$510	
Machine account........................		$500
Profit and loss (sale of fixed assets)..........		10

Instead of the entry:

Cash..............................	$510	
Sales.....................................		$510

And upon closing the books for the period, to clear the machine account by an entry:

Profit and Loss (book value of machine sold).......................	$500	
Machine account........................		$500

may appear to be a different method of measuring. But if the latter two entries are contrasted with the first, it will readily be seen that the measure is the same; the record of the primary measure is merely made in a *different place* in the accounts; and a different means of *expressing* the measure is employed.

A quite different case, as between the merchandise sales and the gains upon bonds receivable, is met. The discounted prospective receipts from sales of merchandise now in stock do not enter into gross income. The whole of the prospective receipts upon the bonds do. In the case of a bond bought within the period, a receipt or a conversion of any kind may or may not have occurred. Income within the period may occur without receipts either during the period or within the period next to follow. (This would occur in the case of a bond bought with certain of the earlier maturing coupons clipped.) What is treated as income is the increase in value of all the receipts up to the time of receipt but not beyond. It is an earning, a growing in value—not a product, not a completion of a stage in production within the period.

Physical Analogue of Gross Operating Income.—Gross income from operations can be illustrated by an imaginary physical analogy. Suppose we have a rope being turned out by a machine. The rope is of varying thickness and is being made of a varying number of fibers. The fibers vary in length and fluctuate in cross-section. The rope is emerging from the machine at varying linear rates per hour. Our problem is to determine the volume or displacement of each hour's output.

The rope could be cut off squarely at the machine at the end of each hour's run. The segments made could be measured with precision once for all. But the segments resulting might not be of convenient length for later use; we should have several ropes—not one. The accountant, too, could make final determination of a succession of annual gross incomes if the proprietor would sell out at the end of each year. But a succession of annually completed, final incomes is not generally so desirable as a continuing though inconclusively measured income.

The rope could be taken out of the machine at the end of an hour's run and a total measure made up to the point of meeting the untwisted fibers. But it might be impossible to start off again without leaving an improperly made section; and certainly a reduction in volume of rope per hour would result. If a proprietor were willing to clean up, to get rid of his whole stock-in-trade and collect the money before beginning again, the accountant could make a reliable approximation. But the loss of income due to winding up would exceed any usefulness of the knowledge of the amount of income.

The volume of the fibers could be measured individually before they are fed into the machine. A summation could be made after each hour's run of the volumes of those fibers, the tail ends of which have entered the finished section during the hour. These successive summations could be referred to the successive hour's runs. This, of course, will not give a precise measure of the rope turned out within each hour. Parts of some fibers may have entered the rope but no part of their volumes will have entered any summation because the tail has not gone through. Some fiber tails will have gone in within each hour's run, and the whole volume of these fibers will have entered the summation for the hour, despite the fact that a considerable portion of each of these fibers may have become embodied in the rope during earlier hours. The aggregate of the summations made will be "conservative" in the sense that it will always be less than the actual volume of rope completed by the end of any hour's run. But if it should be desirable that the measure taken at the end of each hour should be indicative, as nearly as possible, of the actual volume of the actual segment to be turned out during the *next* hour, this kind of measure will be little, if any, better than the corresponding measure taken two or five or ten hours earlier. It gives us no evidence of either the cross-section in the machine at the end of the hour nor of the linear rate at which the rope was emerging. This kind of measuring corresponds to income measuring in "cash basis" accounting.

The summation to be referred to a particular hour may be made up of the volumes of those fibers not hitherto counted that have gone in as entireties within the hour and of those that, having started, are fairly certain to be completely absorbed during the next hour's run. The hourly summations made by this method may be either more or less highly correlated with the actual volumes of the segments leaving the machine than are summations of the previous type. The aggregate of all summations made up to any given hour's run will be less "conservative" than the previously discussed aggregate, in that it will always be the larger. This aggregate may, however, be nearer the actual volume of rope turned out than the other aggregate. Whether or not this is true would be determined by the distribution of lengths and of cross-sections of the fibers being employed.

But the accuracy of the measure of the segment that has just left the machine—or, indeed, of the total that has left it—may be of less importance than a basis for an estimate or partial estimate of what may be expected to emerge from the machine during the following hour. As an incident to making the measure described in the previous paragraph, some useful information about the prospective future performance of the mill is gained. It will have been necessary to observe all the fibers actually *entering* at end of the period; for we must determine, with respect to each, whether or not it will probably be completely absorbed during the next period. Consideration of all the fibers entering the mill gives, of itself, some notion of the cross-section of the rope at that point. Determination of whether or not a fiber will become completely incorporated during the next period implies an estimate of the length to be turned out, which, in turn, requires an observation upon the rate of motion at the close of the period as compared with average rates at end-of-hour runs. It is obvious that this incidental information is of more use in estimating the volume of the next hour-segment than any mere knowledge of the volume of fibers *not further contributing to the rope volume* would be. The more precisely this type of measure can be made—without regard to what it actually measures—the more reliably the next hour-segment of rope can be estimated.

This latter type of measure corresponds to "accrual basis" accounting. Whether gross income is credited for all sales, provided their proceeds can be collected within a year of the closing date or whether income is credited at some earlier stage such as the taking of orders for goods on hand and available, or the completion of goods of standard kinds for which there is ready sale at world market prices, or some other stage, the accounting is "accrual" accounting. Accounting for income at one stage is better than accounting at another if, and only if, it gives a more reliable ground for estimating the future final **receipts.**

No suggestion is intended that the physical illustration is, at all points, analogous to the income-measuring problem. It is resorted to, to point out the direction of the view taken by the writer rather than to give expression to it. The problem of measuring income is immensely more beset with difficulties than is most physical measuring. There is no ground for hope that any such precision and reliability will ever be achieved as is commonly made of engineering magnitudes.

Physical Analogue of Gross Financial Income.—It is possible, too, to illustrate gross financial income by an imaginary physical analogy. Suppose a forest tract upon which two principal kinds of timber are growing. One of these kinds, by reason of its rooting habit and the soils in which it occurs, grows at predeterminable annual rates, rates that, up to the stage at which it must be cut for the intended use, increase with age at a common ratio. The other kind grows at rates closely dependent upon an annually fluctuating and unanalyzed complex of weather conditions. Bulk for bulk, when cut we may suppose the two kinds to be of equal importance. A careful cruise, preliminary to acquiring the tract, has resulted in a report showing a size (or age) distribution of both kinds of trees varying from saplings to merchantable trees. The amount of timber that will reach best cutting size can be expected to fluctuate widely from year to year. Our problem is to determine the volume of tree-growth in cubic bulk from year to year.

Among the means of approximating the measure of tree growth might be included the amount of timber cut year by year. After a long succession of years the total bulk cut, assuming replantings to be made, might be expected to approach relatively close to the total growth within that long period. But there is no reason for supposing that the annual amounts cut would ever become highly correlated with the real amounts of growth in the same year. "Cash basis" accounting for a set of financial investments made for widely differing periods with a widely fluctuating schedule of expected receipts would correspond to this kind of physical measuring. It is a kind of accounting to be resorted to when, and only when, no other practicable kind of measure more reliably approximates the earnings. Annual increment in value of financial holdings has a significance not only greater than that of annual receipts, but also a different kind of meaning.

From the assumptions about the growth rates of the trees, however, another measure suggests itself. If we know a beginning age and size distribution, if we can currently adjust this distribution to account for annual cutting and planting, and if we know the growth rates of the successive age groups, we can readily compute a wood growth each year. But, by our assumptions, we can do this for only one kind of trees. The accountant finds himself in the same kind of position. With respect to investments in bonds or other evidences of ascertained debts, he can and does calculate the increase in value, each year, of each future dollar-receipt and the increase in value during the period but prior to receipt, of each dollar received during the period. No such convenient and simple measure is available, however, for gross income from stocks.

Resort could be had to an annual cruise of the tract. Observations of some known function of wood content could be made upon each tree and the wood growth calculated. This, in effect, is what the holding corporation does. Being in a position to control, it can compel an annual accounting by accountants of its own choosing who are expected to report with special regard to the legitimate interests of the parent company. The small holder is not in so fortunate a position. Professor Ripley's proposal for an annual audit by accountants nominated by shareholders [15] has much more to recommend it than he urged. For not only would all too common abuses of power and acts of bad faith be effectually minimized, but even in the case of honestly and capably managed concerns, all shareholders might expect to obtain a book value figure that would be of first-rate importance to them in their private affairs. At present, even when audits are made by reputable and disinterested public accountants, these latter are usually not charged with a special duty to give their attention primarily to the shareholders' requirements for information. More often still, not the entire report of the auditor, but only selected portions of it, are published to the shareholders.

Summary of Chapter

There are many matters to be kept in mind in employing statistics of gross income if the data are derived from accounts. Chief among these may be enumerated:

1. No measure of gross income made before an enterprise

---

[15] *Atlantic Monthly*, September, 1926.

is wound up either is, or purports to be, a precisely determined matter of fact about the history of the enterprise.

2. The gross income of any person, arising out of any of his relations to an enterprise, is never determined as a matter of fact until that relation has ceased to exist. This is true no matter whether that person be proprietor, shareholder, creditor, or what not.

3. But a final measure of gross income that is a fact and that describes a state of affairs in the real world does inevitably result from the accountant's procedure both (a) when the relation of any person to an enterprise ceases in reality, and (b) when any enterprise is wound up.

4. All measures of income for periods less than the total lapse of time during a relationship or less than the duration of an enterprise are approximate indexes only. These indexes are good or bad to the degree that they enable or fail to enable a future income to be anticipated reliably rather than to the degree to which they approximate the measure that will be, or may ultimately be determined to have been, the real gross income for the period reported on.

5. Gross income for periods less than total duration of a relationship or of an enterprise consist of two distinct and different kinds that have no element in common that is peculiar to them. Only when the accountant's further interest in them *as income* has ceased to exist, only when, merged with preceding periodic measures, they become final enterprise income may they come to have a common significance; and then the interest is historical *only*.

CHAPTER VII

NET INCOME

Attempts to convey in a few words an idea for which the term "net income" is adopted as a word sign are innumerable in the literature of economics and accountancy. One cannot always be sure, of course, whether the ideas sought to be conveyed by two definitions are identical or divergent; but the evidence of the published definitions themselves does indicate that the ideas intended to be expressed are often widely different one from another. Confusion of the ideas is inevitable if the same visible or audible tag is placed upon them. Resort to alternative terms, such as "net profits," "net earnings," "net revenues," "surplus for the year," afford no help; for each of these seems to have many intended meanings. When these expressions are employed as a set of terms to indicate a set of ideas not identical with one another, some assistance to the reader might be hoped for. The hope is an illusory one; for many have resorted to the same set of terms but have failed to agree upon the differences to be implied from their definitions.

Fortunately the writers on accounting and the practising accountants have left a better means of discovering their implied meanings than is afforded by their definitions and their comments thereon. One may examine the whole of the statistical procedure proposed by a particular writer for the ascertainment of net income. So, too, may one examine many reports made by the same accountant or association of accountants. One who does seek the concepts of net income in this way will find a much lesser divergence of ideas among the accountants and the writers on accounting than he will find among the economists. So close together are the notions of the great preponderance of accountants that one may properly speak of accountants' concept of net income rather than of their concepts.[1]

Net Income Has No Qualitative Attributes

It may be helpful, before the positive description of the idea is undertaken, to make some negative assertions about it.

No propositions that assign a qualitative nature to *net* income can be maintained. It is a wholly quantitative thing. This is, of course, to be expected from the fact that it expresses the magnitude of a difference between two summations of non-homogeneous things. Even its numerical value has no significance of any kind except such as is drawn from the nature of gross income, the methods of measuring gross income, and the nature and methods of measuring those things the measures of which are deducted from the summation of gross income. Like amounts of net income in the same enterprise in successive years do not, in general, have a common significance. Like amounts of net income for two different concerns may have widely divergent meanings.

Just as in the case of gross income, there can be a figure for final net income that expresses a matter of fact. Between the entry of a particular proprietor and the termination of his connection with the concern, all those events have occurred the measures of which enter into the summations both of the

---

[1] This, of course, does not mean that, given a free hand under a given engagement agreement, most accountants would be in a substantial agreement upon the *amount* unconditionally to be called net income (or net profits) in the statements for a particular year. Many judgments may have to be expressed, as we shall see, upon important matters that are unique or that rarely recur. The treatment of such matters cannot wisely be reduced to rules of procedure. The amount of net income found is not invariant to the purpose of the statements and the nature of the engagement. A net income may be properly conservative with respect to the interests of bondholders or of holders of preferred shares and still imply an optimism not safely to be shared by those responsible for embarking upon the next year's operating budget. Failure to concur in a given estimate of net income does not create a presumption of diversity of concepts of net income unless the non-concurrence is systematically repeated.

minuend and of the subtrahend. Since what is true for each particular proprietor must be true for any succession of them, there can also be a final net income to an enterprise for the whole period of its existence. Just as with gross income, too, no measure of net income earned in an enterprise in a period shorter than a proprietor's tenure can ever be anything more than an index of progress. The deviations of annually computed net income figures from figures that might, conceivably, be ultimately agreed upon, are, in general, much greater relatively than the corresponding errors of estimate in gross income; for as we shall see, certain of the common deduction items are much more difficult to measure with a given degree of reliability than are any of the gross income items.

Nature of Deductions from Gross Income

One often finds loose expressions such as net income equals "gross income less expenses," or "gross income less costs and expenses," or "gross income less expenses incurred and accrued." But each of these deduction terms, or sets of terms, is also commonly employed to denote classes of items less inclusive than all those items that, as a matter of fact, are included in the summation to be deducted from gross income. There seems to be no brief expression less general than "net income is equal to gross income less deductions" that is wholly true; and this expression comes perilously near being meaningless. It is idle to attach any single term to the whole congeries of items that enter into the subtrahend summation unless some new term wholly free of alternative usages is invented.

Adverseness to Proprietor's Interest.—Though the items have no attribute that is perfectly general among them, there is one that applies to nearly all of them. With very few and relatively unimportant exceptions, the items connote the occurrence of events within the period that are either wholly adverse to the proprietor's interests or that have an aspect adverse to his interests. They record events unfavorable in whole or in part to the holder of the balance sheet assets. The events are not necessarily adverse to him as a person, nor are all events adverse to him as a person reflected. Only those that in whole or in part adversely affect his net estate in the enterprise assets are given place. Thus, if A is a sole trader, the amount of personal income tax paid by him will find no place, nor will any part of it find a place in the income statement of his business. The tax is adverse to A as a person but not to him as a holder of assets. But if C is a corporation and pays a federal income tax, the whole of that tax is shown as a deduction from gross income in ascertaining the net income of the corporation. The corporation has no private life; it exists only to hold enterprise assets; the corporation's accountant deducts the amount of the tax not because it is a tax but because the payment of the tax is an event adverse to the corporation as an asset holder.

The items treated as parts of the subtrahend aggregate include things wholly different from one another in every way except in this one adverseness. Thus an identical statistical effect is given to many things superficially unlike. Dollar for dollar, wages paid for valuable services are treated in the same way as bad debt losses that have no favorable counterpart. Repair charges incurred to obtain the future services of the repaired object are grouped with premiums on expired insurance policies. Outlays for raw materials used in operations are given an effect similar to payments of interest and amortization of discounts on bonds payable. The destruction of fixed asset equipment by casualty is not statistically differentiated, so far as net income is concerned, from the using up of fuel.

Avoidance of Double Counting.—The accountant, in scheduling these adverse events, is extremely careful to avoid double counting. The spoiling of a partly manufactured product is an adverse event; so, too, are the payment for the materials that have gone into it, the wages paid for work done upon it, and the overhead charges incurred in its partial manufacture; but the loss of the article and the cost of the article lost have one, not several, adverse effects. If the damage due to spoilage were to be listed as a deduction item, then the items shown for wages, purchases, and a myriad of overhead accounts would have to be diminished below the corresponding account balances. The outlay for a new factory building is an adverse event just as the acquisition of the building is favorable. But the benefit from acquisition cannot be experienced in a period less than the entire tenure of it. The accountant parcels out the adverse element, the outlay, over the series of years in which the beneficial services are to be received. Just as he avoids counting both the receipt of the building and the receipt of the services of the building but counts only one, he avoids counting both the outlay and the expiration of service value. Depreciation expense is not an expense in and of itself; it is the outlay for the depreciating object that is the primary expense. By the end of the tenure of the building it makes no statistical difference in the balance sheet whether the outlay was treated as a single deduction from gross income when the outlay occurred or as a series of annual deduction items the summation of which is equal to outlay. Obviously, the latter treatment is the more convenient for those who wish periodic information about net income. In the avoidance of double counting the accountant's statistical procedure is above reproach. Definitions of income, common in economic literature, that include both goods and services, do not have this great statistical merit.[2]

The dangers of double counting are not limited to the relations between deductions from gross income and the outlays for assets. There is a corresponding problem involving

---

[2] For an excellent treatment of this phase of income theory, see Irving Fisher, Nature of Capital and Income.

the relation of these deductions and liabilities. The incurring of a liability is an adverse event; so, too, is the parting with assets to discharge the liability. But the sum of the measures of the adverse elements of the two ends of the transaction is greater than the resultant adverseness of the whole operation. If B borrows money from L, and within the year pays him with a larger amount, the accountant does not treat the money received by B as gross income, nor the liability to pay an equal *number of dollars* as a deduction from gross income. When B repays the loan, only the excess of the total payments over the amount borrowed becomes a debit item in the income account. If the borrowing transaction runs through several accounting periods, there will be a series of deduction items; but in every case the sum of these deduction items will be equal to the difference between what the borrower receives, net, at the beginning, and the sum of all subsequent payments.[3]

It should be noted that more than one way of avoiding the effect of double counting is resorted to. In accounting for liabilities only the net debits, the net measure of adverseness, finds its way into the income accounts. But if purchased goods are on hand at the close of a period, the total outlay for them is shown and a valuation of the closing inventory is deducted from the sum of opening inventory and purchases. The difference, usually called "cost of goods sold,"[4] is a resultant that becomes a component of the subtrahend aggregate. Whether the elimination of double counting is attended to in the body of the accounts only or is set forth in the statements as well, seems to be determined solely upon considerations of utility to the reader of the statements. If a double aspect is more convenient to the reader than net resultants, the fuller primary information is given.

---

[3] It is customary but not invariable practice to "prorate" over the lifetime of the debt all outlays at the time of issue, such as engraving costs, legal fees, commissions, and fees of underwriters.

[4] For a discussion of the meaning of this term, see pp. 131, 132.

Some Deductions Not Adverse to Proprietor's Interest.—

On page 127, it was said that not all the deductions from gross income represent the adverse effects of events upon the proprietor's interests. Many single instances in which this is true could be cited. Let it be sufficient to cite one of a type that occurs more often, perhaps, than any other. Suppose a merchant has taken an order for future delivery from a customer for goods at an agreed selling price. Let the quoted price be great enough to give the merchant his usual gross profit ratio.[5] The merchant orders and receives the goods before his inventory date, but has them on hand when his closing inventory is taken. If between the time the merchant ordered the goods and the inventory date, the "market" (replacement cost) of the article has fallen, and if the accountant, following the rule of "cost or market, whichever is the lower," lists these goods at "market," the effect of his procedure is to increase the subtrahend aggregate and to reduce net income to a figure less than the one that would have been found had this whole transaction not been made. "Cost" will have entered the aggregate through charges for purchase, inward freight, etc., but only "market" will be subtracted. The difference between the two will have become a component element in "cost of goods sold." Not only has the favorable and nearly completed transaction been given no weight at all in the gross income figure, but a purely fictitious adverse event has been permitted to diminish the net income. To be sure, a decline in the replacement or market price is, in general, an adverse event to a holder of merchandise; but this can be true only if a decline in selling price, or increase in cost of selling, follows the market decline. In these days of rapid physical turnover and of obtaining sales orders in advance of delivery dates, oc-

---

[5] Roughly defined, the gross profit ratio is the difference between selling price and cost divided by cost.

currences like the illustration are common. This defect in the rule of cost or market may become more important.

"Deductions" Distinguished from "Dispositions."—Care must be taken to distinguish between the determination of net income and what is sometimes called "the disposition of net income." No balance in any income account in the ledger remains open as at the close of business on the last day of the period. The original, currently kept, income accounts, all secondary clearing accounts, and the profit and loss account itself, are all closed at that time. The balances have all been transferred to the balance sheet accounts. In general the "disposition of net income" means only a reconcilement of the previous balance sheet net proprietary accounts with the corresponding items exhibited in the balance sheet on the closing date. Sometimes this reconcilement consists only in showing just what portions of the net income have been transferred to named balance sheet accounts. Thus the amount of net income may be shown and successively diminished by credits to sinking fund reserves, surplus from the sale of capital assets, appropriated surplus, and to some residual account called surplus, undivided profits, free surplus, etc.

Sometimes the reconcilement will require the appearance of items that have to do neither with the amount of net income nor with any disposition of it. Thus, if stock has been issued at a premium during the period, the amount of the premium may be added to the amount of the net income and the aggregate be distributed. Sometimes, too, the amount of net income, by whatever name designated, will be shown, deductions from it of the amounts of dividends be made, and the residual balance distributed. One will occasionally find language in the statements themselves that seems to indicate that dividends paid are to be given the same effect as the deductions adverse to the proprietor. But the writer has never found a certified public accountant who was willing to say that by the payment of dividends it is possible to prevent the occurrence of net income. Payment of dividends can, of course, prevent the year to year increase of surplus, but that is a different matter.

The amount of net income, too, is unaffected by the formal analysis of the year's events in an income or profit and loss statement. Given an analysis of the proprietary accounts that exhibits the opening balances, the debits and credits during the period, and the resulting closing balances, one can readily find the net income figure without resorting to an income or profit and loss statement. This presupposes, of course, that the accounts have been properly kept. But the significance of a figure found in this way cannot be as plain as though it were developed by the usual methods in a detailed income statement.

Qualitative Difference between Gross Income and the Deduction Aggregate.—Attention is invited at this point to a statistical peculiarity of the difference between gross income and the deduction aggregate. Of the latter it has been said that with few exceptions, the items have the common attribute of representing the adverse effects of events upon the proprietor as an enterprise proprietor. Moreover, all such adverse effects both experienced and in probable prospect are taken into account. But in the previous chapter it was said that the items of operating gross income and of financial gross income have no attribute in common that is peculiar to them. The reader may have wondered why it was not said of gross income items that they represent the favorable aspect of events upon the proprietary interest. It is true that only favorable events or favorable aspects of events are reflected in gross income items; but the converse is not substantially true; it is so far from true that even to state it with qualifications would be misleading. For not only are there many kinds of events with favorable aspects that are not reflected in the gross income, but these events, in the aggregate, may be of great significance. An increase in the spread between cost and selling prices, is, with respect to an inventory, a favorable event. Except in the case of certain precious and semi-precious metal mining companies, oil producers and refiners, meat packing companies, a few quasi-monopolies like sugar refining, and some few dealers in grain and cotton, accountants give no effect to this favorable event. The effect will not be recorded until a subsequent period. Fixed assets, particularly land, may increase in value and that increased value may be clearly established, but the accountant usually gives no effect to it. In many instances where an event has both a favorable and an unfavorable aspect, the adverse effect is recorded as soon as it is in sight, but the favorable aspect is left to be registered in a subsequent period— often long deferred.

Accountants over and over assert their general rule to be: Take all losses, expenses, and other deductions as soon as their likelihood is foreseen; take no gains or profits until they are realized. In nearly all kinds of enterprises the procedure of the professional accountant causes gross income, in point of time of recognition, to lag behind the deductions. A small net income followed by a large one does not necessarily imply a belief on the part of the accountant that the events of the second year have, on the whole, been more favorable than those in the first. Gross income and deductions are *referred* to the same set of periods, but the events giving rise to the two measures are not a set of contemporary events.

Since there are many kinds of important favorable events that may occur without affecting gross income, one cannot employ this characteristic as a distinguishing attribute. To have listed or otherwise described all those favorable occurrences to which current gross income is invariant and to have told in each case when, if ever, the gross income account will respond to them, would have been an interminable task. In the chapter on gross income, moreover, the writer was more interested in fixing attention upon what does—rather than upon what does not—enter into gross income.

"**Ideal Income.**"—If effect were given in gross income to all favorable aspects of those events that are contemporaneous with the adverse aspects reflected in the deductions, we should have a more nearly ideal statistical treatment of income. Differences between the debits and credits would be limited to algebraic signs, and we could ascribe common, strictly commensurable properties to the three measures.

But even then we should not have a measure corresponding strictly to that called "standard income" or "ideal income" by Professor Fisher in his "Nature of Capital and Income." For with respect to the appreciation and depreciation of certain asset types, as we shall see in Chapters IX to XIV, the revaluations cannot be true capital valuations. The *statistical* "ideal" or "standard" income toward which we *can* approach would make net income consist of the algebraic sum of six terms, viz.:

1. Receipts that are favorable to the proprietor.
2. Disbursements that are unfavorable to the proprietor.
3. Appreciations in true capital value (where ascertainable).
4. Depreciations in true capital value (where ascertainable).
5. Increases in "book value" of those assets that cannot have true capital value.
6. Decreases in "book value" of those assets that cannot have true capital value.

Of these six terms, three, the odd numbered, are of positive sign; the others are negative. Terms 3 and 4 apply both to certain assets and to all liabilities. (A numerical increase of a liability, since the sign of a liability is negative, constitutes an algebraic decrease in capital value.)

How near to this statistical "ideal" or "standard" we can hope to approach is doubtful.

There are too many pitfalls into which even the wariest

accountant might fall and into which he might lead his followers. But it can be said without hesitation that the commonest procedure nowadays has made the time-gap between the income and the deductions a narrower one than did the most advanced practice of a few decades ago. The most advanced practice of today, too, goes far beyond the prevailing practice. Meanwhile the reliability of accountants' measures has not suffered.

The opportunities for bettering the measures of income, both gross and net, however, are by no means limited to the narrowing of the average time-spread of gross income and deductions. The greatest and most promising field for betterments is in the realm of revaluing assets and proprietorship. Needless to say, this is a great field and the range of possible error within it is great. Every mistake of a dollar in asset valuation, as we shall see later, carries with it a nearly equal mistake in the cumulative aggregate of net income.[6]

The Income Statement

Every one who has frequently to resort to the accountant's statements is aware, of course, that the aggregates of gross income and of the deductions and the difference between them falls far short of giving a satisfactory account of a year's affairs. If only these three figures were wanted, there would be no need for an income statement as a major exhibit in a report. A mere analysis of the balances of the proprietary accounts would suffice. On the other hand, the very great variety of forms and statistical arrangements of income statements must be bewildering to all except those who have made a professional study of accounts. If the writer's experience with students can be taken as an index, many must have sup-

---

[6] But for the existence of deductions that, like the federal income tax, are contingent upon and determined by the amount of net income or that like insurance premiums if full coverage is carried, are contingent upon and determined by asset valuation, there would be a one to one correspondence between errors in asset valuation and errors in the cumulative aggregate (to any given date) of net income.

NET INCOME

posed that the differences in mode of exhibiting the analyses of income imply corresponding differences in concept of net income. This, however, is not the case. The accountant does not *find* the amount of net income by setting up a *pro forma* statement, filling in the blanks, and performing the indicated numerical operations. His statement is an *expository* analysis, not a process of *ascertainment*. The finding of net income begins with and includes the whole of the bookkeeping done by the staff of the concern under audit. The professional accountant coming in at the close of a period to make a detailed audit makes a thorough check of the work done and a complete analysis of every account in the ledgers. For information and verification he goes beyond the records to vouchers, to correspondence, to conferences with members of the management, to records of previous audits, to any source to which he has access and that promises to give him information. He prepares a great many schedules from his analyses of the accounts, and prepares entries for adjusting errors of all sorts that he has found. In every detailed audit a mass of what are called "working papers" are prepared.

Income in the "Working Papers."—Those who, though long familiar with the principal statements and even the full reports of accountants, see for the first time the array of working papers prepared by the professional accountant, are usually astounded at the number and variety of them.[7] But not until one really understands how each of these is made and how each is used does one really understand how the professional accountant finds the components of income and puts them together. One who examines a few sets of working papers carefully can readily understand that indefinitely many forms of summaries of these papers may be resorted to to exhibit the results of the analysis. Accountants, in general,

---
[7] Specimens of these working papers including representatives of all the principal kinds are to be found in Jackson, Audit Working Papers, and in Palmer and Bell, Accountants' Working Papers.

start from a common point of departure and arrive at a common destination area. But they do not follow a road; they explore the country round about both point of departure and point of arrival; and they explore all the intervening terrain. When they have decided from which route the best view of the country can be had, they are then ready to conduct their party of interested spectators from one point to the other.

Classification in the Income Statement.—In general, the number of gross income items in a prepared statement is small in comparison with the number of deduction items. There seems to be a general agreement that the exhibit of a detailed analysis of gross income is unnecessary. Dollar for dollar there *is* little difference among the elements of operating gross income; and there are few differences between one element of gross financial income and another. Quite another condition prevails among the deduction items. These have only a single attribute in common, but there are many characteristics of some of them that are quite as important as the one they all possess. Moreover, the importance of these qualities changes from year to year in the same enterprise and is different as between one concern and another.

Obviously, there are indefinitely many possible bases upon which the items could be classified and arranged. A very great number of these might, in some circumstances, have a considerable usefulness to some class of interested persons. Division on the basis of relative frequency of recurrence would be of assistance to a budget officer. Division on the score of amounts maturing by months or by weeks would to some extent assist both a budget officer and a treasurer responsible for obtaining bank credits. Division on the basis of departmental incidence is useful to a general manager. Classification into operating, financial, and general groups throws some light upon dividend policy, borrowing policy, and credit-extending policy, as well as upon certain operating programs. Segregation of deductions into groups that represent: (1) past fixed asset outlay (depreciation, etc.), (2) outlays made during the period, and (3) items for which undischarged liabilities remain, can throw much light upon prospective solvency. Division on the basis of degree of correlation between the item and gross income brings light to the solution of the many problems involving unused capacity and inadequacies of equipment and personnel, and illuminates the matter of optimum scale of operations. Segregation of compulsory disbursements (taxes, interest on bonds, long-term contractual commitments, sinking fund requirements, etc.) from voluntary and incidental items often indicates the degree of budgetary freedom possessed by the concern and the deficiencies of its capital structure. A mere listing of the balances of all the ledger accounts kept with deduction items, while obviously confusing and inconvenient to those unskilled in the statistics of accountancy, would have great advantages for the economic statistician and the business man skilled in the use of accounting data; for from such a schedule any desired analytical schedules and groupings could be made up.[8]

It is equally obvious that all of these useful bases cannot simultaneously be employed without preparing multiple statements. Not more than one basis of grouping can be *completely* carried through unless a contingency table is resorted to; and even then two bases is the limit if the results are to be exhibited on a single surface. What is not quite so obvious is that no one or two bases of classification are likely to be useful enough to any one to warrant its adoption to the exclusion of others.

What then is to be done? The implied answer of the accountant is: Do not attempt to stick to any one or two bases of

---

[8] In good account keeping it is a constant concern of the chief accountant that no single item entered in any ledger account shall have a dollar for dollar significance different in *any* substantial way from that of any other item in the account. Given the criteria whereby are determined into which account an item shall be entered and a schedule of the adjusted but not closed debit and credit sums of each account at the closing date, the statistical student of enterprise has an almost ideal set of data to work with. But merge the balances, or the debit and the credit footings, of any two accounts and *some* significance of the original data is lost.

classification but exhibit whatever single items or groups seem to be of greatest general interest to those concerned, and arrange these items in the way which seems, in the circumstances, likely to be the best all-purpose order. Very often the evident intent of the accountant is to throw as much light as possible upon the accompanying balance sheet, or pair of comparative balance sheets, rather than to give the maximum of independent information in the income statement itself.[9] To what extent the accountant succeeds in accomplishing his aims is a matter which may be a fact either about the accountant or about those for whom he makes his reports. It ought never to be forgotten that those who are capable of profiting fully by all the information the accountant is capable of giving are a very small number indeed. Nor should it be forgotten that the number who look to the accountant for help and protection is very great. The accountant forgets neither of these things.

In examining some thousands of annual income statements prepared by professional accountants, very few have been found by the writer to follow any one primary basis of classification. In a very few cases, too, where the statement was intended for other than a single person or interest, has it appeared, even superficially, that any single basis of classification could have been better than some mixed arrangement.

Defects from Economist's Point of View.—But the economist, among others, is often interested in some certain problem that manifests itself in many enterprises, or has its roots in enterprise in general. One who, for example, is interested in the problems of enterprise financing may look to the accountant's income statements for a part of his information.

---

[9] The writer has often heard the accounting profession adversely criticised for their statistical procedures. Among others their theory and technique of classification have been unfavorably commented upon. But the writer knows no other information-gathering group who have carried statistical classification to so high a degree of perfection as that exhibited in the ledgers of concerns whose systems of accounts have been built up and supervised by professional accountants.

But unless he is aware that those financial charges, such as interest and discount expense, which are separately expressed in the income statement may not constitute the whole of the financial charges actually present, he is likely to draw wrong inferences from what he finds. The signs of overstrained current indebtedness are not all disclosed by the statements of current liabilities in the successive balance sheets and by the interest and discount expense figure in the income statement. The balance sheets at yearly intervals may be drawn at the season of lowest current indebtedness. Purchase discounts available during the year that were not taken may have been merged with purchases and inventories to find a "cost of goods sold." Cutting down of the scale of operations during the trade's busy season because of insufficient cash resources is not disclosed. Sometimes special fees, broker's commissions for the arranging of loans and the like are not separately shown, or are merged with interest and discount expense. Inability, because of insufficient working capital, to grant the usual credit terms to all the solvent customers who could readily have been obtained, will not be implied in any exhibited figure.

The accountant obtains all this information. It will all be found in his working papers and audit memoranda. Some of it will be commented upon in his report. But he does not put it all into the income statement in plainly labeled items; to do so would, in most cases, inevitably *prevent his conveying effectively* some other information that seems to him more important to communicate. The really fruitful mine of statistical information is in the accountant's working papers and the books after the audit is concluded, rather than in the general-purpose reports. To adopt uncritically data drawn from general-purpose reports of the accountant in the study of any financial problem of a public character is as dangerous logically as to conclude from the fact that a particular index number of wholesale commodity prices has risen that the cost of living in a particular community has risen correspondingly.

What has just been said is not intended to turn economists and other students of public problems away from the accountant's income reports. Much useful and reliable information can be got from them; and much that is significant can be inferred from them. But one who wants to know all that accountants have learned and recorded about any particular problem will never learn it from their ordinary reports. On the other hand, there is an extraordinarily rich mine of information about income and about the problems in which aspects of income are significant, now almost wholly unworked. It is to be hoped that some day qualified economists will gain access to the files of working papers in accountants' offices.

CHAPTER VIII

THE MEASUREMENT OF INCOME

A Comparison and Contrast of the Accountant's Theory with an Economist's

It is the object of this chapter to compare and contrast the accountant's theory of the nature and measurement of income with that theory most nearly allied to it in the writings of the economists. In the earlier chapters an attempt has been made to describe the nature of income implied in modern accounting practice. Description by comparison and contrast has been little resorted to so far. To some extent the measures of income have been brought into the discussion, but only to assist in making clear the various guises in which the concept of income manifests itself and to indicate briefly the significance attaching to the concept. What is common to the theories of the two professions and wherein the theories diverge, remains to be shown.

The greatest difficulty, perhaps, that presents itself is this: The accountants can properly be said to adhere to one highly unified and intricately articulated theory; economists, on the contrary, have brought forth many theories very unlike one another; and at no time can they be said to have been in substantial agreement. To be sure, the theory implicit in accounting has changed and is changing, but implied changes, once they appear, either drop from sight very quickly or else quickly obtain a general following. Numerous diverse and competing theories do not long command contemporaneous adherence. Differences in points of minor technique, differences in finally resulting summations, do exist just as they exist in all branches of statistical inquiry. Such differences will probably always exist. There is some, but not much, indication that economists are coming closer together in their views.[1]

The second greatest difficulty lies in tracing the ramifications of income theory. This is less difficult in the case of accounting than in that of economic theory. The accountants' theory, directly or indirectly, is plainly visible throughout nearly the whole of their work. But in the writings of many economists, one finds definitions of social income, of individual income, of enterprise income, of family (or other group) income, that seem more or less, sometimes wholly, unrelated to one another. And even in the same writings one will find implied concepts of income not accounted for by any of the explicit definitions. In some cases, indeed in a great many, economists neither express nor imply any general concept of income, but proceed to consider the distributive shares, rent, wages, interest, and sometimes profits, each of which, in a sense, is an element of income. Whether or not these shares account for all income or avoid counting items more than once, is often, apparently, not considered.

Were it not for the fact that the most extensive and most fully articulated discussion of income in economic literature is found in the writings of one man, the present writer's task would have been enormously greater. Professor Irving Fisher's treatment of the subject in his books and in numerous papers, whatever the extent of its acceptance by economists, is clearly the most exhaustive work.[2]

---

[1] Some have expressed despair of reaching an agreement. See, for example, Kleinwachter, Das Einkommen und Seine Verteilung, p. 11. Many must silently have shared Kleinwachter's doubt.

[2] Some development of his theory is to be found scattered throughout his numerous writings, but the great body of his work on the subject is to be found in his "Nature of Capital and Income," and his "Rate of Interest." His principal papers dealing with selected topics include: "What is Capital?" *Economic Journal*, December, 1896; "The Rôle of Capital in Economic Theory," *Economic Journal*, December, 1897; "Precedents for Defining Capital," *Quarterly Journal of Economics*, May, 1904; "Are Savings Income?" *Publications of the American Economic Association*, April, 1908; "A Reply to Critics," *Quarterly Journal of Economics*, May, 1909; "Comment on

The reasons for adopting Fisher's theory as the sole representative of economists' views on income are these: (1) his résumé and criticism of the competing theories is sufficient, fair, and clear; (2) he shows more clearly and more forcefully than any other the significance of the income concept; (3) he shows accurately the status of the subject in economists' writings; (4) he has brought within the covers of one book, "Capital and Income," not only the gist of the matters just noted, but his own systematic and complete treatment of the subject;[3] (5) his concept more nearly parallels that of the accountant than does that of any other economist; (6) his mode of exposition is readily translated into the language of the accountant; indeed, much of his work is in that form of language employed by the accountant; (7) finally, the present writer considers Fisher's theory of income to be, by far, the best that has appeared in the literature. Not only does it show more promise of general adoption by economists than any other, but it suggests more that could usefully be consciously adopted by accountants than does the writing of any other economist.

Even though systematic reference is to be made to only one writer the task is still difficult. Obviously Fisher's theory cannot be set out *in extenso*. No synopsis of such a subject, unless too long to be warranted here, can successfully convey to readers an adequate notion of Fisher's treatment; it is difficult enough, in a brief abstract, to be explicitly accurate. The conspectus given here is intended more as a brief restatement for

---

President Plehn's Address," *American Economic Review*, March, 1924, (the address commented upon, "Income, as Recurrent, Consumable Receipts," is in the same issue); "The Income Concept in the Light of Experience," an English reprint (the original paper is in Vol. III of the Wieser Festschrift, *Die Wirtschafttheorie der Gegenwart*, 1927); and "A Statistical Method for Measuring 'Marginal Utility' and testing the Justice of a Progressive Income Tax," printed in Economic Essays Contributed in Honor of John Bates Clark, 1927 (also separately reprinted).

[3] This is not to say that his later publications in the subject add nothing to the literature; they add much; but the additions are more in the nature of applications of the theory than of development of its essentials.

the convenience of those who are already familiar with "Capital and Income," or who will undertake to read extensively in that book, than as a self-sufficient restatement for the purposes of the present discussion.

Synopsis of Fisher's Theory

Income, in its most general sense, consists of services, that is, of desired events of whatsoever nature. All services proceed, ultimately, from existing material objects; but under no circumstance are material things income; these belong to a wholly distinct, though related, category. The economist is not professionally interested in services that may be had at will by all who desire them; services free to all in amounts adequate for all who desire them, are, therefore, excluded from the concept; all scarce services are included in income.

Scarcity of a service implies an appropriation. To the extent to which any one person benefits, others are excluded. The means whereby services are customarily agreed to be appropriated are called property or property rights. These means are made operative through appropriation of the material objects that are capable of rendering the services. The intent of all appropriation of objects is to procure their services, either in whole or in part, during the objects' existence, or during any lesser included period. Rights to, or in, things and persons are, in economic essence, rights to benefit by their services. These rights are divisible and transferable in innumerable ways. It is through the processes of dividing, transferring, and recombining of rights that we chiefly regulate the flow or succession of those scarce, desirable events called income.

The appropriated material objects that are the necessary means to procuring services, or that are the agents or vehicles for conveying services, are called wealth. The appropriation of objects is the evidence that their services are, or are expected to become, both scarce and desirable. All appropriated material objects, including human beings, are wealth. There are several useful modes of perceiving the items of this wealth. Those existing at any point of time can be considered as a stock from which subsequent services can be had. Such a stock is called capital wealth, or more briefly, capital. We can also consider the succession of items that appear and disappear with the passage of time. Changes in the rates at which items appear and disappear may be noted. We can consider the stock of water (capital) in a pipe at a given moment, or the amount of water that flows through the pipe in an hour's time. We can think of the flowing itself, of a rate of flow, or of changing rates of flow, and so on. All these modes of perception are useful, but not to keep them mentally separate leads to confusion of thought. Mental comparisons between two successively existing stocks have a different meaning from comparisons of successive flows and from a comparison between an existing stock and a subsequent flow from it.

There are three principal wealth-income-property-beneficiary relations to be kept in mind. Items of wealth are to be considered in relation to the succession of desirable events (income) which are occasioned by them as time elapses. One may think of a farm in relation to the successive crop-growings upon it. Secondly, any service or set of services is to be thought of as being parceled out in accordance with existing property rights either—(a) among simultaneously running, coordinate rights, such as those of a landlord and a share-tenant; or (b) among successively running rights, such as those of successive tenants of a farm; or (c) in any combination of simultaneous and successive rights such as those of the landlord, a municipal corporation with an easement to run a water pipe through the farm, and a succession of tenants upon the farm. The third principal relation to be considered is that between persons and the avails of their rights. The tenant may be thought of as one to receive the benefits of his rights to the farm's service. By a tacit assumption of the rôle of property the series of relations can be reduced to two: (1) increments of income and the wealth from which the income [4] flows (or wealth and yielding by wealth); and (2) increments of income (incoming) and the persons benefiting by the incoming.

In employing these wealth-income-beneficiary relations, there must be no identification of income with items of wealth acquired. There must be no confusion of the items of wealth that are produced with the services of producing them. The fruit that comes in is neither the service of the orchard nor the income of the orchardist. The fruit is wealth—not income. The *yielding* is the service by the orchard; the *coming in* is the service to the orchardist. It is only an accident that in some cases the *measure* of the new form of wealth is equal to the *measure* of the yielding and the *measure* of the coming in. When water turns a turbine we do not call the wheel the income; we think of the turning as the service; we measure the service by the amount of work done.

Associated with the capital sources, too, there are undesirable events, disservices, the negative of income. To obtain fruit, human labor must be done in the orchard; tools and machinery must be purchased, operated, and repaired; containers for the fruit and means of transporting the fruit to market are indispensable. The performance of the labor and the providing of means with which to obtain the fruit, to assure the coming in of fruit, are all disservices.

Every economic event requires for its completion the participation of two categories of instruments. There must be an acting instrument or set of instruments, and there must be an instrument or set of instruments acted upon. It is con-

---

[4] The word "income," Fisher observes (Capital and Income, p. 122, note) is etymologically inapt in discussing this relation. It is an *outgoing* of service from its capital source, it is a *yielding*, that we are considering; we are looking downstream from the capital-wealth source. When, in turn, we stand with the recipient, looking upstream, the services are perceived to be *coming in*. The present active participles "yielding" and "incoming" more nearly suggest Fisher's meaning than do the noun forms "yield" and "income." The suggested terminology, had it been adopted and adhered to in Fisher's writings, might well have prevented many of the misunderstandings and failures of understanding shown by his critics.

venient to describe these categories as being, respectively, active and passive. But note that *categories not classes* are set up. The employees and the equipment of a tool manufacturer are active in the making of a hammer, while the materials embodied in the hammer are passive during these operations. Later, the hammer in the hands of a carpenter working at house construction is active, the house-building materials, passive. An instrument belongs to one category or the other not by reason of any property inherent in it but because of the nature of the events in which it participates.

The importance of this double-faced aspect of events, of this participation of active and passive categories, is seen when the point of view of the person who brings the event about is related to the event. That which is done by the active category at the will of the owner constitutes a service of the *active instruments* or *agents* to their *owner*. But the fact that the operation must be performed upon the passive group is a disservice of the latter. When a house owner hires a plumber to repair a leaking pipe, the plumber and his tools render a service to the house owner. On the other hand the leaking pipe, not by reason of its *leaking*, but by reason of its *having to be repaired*, has performed a disservice to the house owner. There has been only one economic event, the repair of the pipe, but the participation of one category is favorable, whereas the part played by the other is unfavorable. To these double-faced events Fisher gives the name "interactions." An interaction is a service of the acting instrument, a disservice of the instrument acted on.

In some events the owner, whose point of view is the significant one, is himself a participant. A man may work at building his own house. His work is a service of his person and a disservice of the house under construction. He does not bring the house into existence in order that he may work at its construction. When, later, he lives in the house, the house renders the service of sheltering his person, but it is a disservice of his person that he must have a house to shelter it. The owner is adversely affected when he acts as a laborer; he is beneficially affected when he obtains final objective uses.

But in the great preponderance of events that occur in modern roundabout economic processes the owner, whose income is in question and whose point of view is determining, does not participate directly either as an active or a passive instrument. He is not an agent nor is he immediately acted upon. He is, rather, an interested bystander.

It is of the utmost importance that those events in which the owner, or person in whose income we are interested, is a participant, be considered apart from those in which he is a bystander. For we shall see not merely that there are both a service *and a disservice* in every interaction—a thing which many economists have failed to see in their analysis of productive processes—but that in those events in which the owner does not directly participate there is a complete cancellation of all services against equal and offsetting disservices. These mutually canceling items are called "couples." We shall see further that the cancellation is one not of equally valued, but different, things; the cancellation is rather of the same event, however valued, that is looked at in opposed ways. We shall see, on the other hand, that there can be no canceling either of labor costs (to the laborer) nor of final objective uses (to the user). That is to say, all cost or disservice ultimately will be found to resolve itself into labor cost, and all income or service into final objective uses. The fringes of the income fabric are to be looked for in those events in which the person whose income is in question is a direct participant.

Each of the concepts, wealth, capital, services, and disservices, can be dealt with quantitatively as well as qualitatively. Each can be measured in appropriate units. Wealth of each kind can be enumerated, or measured in surface exposure or weighed, and so on. Capital, since it consists of items of wealth, can be treated in the same way. Property rights can be enumerated or expressed as rights in so many pounds, yards, acres, etc., of particular kinds of wealth. Services or disservices can be measured in terms of work done (or occasioned) or wealth that has come in (or gone out) as an incident to the operation of productive agencies, or to the holding of property rights. But all these are measurable, in some degree at least, in terms of a common unit, money value. If a quantity of money is exchanged for a quantity of wealth, the money price is found by dividing the measure of wealth into the measure of money exchanged for it. Money value of a quantity of wealth is found by multiplying the price by the quantity. Price and value of property and of services (or disservices) are found by like operations.

The principal concepts thus far introduced summed up in Fisher's own words [5] are that:

... wealth consists of material appropriated objects, and property, of rights in these objects; that wealth in its broadest sense includes human beings, and property in its broadest sense includes all rights whatsoever; that services are the benefits of wealth, ... that prices are the ratios of exchange between quantities of wealth, property, or services, and, finally, that value is the price of these multiplied by the quantity.

The primary analysis of income may be made either with respect to income and its capital source, or with respect to income and its recipient. "Capital and Income," concerns itself chiefly with the former aspect.[6]

From a social point of view neither what we call the productive processes nor any transfers of interests in things or in future services can result directly in any final income. A cotton-growing enterprise, the land, the tools, the farmer himself, and so on, yields raw cotton. If we stop here, there seems to be a yielding and an incoming; but if we did stop here, the incoming would be of little or no importance. After ginning, the

---
[5] Capital and Income, p. 51.
[6] Pp. 121-122.

previous incoming, measured by the raw cotton, has become an outgo. We have no raw cotton left; the farm enterprise and the gin enterprise have yielded baled fibre cotton and seed. To follow one of these joint products only, we will successively see cloth appear and baled cotton vanish, cloth vanish and clothing appear. Finally, the clothing will be worn. All the former services will cancel out against equal and offsetting disservices. But there is no objective cancellation of the final service, the use of the clothing.

With respect to human beings all objective income is ultimately resolved into the final uses of material objects just as all costs or disservices are ultimately resolved into labor sacrifice costs. Between these limits, but excluding both, there is nothing mysterious about the *complete* offsetting or cancellation of all service and disservice items; nor is there anything arbitrary in asserting the equality of the single items canceled against one another. The equality is not a mere conventionally assumed or asserted equality; for the items are *identities*; each *pair is merely one item looked at in two ways*.

The necessity for using up raw cotton in order to get the segregated fibre and seed is a disservice of the two latter items. This disservice is measured by the value of the raw cotton utilized. But the value of this *same* raw cotton, as an *outgo* in ginning, *also* measures the service of *bringing in* raw cotton by the farm enterprise. The ginning of the cotton is a service of the *gin*, but the ginning, which is indispensable to separating the raw cotton into fibre and seed, is a disservice of the *fibre and seed*, an undesired event incident to the *coming in* of these commodities. Ginning is the *same* operation whether *considered* in relation to the machinery or in relation to the products. If the farmer sells his raw cotton, or the ginner, the ginned products, the price paid is identical with the price received.

Every item in the series can be considered in the two opposed ways; and if we are to avoid statistical distortions and falsehoods, every item must be so considered. To assert this complete cancellation is not to set up a mere hypothesis nor to assume a simplified state of facts; it is rather to describe the facts of experience. No social income arises *directly* and *immediately* from any of these intermediate operations. Only final uses appear in gross social income and only labor sacrifice costs appear in social outgo.

Interactions may, and usually do, result in an increase of total utility. This is true whether the interaction consists of a transformation, as of cotton into cloth, or of a transportation, as of sawed lumber from the mills to a building under construction, or of an exchange of one good for another. In these interactions either the services of wealth are applied where they are most needed, or the wealth itself is put into the hands of those who can use it to better advantage. The values to be canceled, however, are connected not with total utilities but with marginal utilities. It is because they have to do with marginal utilities only that the cancellation described is an unassailable statement of fact; for each interaction consists of one event only; and the (marginal) value attaching to that event is numerically invariant to the direction from which it is regarded.

A like result is found from an individual point of view. As a result of his own labor and of the services of his tools, the farmer receives cotton. He and his tools have rendered a common service—the bringing in of cotton. But his cotton has occasioned a disservice—the necessity of working and of using his tools. When the cotton is sold, it performs a service— the bringing in of money. With this is paired a disservice— the loss of rights in the cotton. The farmer buys groceries. His money performs a service, the groceries a disservice. But when the farmer uses the groceries, he obtains a service for which there is no objective offsetting disservice [7] apart from the farmer himself.

---

[7] Fisher does, indeed, carry the analysis one stage further. In his chapter on psychic income, he regards the human body as a transforming agency.

All objective services cancel out against equal and offsetting disservices except final uses, stimuli to our senses and prolongation of our lives. All objective disservices cancel out against equal and offsetting services except the labor of our persons occasioned by our attempts to procure ultimate objective service.

This cancellation of service against disservice in interactions underlies the accountant's rules of debit and credit in his income accounts. When an operation is performed the operator is credited and the product operated upon is debited. When a sale is made, the thing sold (which has caused funds to come in) is credited and the thing received, which has occasioned the giving up of goods, is debited.[8]

There is one primary measure of income and of outgo called "realized income"; and there are two derivatives (or derived measures), called respectively "capitalized income" (or capital value), and "earned income" (or earnings).

If the successive desirable events proceeding from a wealth source can be expressed in money valuations, the time-schedule of these money valuations constitutes a measure of gross realized income. A like time-schedule of the negatively-valued disservices may be prepared. If these schedules are laid out in identical periods of time, the algebraic sums of the items entered in the successive periods constitute a measure of net realized income. If any such algebraic sum is negative, it is called a net outgo. The periods adopted may be of any length,

---

The final form of income is the stream of consciousness itself. To provide a desired and long-continued stream of consciousness requires the provision of stimuli to our persons as transforming agencies. The requirement of means of stimuli, e.g., food, clothing, entertaining spectacles, etc., is a disservice of the body. The text discussion is here terminated with final objective income not because subjective income is of no consequence, but because there is no reason to suppose that accountants will ever need to have professional regard for it.

[8] The accounting principles governing debits and credits are too often looked upon as mere arbitrary, empirical rules. Expressed as instructions to a clerical worker they are empirical rules. But these rules imply a theory of income and expense and of measuring income and expense that economists have been slow to recognize and to appreciate.

THE MEASUREMENT OF INCOME

or may aggregate to any length, not in excess of the duration of the wealth source.[9]

Having a realized income from any item of wealth in the form of a time-schedule of all future dollar-items, the series can be valued as an entirety by the familiar process of discounting the items. This amounts to scaling down each future dollar-receipt to an equivalent present money value and to taking the sum of the terms thus scaled down. This sum is at once the capital value of the item of wealth and the capital value of the income from it, the present worth of the money-valued future services.

Evidently a capital value of an item of wealth, or of the income from that item, can be found both at the beginning and at the close of any period of time during the existence of the object. If to the realized net income within that period is added the increase, or decrease, in capital value during the period, the algebraic sum is the earned income, or earnings of the period. In other words, net receipts plus appreciation or minus depreciation, is the measure of earnings from a given source during a period.

Of the three measures realized income is the elementary and primary one; the others are derived from it and cannot be independently derived.[10]

---

[9] This "realized income" is different from the accountant's "realized" income. Indefinitely many of the items in it may be future items. The accountant reserves this term to denote increments which have been received or, at most, to denote increments that will be received within one year. The accountant is, of course, familiar with Fisher's ideas, the schedule of future nominal interest receipts and of the principal of a bond owned is a common instance of a realized income.

[10] The statement that realized income is the elementary, fundamental concept is often challenged, in the writer's teaching experience, by excellent students. The doubt does not arise wholly from the ground which Fisher anticipates and quite successfully deals with in his chapter on earnings and income, viz., our common habit, not consistently adhered to, of thinking in terms of earnings or standard income. Let the aggregate of wealth that is to be valued (or the income from which is to be capitalized) be an orchard. Its natural income (its yielding) consists of bringing in fruit. The realized (gross) money income terms consist of the money valuations placed upon the successive fruit crops. That is to say, we adopt the value of the *fruit yielded* as the value of the *yielding*. But the fruit is wealth; and the value

Certainty or foreknowledge of realized income is not essential to its effective valuation. If we can form a judgment of the probability, p, that a five-dollar increment of income will occur, that increment is mathematically worth $p \times \$5$.[11] To be sure, we are unable to set down numerical values ranging from 0 to 1, i.e., from certainty of failure to certainty of success, that correspond precisely with the mathematician's degrees of probability. But we can and do experience effective impulses to act upon non-precise estimates that are very like a decision to act upon some stated probability. This state of mind and the resulting valuations that are acted upon may be suggested by a simple case. Suppose an owner of a parcel of unused land offers it to a prospective speculative buyer for $1,000. The buyer in question mentally fixes an earning at the net certain rate of 6% compounded annually as the minimum rate at which he will buy. The buyer feels *sure* that he can get $1,200, free of selling and conveying expenses, five years hence; he feels fairly confident that he can get more by that time; he thinks there is hardly an outside chance of getting as much as $2,000 for it. One can represent such a state of mind with respect to possible prices five years hence as follows:

---

placed upon it is a capital value assumed to prevail at a future time. If we draw up a schedule of such valuations for the yielding life of the orchard, it is a schedule of capital values. If we capitalize this schedule, we have capitalized a series of capital values, a time-series of wealth valuations. As a description of statistical *procedure*—not only that of accountants, but that of all others who do actually value incomes—Fisher's assertion (Capital and Income, p. 236) that realized income is the most fundamental concept and measure is not true. But this is a fact about statistical procedure—not about Fisher's philosophical analysis—for statistical procedure is always incomplete. The basis for the value of the fruit is the value of the uses to which the fruit will ultimately be put, that is, the value to the consumers, whoever they may prove to be and whenever they chance to use the fruit. A schedule of these valued final uses—however many items might appear in it and however these items might be distributed in time—can be conceived with respect to each fruit crop. Whether these schedules are separately capitalized or simultaneously capitalized is philosophically a matter of indifference. Within the limits of its accuracy, which are imposed by the accuracy of prediction of the final users' judgments in any event, a schedule of the capital values of the crops can be treated statistically in exactly the same way as the schedule of valued final uses.

[11] A caution factor, q, is neglected for the moment.

THE MEASUREMENT OF INCOME

Prices possibly obtainable 5 years hence	Excess of price over that previously considered (I)	Estimated chance of getting the increment (C)	Effective future worth of the increment (C × I)
$ 0	$ 0	1.00	$ 0
1,200	1,200	1.00	1,200
1,400	200	.95	190
1,500	100	.90	90
1,600	100	.80	80
1,700	100	.65	65
1,800	100	.40	40
1,900	100	.10	10
2,000	100	.00	0

Summation of the increment values.................... $1,675

Since each increment is multiplied by the estimated chance of getting it, the summation is the equivalent of a price certain five years hence. If this resale price, assumed to be net of reselling and conveying costs, can be had at an annual carrying expense of $25 for taxes and the like, the offer, subject to the caution factor, will be acceptable. For at 6% the present worth of $1,675, deferred five years, is $1,251.66 and that of the carrying charge annuity is $105.31, leaving a net present worth of $1,145.35, nearly $150 in excess of the offer price.[12]

If, however, the buyer in question is a person who greatly prefers "safe" investments to risky ones, even though a proper allowance for the risk itself has been made, he might be unwilling to buy unless some other prospective use offered a greater gain than that implicit in the risk-free, five-year price. Perhaps the most familiar manifestation of the existence and operation of this "caution" factor is that inherent in insurance

---

[12] In the foregoing case no opportunity, open to the prospective buyer, other than resale at the end of five years, was considered. It is not necessary, in general, in purchases actually made for the purchaser to consider all possible future opportunities. If, at a price asked, *any* available employment promises a present worth greater than the quoted price an exchange will occur. A decision to sell at an offered price is not, however, so easily made. Such a decision implies that *no* optional employment open to the seller has a present worth as great as the price offered. Much of the accountant's reluctance to express a valuation of a fixed asset greater than its cost is attributable to the lack of evidence, or the unreliability of the evidence, that even the holder values it at a higher figure.

premiums. The value of a unit of wealth multiplied by the probability that it will be destroyed within a unit of time by a given peril closely corresponds to what is called a "net natural premium." Private insurers must, of course, charge more than this amount—the costs of carrying on an insurance business are not limited to paying damage awards. Assuming correct estimates of the probabilities of loss, the odds at quoted premiums are always against the insured. His willingness to insure at odds in excess of the risk of loss discloses the existence of this valuation factor in valuations. Not only must the purchaser discount for time preference and for risk, but for some degree of caution also, if the discounting is to account for the characteristic spread between a maximum purchase price and a prospective future resale price. The coefficient of caution may, of course, be equal to or greater than unity in some cases.

We have seen that the valuation of each and every unit of a realized income that is not foreknown or assumed, is a product of three factors: the unit under valuation times a chance factor times a caution factor. The resulting product can then be treated, in capital valuation and in earning valuation, precisely as though it were a foreknown item. This does not assert, it should be noted, that the whole future course of valuation can be predicted, for later evidence may bring within the range of possibility items of realized income not hitherto thought of; rates of time-preference change with the changing circumstances of the valuer; degrees of chance are not invariant to new evidence; nor is a caution factor (or schedule of caution factors) a stable quantity. The only assertion made is that at any given moment of time the product of the three factors prevailing at that time can be treated as a foreknown increment.

Fisher's Theory and the Accountant's Compared

The chief differences between Fisher's concept of income and that of the accountants are attributable to three factors:

(1) scope of subject matter contemplated; (2) method of analysis pursued; and (3) point of view taken.

Scope of Subject Matter.—Fisher's treatment may be called general and comprehensive; the accountant's special and incomplete. All scarce services of whatever nature are included in Fisher's concept. He is equally interested in the sources or origins of services, the manner in which services occur, the manifold transformations and interactions of services and disservices that occur between origin and destination, and in the way in which services become finally effective. He considers the totality of primary or immediate services to be had from a given object, the time-distribution of these services, and the dispersion of the ultimate benefits of these services among persons having rights in them. He discusses the mechanism of exchange whereby the flow or time-distribution of final services is adjusted to the requirements of persons. He is equally interested in the complete time-distribution of the final incomes of individuals and of society.

The accountants, on the other hand, are interested in the phenomena of income only to the extent to which these appear in a particular enterprise—though these enterprises may range from the gainful occupations of individuals or groups to domestic establishments or from purely private concerns to national undertakings. Seldom, if ever, does the accountant have occasion to treat professionally all of the income interests of any one person; he never has to treat social income. The accountant deals with the *acquisition and relinquishment of the means whereby final income is to be procured*—not with the primary origins nor with the final enjoyment of it. When the accountant prepares an income statement for a private business enterprise, he describes the extent to which past activities in the enterprise have enhanced the ability of those beneficially interested in the proprietorship to command future final income. Present power to command future final income is a matter of capital valuation; and changes in this power during a period of time is a matter of what Fisher calls earnings or earned income rather than of realized income. The accountant observes the progression of income phenomena in particular component channels; only incidentally does he explore the channel to some of its primary sources or follow down the stream to any of its ultimate delivery points. A fuller treatment of this difference between Fisher and the accountants is reserved to a later chapter.

Method of Analysis.—Fisher's analysis is one of conception. No bounds are set to it by obstacles insuperable to statistical procedure; though he does, of course, recognize the practical *impossibility of a complete statistical analysis of income.*[18] He is chiefly concerned with establishing a self-consistent foundation and with planning a logical framework to carry whatever statistical building material may be or may become available for clothing it. His work is architecture—not construction.

The accountants have no complete philosophical system of thought about income; nor is there evidence that they have ever greatly felt the need for one. Their generalizations about income, to the extent that they go beyond procedure at all, are too inchoate, in comparison with the structure of procedure they have built up, to permit one to suppose that they have ever seriously put their minds to the philosophical task. They have built up their structure of theory only to the extent that they found suitable and convenient statistical material to clothe it in. Their advances in theory seem unlikely to precede development of practice; and practice will develop only when inter-

---

[18] In his essay in the John Bates Clark memorial volume he makes an admirable statement of the limitations of statistical procedure (p. 159) and of the difficulties of appraising statistical results (pp. 179-184) in one topic within the general subject of income.

ested persons become willing to pay for pushing statistical inquiry further than it has hitherto been pushed.[14]

Point of View.—The greatest difficulties experienced in passing back and forth between Fisher's theory and that of the accountants arise from differences in the point of view, or direction in which the observer is asked to look. If one explores a stream from mouth to source and keeps his vision focused upstream, he will recall a very different succession of images from that which he would remember if he worked downstream. Something very like this confusing difference must be experienced by the professional accountant who reads Fisher for the first time; and the economist who is familiar with Fisher's treatment is likely to be bewildered by the work of accountants. Both are likely to get an impression of materially different notions about income that are more apparent than real. In Capital and Income, Fisher says:[15] "In this book we shall need to consider income chiefly in its relation to the capital yielding it rather than in its relation to the owner receiving it." Not only in the book referred to, but throughout his writings, the emphasis is heavily upon this relationship. He follows a downstream course. And even when, in his pursuit of an item, it nears the final recipient, he chiefly looks at it as *going* toward rather than as *coming* toward that individual.

The accountant prevailingly looks upstream from a point slightly above the mouth and observes what is coming down. All income looks alike to him as it passes his reviewing stand. Where it ultimately came from is a lesser concern than how

---

[14] Many recent tendencies support the view taken here. Willingness of accountants to recognize appreciation of fixed assets, when certified to by competent, disinterested appraisers, the increasing number of extensive financial and industrial examinations or surveys being made, and the lively interest in budgetary procedure that is now to be observed, and many other developments, seem to have gathered great strength within the last fifteen years. All of these result in an expansion of the statistical treatment of income and lead to a reformulation of the implied theory of income in more general terms.

[15] Pp. 121-122.

much of it appears recently to have passed and how much of it appears to be coming and when it is likely to arrive. Sources, as such, are a matter of indifference. If a long succession of income elements is in prospect, it is only of secondary importance to know whether the succession of incomes is from a long-lived source or a succession of short-lived sources. It is statistically possible to make summations of that which has gone past and of much that is in sight and on its way down. It is not possible to make statistical observations of all primary services that have left all primary sources, to trace each increment of such service through all its devious wanderings, transformations, dispersions, and interactions, and to make year-by-year summations of all this infinitely complex mass that has run its course or reached any particular stage in its course.

One can mentally picture the yielding of logs by a forest tract, the yielding of sawn lumber of many varieties by a sawmill, the indefinitely great dispersion in space, and in time of use, of these mill products, the infinite variety of final uses to which the products may be put, and the succession of persons who benefit by these uses. One can even go further and picture some of these recipients (they, too, being wealthy) devoting their efforts to growing forest trees, and so repeating the cycle. But one cannot carry statistical procedure to the enumeration of infinitesimals indefinitely dispersed in time, space, and money value. A slice of bread may contain wheat content grown on 10,000 different farms.

Statistically, observations can be made of the relations between an existing source, the immediate service rendered by it, and the proximate beneficiary. One can observe and measure the progress of a band saw through a log and determine whose lumber is yielded by the cutting. And when many immediate sources are conveniently congregated under the control of one owner or set of owners one may make many like statistical observations at successive stages. All the simultaneous and successive processes that occur in the sawmill can be observed and measured from day to day. But the moment the lumber passes to purchasers or dividends pass to stockholders or wages to workmen, the statistical procedure ceases; for the subsequent measuring is too widely dispersed and the lines of communication to the account books are broken. The accountant does not attempt to go beyond the closed transaction. That which has passed beyond the control of one enterprise, e.g., the lumber sold by the owner of the sawmill, becomes subject matter for the accountant serving another and separate enterprise or establishment.

If due allowance is made for the difference in scope of subject matter contemplated, kind of analysis made, and point or direction of view taken, there is very little discoverable difference, within their common ground, between Fisher's theory and that of the accountants. How small the real difference may be is easily shown by selecting a stage or two in the income cycle and observing the measures made by the accountants and contemplated by Fisher.

An accountant, asked to ascertain the amount, in money value, of the final objective income of an individual without dependents during a specified year, would be likely to set up, as a first approximation, what he would call that person's "living expenses," or "cost of living," or "expenses incurred to obtain this year's living."[16] This first approximation is based upon the assumption that value of service received in most cases corresponds closely to the value of consideration given; but no accountant asserts a universal identity of these amounts.

If the person in question has kept adequate and convenient memoranda that permit the exclusion of all occupational or

---

[16] The term "expense" as used in accounts must always be distinguished from "expenditure" or "disbursement." It is a matter of indifference to the accountant *when* the house rent is *paid*; the rent "expense" is concurrent with the house service. The amount of the expense is the value of the consideration paid, or to be paid, for the service enjoyed during a given period.

gainful operations, the most probable procedure of the accountant would be as follows:

1. Verify the inventories of household personal effects and personal debts at the beginning of the year. This results in three schedules: (a) a schedule of residual use-values (based on cost) of those objects, such as stocks of clothing, food supplies, furniture, and so on, procured earlier, but, to some extent at least, to be used later than that date; (b) a schedule of future services, such as house rental paid in advance, etc., not attaching to owned objects; and (c) a schedule of personal debts then existing, i.e., debts incurred either in procuring previously enjoyed services or in procuring consumption goods whether these latter have been wholly used or not. The net sum of these schedules would be found.

2. Verify the corresponding inventories at the closing date of the year.

3. Verify the sum of payments made during the year and of debts incurred during the year that were not paid during the year.

To this latter sum he would add the net amount of the beginning inventories and deduct the net amount of the closing inventories. The resulting numerical value will be the "expenses of living" for the year. To the extent that outlay, *whenever* made, can be taken as a measure of that which is received, the figure that the accountant thus finds is exactly equal to the figure that Fisher would find for final objective income. No use occurring during the year that has been or is to be paid for, whether directly or indirectly, is omitted; and each such use is valued at the outlay incurred or to be incurred to get it. No use that occurred in a previous period or that is to occur after the period, has been permitted to affect the final summation.

To be sure there are some elements in this procedure that look, superficially, like that which Fisher calls earnings. Suppose there appears in the first inventory valued at $760 a piano bought six months before the year began at a cash price of $800. It is "valued" in the closing inventory at $680, or $80 less than the year before. The outlays made, with respect to, or occasioned by, this piano (tuning, taxes, insurance, care by servants, etc.) amount to $30. There is, therefore, an "expense" component with respect to this piano of $110. Of this, $80 is for "depreciation" (but no "depreciation fund" has been created) and $30 represents current outlays.[17]

There appears to be a (negative) earning amounting to $110 and consisting of $30 of "realized" (negative) income and $80 of decline in value. This appearance would be real if what the accountant were really trying to do were to measure the unfavorable events that occurred during the year and that were occasioned by the ownership of this piano. But this is not what the accountant is trying to do. He is trying, rather, to place a (negative) value upon the adverse events occasioned by *this year's use*. A long series of adverse events, payment of purchase price, of taxes, of insurance premiums, of tuner's and repairer's wages, servants' wages, and so on, has been and will be incurred in order to get, not a piano, but piano use. Some use has been made this year. Some of this series of adverse events is referable to this year's use. And, finally, the amount of this series referred to this year's use is supposed to be approximately equal to the value of this year's use. The $110 becomes a measure of the year's use.

During the year the person may have contracted to buy an automobile and may have paid for it, but the machine may not yet have been delivered by the dealer. This transaction will

---

[17] But this $30 is not necessarily put down as a separate item, because it was spent in this year; certainly the closing inventory value of the piano is higher than it could warrantably have been put if the piano had not been tuned and cared for. As will be shown in the chapters on valuation, depreciation is not, in reality, independent of maintenance, upkeep, and repair either with respect to past operating charges or with respect to future charges. Only where crude approximations are all that the client wants made and are all that the public has a right to expect does the accountant treat depreciation as though it were independent of other charges.

have no effect at all upon this year's living expenses. The amount paid will appear in the summation of payments (item 3 above), but it will be canceled by a closing inventory item of like amount. There has been an adverse event occasioned by automobile ownership, but there has been no automobile use; hence no expense for the use of this automobile.

If the accountant were asked to make a closer approximation to this person's final objective income within the year, he can readily do so without departing from recognized procedure. Suppose the person to have received gifts, valuable in money, that have been in use during the year. If some valuation of these gifts can be supported by *as good evidence as actual payment* of that amount, no accountant would balk at treating that amount precisely as though it were a price paid. If the person bought and paid for a vacuum sweeper that wouldn't sweep, no accountant would hesitate to eject the item. This is not an expense of sweeper use, for there has been no sweeper use. If proper and sufficient evidence can be brought to show a discrepancy in either direction between the value of a service-use and the outlays necessary to obtain it, there is abundant precedent in accounting procedure for making an adjustment of the first approximation that would have exactly the same effect upon the measure of the person's final objective income that Fisher's analysis would yield.

One difference, only, in this particular field, would be found. Fisher, apparently, would permit effect to be given to the person's own asserted valuations of the final objective income. The accountant would not; for he is acting as an independent responsible principal. He is asserting *his* opinions about the affairs of others; and since he cannot penetrate another's mind to distinguish between anticipated benefits and remembered experiences of benefits, nor altogether rely on every one's good faith, he always requires the corroboration of actions or of general traits of human conduct. But this is a trivial difference. Fisher does not say that if *he* were valuing some one *else's* income, he would accept that person's appraisals. The accountant, on the other hand, does not object to having his client disagree with the valuations he adopts. Both Fisher and the accountant would readily admit that there are many much desired final objective incomes, for which no money valuation whatever can or ought to command general acceptance.

There can be no doubt that the results of the accountant's procedure are often misunderstood. Even in the field of household accounts, where the subject matter is all of a kind that enters the experience of all mature persons, many wholly fail to see more than the obvious superficial character of the data employed and the numerical operations performed upon them. They see the accountant putting down the outlay cost of the clothing and of the food, the depreciation on the piano and the automobile, the taxes and insurance paid, and so on; it seems to occur to few only that there may be a reason for adding a decline in value to an outlay and for including some but not all outlays. But if the intention of the accountant and his concept of final income can be determined by the properties of his finally resulting measures, there can be no doubt that his primary interest attaches to uses enjoyed rather than to outlays made or to objects acquired. When he prepares an adjusted statement of living expenses, he is preparing it as an index of living income. The economist does exactly the same kind of thing in another field. When he prepares an index number of wholesale prices, he is studying money, not commodities sold at wholesale. His chief interest is in the fluctuations of the *purchasing power of money,* a thing which cannot be directly measured. To study it he observes a few of many price series that, in conception, are reciprocally related to the purchasing power of money.

When the accountant is working in the field of final objective income, his procedure enables him to find, when the occasion requires it, exactly the same numerical valuations that

Fisher contemplates. Moreover, his procedure enables him to find this income without reference to any but immediate (or late) sources. He need pay no attention to his client's gainful occupation except to exclude all gainful operations from the domestic accounts. Whether the collecting reservoirs from which the person's future incomes must be drawn have been filling or have run dry, does not in the least matter. But when, on the other hand, the accountant is preparing the income account of an enterprise (one of these collecting reservoirs), the mode of living of the proprietor or of those beneficially interested in the proprietorship in the enterprise is none of his concern.[18]

In accounting for enterprise income, that which is reported is neither a measure of what Fisher calls realized income nor of earnings. It is a mixed index of the two. If the enterprise holdings included a few shares in a corporation the affairs of which are not known to the accountant, the income increments will consist of the realized increments, cash dividends, as they are received. If a manufacturing plant has been held for years without reliable, going-concern reappraisals, the annual income accounts are likely to contain depreciation charges based upon an original outlay cost. Even this first cost is not a true capitalization. The plant may have cost more, but is likely to have cost less, than its maximum service value to the proprietor. The arbitrary distribution of this outlay cost over the expected periods of service-life and the concurrent "writing down" of the plant's "book value," do not constitute true revaluations; nor do they result, necessarily, in a succession of strictly homogeneous valuations. In Fisher's terminology, neither a true

---

[18] Though the accountant can, he seldom, if ever, does merge the two fields. He may merge all the gainful activities, whether or not they amount to going-concern enterprises, in a report on an individual's financial status. He may prepare capital accounts of both domestic and enterprise holdings, as in bankruptcy cases. He may merge some of the personal income elements, e.g., interest paid on a debt incurred in the purchase of a dwelling occupied by the taxpayer, with most of the data on gainful activities in personal income tax returns. But in the great preponderance of cases the fields are carefully segregated.

realized income nor a true earning is reported. But the income element attaching to the plant service that arises from the "book value" rule of "cost less allowance for depreciation," shows a much closer statistical *resemblance* to earnings than it does to realized income. In the case of "safe" bonds held the accountant reports earnings.[19]

This mixed measure is clearly not the result of choice on the part of the accountants. All recent development in accounting procedure is consistent with the proposition that accountants wish to ascertain enterprise earnings rather than enterprise realized income. There are two principal reasons why they do not approximate true earnings more closely: first, the unwillingness of their clients to pay for better approximations; and second, the very great difficulty of obtaining reliable data upon which to base the requisite revaluations. There is, in the case of some professional accountants, a third reason: they are not well enough founded in statistical theory and method to grasp *fully* the nature and meaning of the specialized statistical procedure in which they habitually work. That is to say, there are some accountants, just as there are some in every profession, who are pattern followers.

There is no reasonable ground for doubt, however, that earnings (earned income), to the extent that they can be economically measured, constitute a superior and more immediately convenient measure of income. Realized income, in Fisher's sense is, indeed, the more elementary and fundamental measure. But not only is it often impossible to lay down approximate future schedules of it, but also these schedules would need to be interpreted by conversion into successions of capital value and of earnings. The proprietor and those beneficially interested in proprietorship wish chiefly to know what

---

[19] Certain self-canceling pairs are, however, usually omitted. The increase in value from zero (before purchase) to the value of the consideration given is canceled, though without entry, against the consideration outgo in the period of acquisition. A corresponding couple is omitted when the bonds are resold or are paid by the debtor at maturity.

net changes in power to command future final income have occurred within a year by reason of the enterprise activities. Not only is this information requisite to a proper determination of shareholders' investment policy, but to considered decisions about their scale of living income to be planned for the near future. Those responsible for the administration of the internal affairs are better able to plan and control their policies on the basis of earned income than on that of realized income. The interests of creditors are best served by the pursuit of policies that most greatly enhance earnings. In short, for every major purpose for which information about enterprise income is wanted the earning figure is more immediately significant than is the figure for realized income.[20]

There is one apparent but not real difference between Fisher's theory and the accountant's that seems to be attributable to the difference between the accountant's mode of expressing income measures and Fisher's more complete "conceptual" accounting. He resorts to a "method of balances" (Capital and Income, pp. 152-158) to describe schematically how the "natural" uses of capital succeed one another in the many stages intermediate between primary origin and final use. He shows the logging camp yielding logs, the sawmill yielding lumber, the warehouse, made of the lumber, yielding protection to a stock of cloth, the warehouse cloth yielding tailor's cloth, the latter yielding clothing, and finally, the clothing yielding use. In the writer's teaching experience many able students of accounts

---

[20] Fisher is of the opinion (see Capital and Income, pp. 250-254, and elsewhere in his writings) that earnings taken as a measure of a tax, whether proportional or progressive, is inequitable and harmful. The tax burden imposed under a given schedule of rates as between earnings on the one hand and final objective income on the other, is undoubtedly different, and different to exactly the extent that he describes. But there may be more than one tenable view upon the fiscal propriety of a tax on earnings. This is especially to be considered if the tax in question is only one of many taxes in a fiscal system. Nor is the question of propriety or social excellence of a particular tax to be decided without reference to the character of public expenditures to be made. The present writer wishes to reserve expression of his views on this subject. An adequate treatment would be a major digression.

think they have found in Fisher's discussion an implied specific productivity theory of income—a theory quite at variance with the accountant's views. But no such theory is necessarily implicit in Fisher's exposition. The proper valuation of the use of a given stock of clothes is wholly unaffected by the *de facto* antecedent stages. The figure would be the same whether the clothes were a miraculous gift from heaven or resulted from a criminally wasteful use of other and earlier forms of capital. Successive contributions may, as a matter of fact, occur, and the method of balances suggests a mode of occurrence. A thinkable scheme of reconcilement is quite a different matter from a statistical summation or analysis.

There is, of course, a popular fallacy that income, even in the sense of final objective services, can be traced statistically to remote capital sources. Not only is it seldom, if ever, possible to do so, but no purpose could be served by doing it. Suppose B and C simultaneously give A $5 each. A notes the serial numbers on the banknotes and observes that he pays out the one given him by B for a ticket to a football game, which he attends. He later sets the value of the spectacle at $6. The state of facts supposed warrants A in saying that he got $6 worth of final income. In a sense he can truly say further that B contributed $5 toward this and C nothing. But it is not true in an economically significant sense. If A had first deposited both notes in his bank in which he had a prior balance of $100, and had later drawn a check to pay for his ticket, his "final income" is unaffected, but he cannot say, except as an arbitrary and meaningless form of words, that any specified amount of his final income, with respect to the game, is contributed by either B or C or by any other person or thing. Increments of service performed by objects remote (in stage of causation) do not preserve their continuity and identity through successive stages in the income sequence, any more than drops of water falling at a stream-head preserve their continuity, form, and identity until they reach the stream mouth.

To speak of the *receiving* of a money rent upon an annuity, or of a dividend, or of month's wages as income, and of a money bequest of $100,000 as not-income, is wholly without propriety. If we stop at the *money receiving* stage, they are all income in the gross, and for exactly the same reasons; each implies a servant, a service done, and a beneficiary. If in the period in which these receivings occur, we seek for the recipient's final objective income, there is no necessary reason why we should have regard for any of these items. We look at the last stage only. These earlier stages of receiving can have no *direct* influence upon final income in the period of their receipt. And, except to the extent that the amount of the receipts, together with the amount of other holdings previously in hand, influences the decision of the recipient to enjoy final income in that period, receipts have no *indirect* effect. The extent of such an indirect influence is not practically measurable.

The Relative Merits of Fisher's and the Accountant's Treatment of Income

It may not be amiss at this point to put forward a comparative appraisal of the accountant's views and those of Fisher. And it may be convenient to make that appraisal upon the bases adopted for comparison, viz., scope of subject matter contemplated, mode of analysis pursued, and point of view taken.

With respect to the first there can be no possible doubt that Fisher's work is immensely superior. How much of his views will ultimately prevail among economists and among accountants no one need consider. Only a guess could be made. What the event will ultimately prove, too, might as readily be a fact about the two professions as a fact about Fisher's theory. But as a general, comprehensive treatment of the theory of income, there is nothing to compare favorably with it in either literature.

On the score of mode of analysis pursued, no relative advantage can be asserted and shown. Both the conceptual and the statistical modes are desirable. In scientific work the philosophical analysis usually—though not always—precedes the statistical in point of time and often very greatly accelerates the benefits of the statistical follow-up. The statistical mode as a sole mode, has in general, to spend many years in rule-of-thumb work, which grows better slowly and becomes increasingly difficult to change radically. It proceeds by a series of patchwork and tinkering. Even when the faults of a special procedure become apparent, it is often very difficult to make a fresh start. By the time that the intricacies of the procedure are learned by a student, he may have long been carried past the point at which he, left to his own devices, could have made a betterment.[21]

The philosophical theorists, on the other hand, run the very great risk of creating an imaginary world of affairs and of mistaking it or causing their readers to mistake it for the real world. Even when they are ever conscious that their theories describe an oversimplified situation, they cannot be sure how bad the distortions are. There is a tendency for such work to become a fabric of rational processes based upon plausible guesswork.

Rightly combined, the two modes are immeasurably superior to either alone. The imaginative mode sketches in patterns of thought to be checked by statistical measuring. The statistical measuring suggests reformulation of assumptions more nearly in accord with the facts found. Fisher, as is well known, deserves high rank both as a statistician and as a theorist. It may or may not be significant that his rank as a statistician is not to any considerable extent enhanced by work

---

[21] My colleague, Professor H. F. Blichfeldt, once expressed the view that full knowledge of the literature of a problem upon which he may be working is sometimes of dubious value to a research mathematician. Left to his own devices, he may avoid those manipulations, easy and obvious in their early stages, that lead inevitably to difficulties too great to be surmounted.

in income statistics. His work in money, backed up by his work in price statistics, particularly in index numbers, presents a much better *consolidated* treatment than does his treatment of income.

In the matter of point or direction of view a decision is difficult to make. The accountants predominantly focus upon what is *coming*. This is true both with respect to final income and to the earlier phenomena whereby final income is got. They do, to some extent, reverse this process at times, and there are decided gaps, capable of being filled in, between their treatment of final income as manifested in household accounts and their treatment of the income of single enterprises. Fisher begins with the origins of services and traces them through to the stream of consciousness resulting from final objective services. Very often, of course, he refers his reader back to the ultimate beneficiaries' point of view. He, like other economists, begins with wealth and the phenomena of production, continues with property and the phenomena of exchange, proceeds next to income and its distribution, and concludes the schematic development with consumption or the enjoyment of income.

The question of superiority, as between the accountants and the economists, with respect to point or direction of view, turns upon the answer to a more fundamental and elementary one. At what point can the analysis of income most advantageously be begun? Should the beginning be made in the stream of consciousness of the ultimate beneficiary of income, or as close thereto as possible, or should it begin with the ultimate origins of services? Is there some middle point that is more convenient?

In general, a beginning can most easily and advantageously be made with the most elementary concepts, with concepts that cannot be explained in terms of ideas simpler than themselves. It is desirable that these first introduced concepts should throw as much light as possible upon the more complex ideas later to be brought under consideration. Geometry does not begin with hyperspheres, nor chemistry with living tissues, nor physiology with the functions of the human brain. Points and lines, elements and simple compounds, and unicellular creatures are better points from which to take off.

In a late article Fisher says: "I believe that the concept of income is, without exception, the most vital central concept in economic science and that on fully grasping its nature and interrelations with other concepts largely depends the full fruition both of economic theory and of its applications to taxation and statistics."[22] If he had written instead that *income is, without exception, the simplest and most fundamental concept of economic science, that only by means of this concept can other economic concepts ever be fully developed and understood, and that upon beginning with this concept depends the full fruition of economic theory in economic statistics,* it would have been an equally true and a more significant statement.

There is no simpler concept in economics than income if the essence of income be "a desirable event." No other concept in economics throws any light upon its nature or significance. If it can be explained in terms of concepts more elementary than itself, that explanation must come from the psychologists and the physiologists. Economists are prone to begin their theory writings with a discussion of wealth. The wealth concept is, without exception, the most complex and most difficult of comprehension to be found in the science. Its full significance can never be seen until the notions of income, of distribution of property, of exchange, and of production, have been set into their proper relations to it. It is not asserted that wealth is difficult to define in the sense that the student experiences difficulty in determining, from the definition, just what things are, or are not, wealth. What is meant is that neither intuition nor direct experience can be relied upon to clothe the concept defined either with a comprehensive and

---

[22] *American Economic Review*, Vol. XIV, p. 64.

properly proportioned sense of its great significance, or with an appreciation of the extremely intricate relations between wealth and the problems of economic experience. Both of these must wait upon a treatment of income.

The motivation of human conduct with which the economist has chiefly concerned himself is directly associated with income; it is only remotely connected with wealth and the infinite complexity of forms that wealth takes in the modern world. One cannot explain what men do in their mode of living in terms of what they desire to do in enterprise, but one can explain a great deal of what men do in enterprise in terms of what they desire to do in their private lives.

Direct appropriation, properly understood, is not an exceptional mode of life; it is the only one available; no one else can enjoy events for us; but it is a direct appropriation of services desired for their own sake. It is a direct appropriation of ends—not of means to an end. The development of economics should begin with objectives, with consumption, and should end with production—not, of course, in point of time with respect to a chain of events ordered in time, but in order of contemplation and in order of exposition. We do not order our living to suit existing wealth. We order the wealth sources at our command to suit our future income. The general nature of final objective services—nourishment, housing, amusement, and so on—survive through civilizations; the means whereby these services are had, change too fast to permit any science to make an exhaustive study of them.

The present writer believes that had Fisher written "Income and Capital," beginning with a chapter on the topic of psychic income and ending with a chapter on wealth considered as a kind of embodiment of services directly or indirectly to become income, his work would not only have been more useful to the thoughtful reading public at large, but also, and most particularly, to accountants and economists.

There is very real occasion for regret that the professional accountants have found so little occasion to work in the subject of final objective income. It can hardly be doubted that, in their enterprise income accounts they, at times, lose sight of the fact that such statistics are wanted primarily for the ordering of the mode of living of the persons interested. For example, it is usually pressure upon shareholders for the wherewithal to meet living expenses that excites the clamor for larger dividends. Full statement of the earning prospects that condition the upbuilding of surplus would, at least, prevent their urging dividend payments contrary to their own best interests. Full statement, too, even though no dividends are forthcoming, may put the shareholders in a favorable position—through selling part of their holdings or borrowing upon them—to maintain their customary scale of living. By keeping more constantly in mind the gap between the enterprise earnings and the mode of life of the persons interested, the usefulness of their income statistics could be greatly enhanced.

From the economist's point of view, and for the good of the public, it is of very great importance that the accountants should make their income statistics as full and as complete as the conditions of their professional practice will permit. The professional accountants as a whole are abundantly able to give us better statistics than they do. It is to be hoped both in their own interests and the interests of the public as well as in the interests of their clients, that they will continue to press upon the notice of their clients the very great importance of better and fuller measures of income. The world must, at least for a long time, look chiefly to the professional accountant for what is known about income. That the work of this chief of our income intelligence services should consist so largely, as it now does, of what are called "balance sheet audits," amounts to showing that our professional public accountants are inadequately employed.

There is little room for hope that statistical methods can ever furnish inductive verifications of what are commonly called the "laws of economics" as many of them are now formulated. They were not invented with a proper regard for what can be done statistically. If economics is ever to become essentially a statistical science, it will be necessary, in economics just as elsewhere, to begin with simple measures of elementary things that most frequently recur. That beginning point is, in the present writer's opinion, most likely to be income—income as close to the recipient as possible. There will always be room for the imaginative economist. Shrewd intuition is as necessary as ever, but it is not sufficient by itself.

CHAPTER IX

FINANCIAL POSITION

In the foregoing chapters, attention has been given to the nature of the elementary ideas of accounts. Assets, liabilities, proprietorship, and interrelations of these ideas as implied in the equation of accounts have been looked into. The nature of income, both gross and net, has been considered and compared with the notions held by some economists. As much of the elementary processes of measuring of income as seems necessary to understanding the special meaning of the income statement has been set forth. But as yet, no systematic consideration has been given to the accountant's chief objective, viz., the determination of financial position. This chapter addresses itself to the task of explaining the meaning of financial position and showing how and to what degree the major end-product of accounting, the balance sheet, does reflect or disclose an existing financial position.

"Financial Position" Undefined in the Literature

Every writer on accounts and every accountant asserts that the balance sheet is intended to reflect the "financial position" or "financial condition" of the enterprise reported on. In accountants' usage the two terms are substantially interchangeable. The former seems, however, to be displacing the latter. Literally considered, the prevailing term seems preferable; financial "condition" to many persons, seems to imply too much. Curiously enough, neither the writers on accounts nor the accountants seem to have given much thought to defining either term. A few scattered propositions about the idea are to be found, but no systematically considered definitions appear. Is this state of the thought due to an assumption that every one understands the meaning of the term? Or is it thought that the term is incapable of definition? If both these questions are to be answered in the negative, just why has the term gone so long undefined?

Concept Not Undefinable.—Clearly, an assumption that the term is undefinable cannot be made without discredit to the accounting profession. Nor is the assumption that every one knows the meaning of the expression tenable. Ask the first ten bankers or merchants or professional accountants you meet to tell you the meaning of the term. Before you have reached the tenth you are likely to discover that there is not a common understanding. The responses of the accountants will most nearly approach one another in form, but they will not be of great assistance; for they will amount to saying that financial position is that which the balance sheet is intended to reflect. Properly considered, this is not a bad answer. The meaning of any statistical summary is dependent upon all of the statistical operations that have been resorted to in its compilation. Whether or not financial position can be said to have a substantial core of meaning is dependent upon the extent to which a common set of procedures prevails. The importance of the term is dependent both upon the degree to which common practices prevail and upon the judicious devising and selecting of the measures employed. It is quite possible for a term to have a definite meaning that is of little importance or convenience.

The phrasing of the term implies that it has to do both with some phase or phases of finance and with a status with respect to those phases. It seems to refer to the status of some specified concern at a specified time with respect to procurement of funds and to distribution of funds. All recognized branches of finance have regard for both procurement and distribution of funds; and what we call financial businesses or financial institutions have corresponding activities. Thus corporation finance deals with the procurement of funds by means of corporate issues and with the distribution of funds among the holders of these issues. A bank procures funds of others for which the owners have no employment for the time being, and distributes funds among those who have temporary need for funds in amounts greater than their present possessions.

The internal employment or application of funds is generally comprised under the term, operations. Just what particular activities are carried on by means of conversion of funds is not subject matter of finance. This does not amount to saying, of course, that the applications made and the activities carried on are without financial significance. The mode of conducting a service of transportation by a railway company is not a matter of finance, but the revenue receipts and the disbursements have a financial effect.

Sources and Distribution of Enterprise Funds.—Enterprise funds are procured from two categories of source: (1) the excess of receipts over disbursements that occurs in enterprise operations; and (2) the contributions of persons—creditors upon loans, subscribers to shares, etc. Of these the former is obviously the more significant. But for the prospect that operating receipts will, in the long run, considerably exceed the disbursements incident to operations, no contributions would be made to business enterprises. To speak of a business as self-financing is to say that its operating receipts suffice both for its conduct of operations and for its current distributions of interest, dividends, debt retirements, etc.

Enterprise funds are distributed according to the tenor of contribution agreements and according to public law. In general, of course, more funds are distributed to contributors than are contributed by them.

Four Possible Meanings of "Financial Position."—A "position" to be "financial" must, therefore, be a position with respect both to fund procurements and to fund distributions. Fund procurements, with reference to any specified date, may be either past or future procurements; so also may distributions be past or future. There are, therefore, four possible pairings which may be shown schematically thus:

Fund procurements that:	Fund distributions that:
1. Have occurred	1. Have occurred
2. Have occurred	2. Are expected to occur
3. Are expected to occur	3. Have occurred
4. Are expected to occur	4. Are expected to occur

To which of these pairings does the balance sheet most nearly conform? What rôle is played by assets? Clearly the first pair will not answer. If this pairing were adopted, the balance sheet would have to exhibit a sum equal to the total of cash receipts since the founding of the enterprise. Likewise, it would have to exhibit the total amounts paid to those who have been contributors, e.g., the totals paid to shareholders in the form of dividends and redemption of shares and to creditors, who have loaned funds, in the form of interest and principal payments. Nor will the second and third pairings answer; for each of them implies one of the cumulations implied in the first. There remains the fourth pairing. This is the one sought—not, to be sure, merely because it is the only one left, but for independent, positive reasons.

Direct Valuations.—These independent reasons, with respect to expected fund procurements, or power to procure funds in the future, may be indicated briefly by a few items. Consider the cash item.[1] It consists of funds available at will or on demand. The future time implied is numerically zero or

---

[1] "Cash" is not interchangeable with "money." Not all money is cash nor is all cash money. Money in the hands of an escrow agent awaiting the performance of a condition is not available at will or on demand to either party. An unpledged demand deposit with a solvent bank is not money, but it is cash, i.e., an absolute right to obtain money on demand that the business community agrees to treat as the full equivalent of money that is in hand and that is disposable at the will of its owner.

greater, at the will of the asset holder. Accounts receivable obviously express an expectation of funds within a brief interval. No event need be intermediate between the present asset form and the realization of funds. Finished goods inventory likewise expresses an expectation. The waiting interval to a concern that sells on credit is longer for inventories than that for accounts receivable. Note, however, that there is only one stage of operation, one interaction, to occur, viz., an exchange of goods for money. The two transfers may not be simultaneous. There may be a waiting period between the transfer of the goods and the transfer of money. For partly manufactured goods the waiting interval, on the average, must be still longer. But the chief difference between the valuation of these goods and that of finished goods is that some additional transformation or transformations must occur before the final interaction, the exchange for money, takes place. It is still possible, however, to make what may be called direct valuations. For the amount and character of finished merchantable goods to result from the manufacture that has been begun can be determined; allowances for residual costs to complete the process can be estimated.

The items just discussed are all capable of a direct money valuation that is more or less reliable. Cash involves no estimate. Accounts receivable involves an estimate of collectibility only. Merchandise involves likewise merely an estimate of funds to be collected as a result of sales, though, of course, a highly reliable estimate is not always possible. In the case of cash the enterprise services have all been rendered. In the case of the accounts receivable and the merchandise, only one service, the bringing in of money, is involved.

Indirect Valuations.—But not all assets are of this kind. In a manufacturing establishment many kinds of machines are employed each of which renders a kind of service peculiar to itself. None of these services consists in the direct and immediate bringing in of money. And while no one will question the proposition that the value of a machine is derived from the value of its services and from the outlays incident to procuring its services, no one can make a direct money valuation of those services unless they are to be sold separately.

The two general classes shade imperceptibly into one another. Raw materials that can be used for one kind of product only, or materials that have been earmarked for some particular manufacturing order that must be executed, either by reason of contract or to prevent loss of sales, can be valued in the same way as partly manufactured goods, though, of course with a lesser degree of reliability. Raw materials that may be used in the making of any of several products and that have not been earmarked for any certain use are still more difficult to value in terms of the direct money return that is expected to result from the sale of goods into which they enter.

Somewhere in the scale a shift from direct to indirect measuring of funds to be provided must be made. No indirect measure of the cash and accounts receivable seems desirable; no direct measure of the value of machines employed in manufacture is possible. Just where the shift should be made is partly a matter for theoretical (or ideal) consideration and partly one of practical possibilities.

Direct Valuations Preferable if Reliable.—Ideally, of course, it would be desirable to have direct measures throughout. If we could by any means obtain future manufacturing and sales data in the forms and amounts that are later to eventuate, we should be able to prepare a balance sheet that would be an instrument of precision. We should be able in a true and realistic and reliable sense to disclose a financial condition with respect to the capital value of an enterprise. But to carry direct valuation much beyond the inventories, under conditions that now exist, runs too close to the work of the clairvoyant and the astrologer to appeal to the professional accountant. In attempts to disclose financial condition we must either stop short with those valuations that can be made directly and with sufficient reliability, or we must resort, willy-nilly, to piecing out our direct valuations with some mode of indirect valuations. Accountants choose the latter alternative.

Specific Productivity Not Measurable.—If indirect measures are to be resorted to, it would be desirable to have some hypothesis of specific productivity that is capable of statistical application, and that, applied statistically, would prove to approximate the facts of experience as time reveals them. Unfortunately no such hypothesis has been proposed. Just how much of the money value of a basket of pears is attributable to the light and heat of the sun, how much to the work of earthworms and soil bacteria, how much to the chemical content and physical mixture of the soil, how much to the bole and leaves of the tree, how much to the man who cultivates the soil and picks the fruit, and how much to the tools used in cultivation, is still a mystery. The services rendered by each are capable of definition and measurement by means known to us; we lack coefficients of conversion. All these services are income, but they are income of incommensurable orders. Hypotheses of specific productivity have their place, if any, in the realms of conception only. The students of the calculus of variations have not yet solved problems of the order presented to us in our daily economic activities.

But indirect valuations, if they are to be better than random guesses, must be based upon some relation that actually exists between the future series of fund receipts and disbursements and some other series to the values of which we have present access. That is, we must find some series of which a sufficient number of terms are known that is correlated with the future receipt series.[2] The accountant's indirect measure of funds to

---

[2] Correlation is used here in its most general sense rather than in the narrower sense of a linear contingency such as is disclosed by the Pearsonian coefficient. Knowing the age of a human being, one can make a better

be provided is based upon a relationship of this general character.

Just what series is supposed by the accountants to be most nearly related to the future receipts series, and just what relationship they suppose to exist, cannot, of course, be determined. Accountants have never been given to expressing systematically the hypotheses upon which they proceed. Both the identity of the series and the supposed relation can be approximately determined only by examining what the accountants actually do. That task will be undertaken here, but with no hope of saying a last word. It is hoped only that the degree of approximation achieved will be greater than any hitherto published.

Cost and Value or Valuation.—Economists and others have often made the gross mistake of attributing to accountants a confusion of cost and value, or of identifying cost and valuation. No such crude association can be shown from the facts of modern accounting procedure. Others, particularly the writers on accounts, have said that accountants adopt cost less depreciation as the measure of valuation. This is much nearer the mark. But even if depreciation be defined in the most refined and accurate sense, with respect to that which is found in practice, the statement is still wide of the mark. Modern accounting procedure abounds in instances that do not conform to this oversimplified description. To make this assertion about accountants' valuations would make the modern balance sheet assert things that the underlying procedures do not assert at all and would make it omit saying many things that it does assert. Cost is only one class of evidence considered; depreciation, however defined and measured, is only one class of evidence among many. In a multitude of cases, initial valuations greater than cost are recognized; in a like multitude, increases in value are exhibited.

---

estimate of his stature than if one knows only the number of letters in his name. Stature and age are correlated. Stature and length of name are not.

Valuation of Objects vs. Valuation of Services.—Much of the failure to interpret the work of the accountant is due to the supposition that he is primarily concerned with objects and the valuation of objects rather than with services of objects and persons and the valuation of those services. To be sure, much of this failure is chargeable to the accountants themselves; they do not always accurately describe just what they have done in their underlying procedures, but the procedures do more clearly imply a much greater emphasis of thought upon services, upon income in its most general sense, than upon what the economist calls capital goods.

Hypotheses Underlying Accountants' Valuations

The argument of the hypotheses implied in accountants' valuations of funds to be provided by enterprise operations seems to be somewhat of the following order:[3]

1. **Capital Value of an Enterprise.**—If all the various and sundry services that are necessary to putting a product into the hands of the buying public and to collecting the accounts can be had for a schedule of outlays sufficiently less than the schedule of operating receipts, this aggregate of services can be said to be worth as much as it costs. Put in another form, if the present worth of all future receipts of an enterprise is greater than the present worth of all future operating outlays, the *enterprise* has a capital value equal to that difference.

2. **Value of Essential Services.**—If a capital value exists in an enterprise, it can be said of any *essential service* still to be obtained that it is worth as much as the *minimum present outlay* at which it could be had in a *free market in the quantity required*. That service can never be worth more than an amount thus determined in the sense that any one acting for himself and in his own interest could rationally elect to pay more for it.

---
[3] For a detailed analysis of these hypotheses and an application of them see pp. 206 *et seq.*

If this second proposition is true, a related proposition can be derived from it. If the necessary service in question is to be procured through control of the agent rendering it (e.g., a machine), a valuation of the agent can be found. The agent is worth no more and no less than (1) the present worth of future outlays necessary to obtain like services in like amounts by the *best available alternative means*, less (2) the present worth of future outlays necessary to obtain the agent's future service in the *most economical manner*. But it is the assured, separable service-series, not the agent rendering them, that constitutes the essence of enterprise assets. This is of especial importance in considering the valuation of those assets for which a direct and immediate, i.e., not indirect and not remote, going-concern valuation cannot be made.

Upon the grounds of the first two propositions, two others of prime importance may be based.

3. Goodwill May Be Positive.—The capital value of an enterprise may be greater than the sum of the values of all the services necessary to carrying on the operations of the enterprise. That is to say, a goodwill can exist.[4] At any given date the present worth of anticipated future receipts may be greater than the sum of, (1) the capital value of anticipated future outlays, and (2) the capital values of outlays made in the past to procure services not yet received or realized.

4. Goodwill May Be Negative.—The capital value of an enterprise may be less than the sum of the values of all the services necessary to carrying on the operations of the enterprise. That is to say the negative counterpart (or a credit balance) of goodwill can exist. At any given date the capital value of anticipated future receipts may be less than the sum

---

[4] Despite the many and varied definitions of goodwill that are to be found in the older literature of accounts, in legal decisions, and in the writings of economists, the prevailing meaning of "goodwill" among accountants can be said to be the value of the power to earn in excess of the rate on cost that is necessary to induce men to engage in the enterprise under consideration.

of (1) the capital value of anticipated future outlays, and (2) the capital values of outlays made in the past to procure services not yet received or realized.

The "Paradox" of "Going-Concern" Value.—There may seem, at first thought, to be a paradox in the four propositions just made, but there is none. Two related but not identical things are being measured. The value of a service is related to the capital value of the enterprise in which it is to be employed, but an enterprise is not a service, nor is it a mere aggregate of prospective services or of present serviceable agents. The capital value of an enterprise is determined by reference to gainful opportunities available in other enterprises and by reference to the time preferences of persons in the market for shares in enterprise gains. The value of single services or of separable sets of services, is determined by (1) the *existence* of a capital value in the enterprise in which it is to be employed, and (2) the best available terms on which such a service can be had in a free market in the required amounts. Some particular congeries or aggregate of services is requisite to every enterprise, but no such set of services is limited to any particular set of sources or serving agents.

The matter in the preceding paragraph is readily illustrated. The service of a pair of shoes is worth more than twice as much as the service of either shoe worn alone. The service of a pair of shoes alone and of an outfit of clothing not including shoes adds up to less than the service of a complete outfit of dress. Having only one shoe of a pair, one could, if necessary, rationally pay for the mate as much as the difference in value of service between that of one shoe and that of a pair, but he could not rationally pay that much apiece for shoes.

A corresponding, though extreme, illustration in the field of enterprise may throw additional light upon the nature of the asset valuation problem. Suppose a mining plant to be newly and completely constructed and developed, and ready to begin milling operations except for one missing boiler tube. The plant is at such a distance from markets that no substantial element of the plant can have a scrap value. Suppose that, the tube being installed, the enterprise has a capital value of $100,000. What is the *maximum* price that the mine owner could rationally afford to pay, *if he had no alternative,* to obtain the installation of the tube? Obviously he could afford to pay $100,000; for he could then earn interest on that amount as against nothing at all if he did not operate the plant. But it is equally obvious that he could not now afford to pay $100,000 apiece for two tubes; nor could any one afford to pay more than $100,000 for the entire establishment completely ready to operate.

If in the whole program of construction and development the mine owner paid no more for any service than the minimum necessary to obtain it, and if he chose the best alternatives available to him, no single element of the structures, shafts, drifts, etc., can rationally be said to be worth either more or less than was paid for it. Nor can any element of service rendered by these be said to be worth more or less than the price impliedly paid for it.[5] This is true no matter whether the capital value of the enterprise implies a rate of return on the whole investment, past and future, of 1% per year or of 20% per year.

There is, of course, no intention of asserting here that the foregoing hypotheses underlying indirect valuation are anything more than hypotheses—though they are as good as any proposed. They are quite probably capable of changes that would make them fit more accurately what the accountant

---

[5] Note that the ore deposit is omitted from this list. Because the concentrates or the recovered metal in the deposit will be sold, the ore deposit is in some degree capable of direct valuation. But that valuation can be reached only upon assuming some schedule of future prices, future physical yield schedules, and total future costs of exploiting the deposit and effecting the sale of mine products. It is doubtful if such a remote degree of direct valuation can ever become reliable. Engineers' valuations of ore bodies are direct valuations, but high statistical reliability cannot be claimed for them.

actually does. Certainly no belief is expressed that the detailed technique of valuation ever finds precisely the asset valuations contemplated in the phrasing of the four propositions made. All that is asserted is that the propositions do approximately declare the nature of what the accountant calls "correct" valuations in so far as he resorts to indirect valuations. The accountant's rule of "cost or market whichever is lesser," applied to finished goods inventories is an indirect valuation of this kind. If accountants are to be criticized for this inventory rule, the criticism should take the form of suggesting a direct valuation like that made of cash, accounts receivable, notes receivable, temporary investments, bonds receivable, and so on, rather than in suggesting some other rule of indirect valuation. It is more than doubtful that a better *indirect* rule has ever been proposed.

"Ideal" Meaning of "Financial Position"

Beyond doubt the accountants would like to mean by "financial position" a position declared by direct positive measures of funds to be provided by enterprise operations. It is equally beyond doubt that this can never be done before the gift of prevision of all future sales and outlays becomes general.

"Financial Position" Defined.—With respect to procurement of funds, then, financial position as disclosed in the balance sheet means "regarded from this date, future fund procurements by means of enterprise operations will occur to the extent of the directly valued assets. Toward the procurement of further future funds there are certain correctly, but indirectly, valued assets, future necessary services now subject to control, in the amounts set out." In general, financial position is a position with respect to asset valuation and constitution rather than with respect to capital value of the enterprise.

Possible Betterments of Practice.—It is, of course, within the powers of public accountants much more closely to approximate the financial position with respect to capital value of enterprises than they do. If, year after year, a concern exhibits a ratio between (1) the sum of net income and of interest payments, and (2) the book value of assets, that is greatly in excess of any commonly enjoyed rate upon properly valued assets, a substantial goodwill probably exists. No accountant will deny this. But it is quite another matter to ask him as a disinterested, responsible principal to put down an amount in figures, or to adopt some one else's figures and solemnly declare them to be reliable. Properly to value goodwill amounts to determining the capital value of an enterprise. To do this requires an extent of intimate knowledge of the affairs and circumstances of an enterprise that the ordinary conditions of the accountant's engagement do not permit him to obtain. Under a proper engagement an accountant will advise his client concerning a goodwill valuation contemplated in bargaining for the purchase or sale of an enterprise.

There are, however, conditions under which an accountant will adopt a goodwill valuation. If in the purchase of an enterprise the buyer and the seller were strangers in the sense of having opposed self-interests, and if a price for goodwill was agreed upon and paid, then in a subsequent engagement with the buyer if the accountant's examination of affairs discloses no good reason for supposing the goodwill to have been improperly appraised, he will adopt the valuation and certify his statements without qualification. Many have felt that the brief dogma frequently expressed by accountants that goodwill should not be certified to unless paid for, is trivial. And so it would be if the mere *fact*, or alleged fact, of payment were thought to be decisive. Many accountants and writers on accounts have exposed themselves to this interpretation of their words. But a more favorable view may be taken. The significant matter is not the mere fact or form of payment, but it is the fact that real payment, when the interest of buyer and seller are really opposed, constitutes a penalty too heavy to be ignorantly assumed. Ascertained good faith and corroborated prudence, evidenced by payment to a stranger in interest, is by no means a trivial ground.

For precisely the same reasons and upon precisely the same grounds, other valuation accounts of the same order as goodwill are recognized. Necessary services in organization, if actually paid for in good faith, may be shown. The same kind of services actually donated and later merely asserted by the donee to be worth a specified figure, will not be adopted. What a man honestly thinks he might have paid is a different thing from what he really would have paid if actually called upon to do so.

Possible Uses of Reports in Series.—Those who are often ready to criticize the accountant for his failure to express an opinion about goodwill and other intangibles often neglect to use the information with which the accountant does supply them. If a concern has been operating many years and has regularly had its affairs reported on by professional public accountants, the series of annual balance sheets and of annual income statements will present a great deal of useful evidence. If, year after year, the sum of financial charges and of net profit are stable, and, converted to a rate of return upon the book value of assets, show a high rate of gain, there is a strong presumption that a positive goodwill exists. If, on the other hand, the rate is low in relation to the rates prevailing in the industry, the presumption is that the goodwill is negative, that is, that the capital value of the enterprise is less than the sum of the asset valuations. But these are no more than *presumptions*; for it is always possible that the technique of valuation pursued for years has too rapidly been writing off the value of fixed assets. Value return rates are, therefore, too low and a "secret reserve" is accumulating that must, of necessity, bring about higher future rates after fixed assets are reduced to a minimum book valuation. Valuation errors in the reverse direction are associated with correspondingly displaced income. Some evidence that both classes of error are fairly common can be gleaned from the amounts of net income upon which corporations have paid the flat-rate federal income taxes.

Fund Distributions.—Little need be said of the other aspect of financial position. Observance of the so-called balance sheet equation requires the amount of distributions shown to be equal to the amount to be procured. The classification of distributions amounts to little more than a direct valuation of financial debts and an allocation of the difference to the proprietary interests.

The "Ideal" Balance Sheet.—To say that the conventional balance sheet, with its associated statements, falls far short of accomplishing its ideal purpose is rather to express a confident hope for betterment than, necessarily, to imply an adverse criticism of the accounting profession. In the concluding chapters certain of the influences leading to betterment will be discussed and appraised. Let it suffice here to say that to reap the full benefit of what can be done by professional public accountants will require the working together of an active and aggressive public interest in the conduct of affairs, of a livelier appreciation of the monetary value of good accounting service, of a rationalizing of business, and of an improved theory and technique on the part of the accountants.

CHAPTER X

THE ACCOUNTANT'S PROBLEM OF VALUATION

Restraints upon the Accountant

It has been made apparent in the previous chapters that the accountant's problem of valuation is not coextensive with that of the economists. But even within the common ground of the two fields, the accountant is less free to express the valuations that he thinks ought to be found and expressed than is the economist. Clients are not always willing to pay for adequate service. Certain statutory enactments prescribe modes of valuation that do not always accord with the accountant's views. The absurd "cost of reproduction new less depreciation" rate-base rules in the field of public utilities remove the incentives to good valuation work.

Revenue acts set up ill-considered and changing statistical determinations of taxable income and provide awkward and fluctuating systems of tax-rate progressions. Ill-considered phrasings in corporation charters, unwise by-laws, errors of judgment expressed in directors' resolutions, arbitrary covenants in indentures of stock issues and bond issues that bind the corporation to a specified mode of valuation procedure—these and a host of others either constrain the accountant to give effect to a mode of procedure to which he does not necessarily subscribe, or, at best, offer strong inducements to deviate from good procedure. The accountant has his living to get by that to which he gives expression in his reports. The economist has a freer hand in what he does, though, of course, fewer opportunities to participate in valuation programs.

Restraints Imposed by the Engagement.—It is not always possible in reading the report of an accountant to determine what special restraints were imposed upon him in his engagement. Nor can one be sure always that an expressed or an implied hindrance to which the accountant has given way is a hindrance that the profession would recognize as a legitimate one. When one reads in the accountant's "certificate" of the balance sheet of a very great corporation, "The minutes of the Board of Directors were not placed at our disposal," one may have to make a blind guess at the extent to which additional caution was taken in verifying the valuations of assets and of liabilities. Since there may be indefinitely many hindrances to good valuation, and since most of these are operative temporarily or locally only, no attempt will be made to consider critically even the principal divergences from what is loosely called "good practice."[1] But in attempting to discuss that which is generally done where circumstances permit a fairly free hand to the accountant, it is clearly recognized that many inadvertent minor errors will be made. There is no possible way of determining to what extent an accountant has been free to act as he would choose to in the joint and common interest of his client and the public.

Restraints Arising Out of Lack of Data.—Certain portions of the problem of valuation will have to be omitted, not because the accountant is not interested in them, nor because he is not free to consider them, but because he cannot possibly obtain the data requisite for their consideration at the time he requires them. Accountants are fully aware of the difference between "dollar accounting" and a conceivable "purchasing power accounting," and would prefer, just as the economists do, a purchasing power accounting. But the adjustment

---

[1] "Briefly defined, the term 'good accounting practice' means accounts and methods of accounting which correctly reflect the financial position of a concern and its gross and net income." Montgomery, Auditing Theory and Practice, 4th ed., Vol. I, p. 345.

data can never become available at the time records are originally made, nor do they become available in time for report-making. Whether or not it would pay to make such an accounting currently, is doubtful; but the cumulative effect of a depreciating currency upon valuations of long-lived assets and debts may be such as to require partial readjustments at relatively long intervals.

Theory of Value vs. Theory of Valuation

Economists often assert that the accountant's theory of value and of value determination are markedly different from their own. Often, apparently, they base that assertion on no better ground than that the numerical valuations expressed by the accountant do not conform to the economist's definitions of the nature of value and of the measure of value. Such an inference is of dubious validity. The economist, in general, calmly assumes the existence of data that never have been available and never will be. Having defined value and rent, the economist says of a parcel of land that its value is equal to the present worth of its future rents. He observes that an accountant is carrying it at cost in his successive balance sheets. Before he infers that the accountant has a different theory of value, he should ask himself what particular figure he would adopt and how he would get it. These future rents constitute an infinite series that can, term by term, take on a very great range in value and may be either positive or negative in sign. The series of present worths of these terms is also an infinite series. Each term in the series is itself a summation. The economic rent series simply has no real existence. Nevertheless certain approximations can be made to land valuations good enough to serve for practical purposes. The actual taking of a price by the seller and its payment by a buyer, each acting irrevocably in what he conceives to be to his own interest and each presumably having some skill in appraising *the practicable options available to him,* provides a working valuation for the land. The accountant merely adopts this "prudent investor" figure until he obtains equally reliable evidence to support a different valuation. Whether or not the accountant is always sufficiently skeptical about "cost" valuations, or sufficiently eager in his search for new evidence of greater merit, is a fact about the importance that he attaches to "correct" valuations rather than a fact about his theory of value and value measure.

No Theory of Value Professed by Accountants: Valuation Practice.—To what extent the accountant's theory or theories of value differ from any held by the economists is not the subject matter under inquiry here. Whether or not accountants as a class subscribe, or would subscribe, to any theory of value is not known. They do practice valuation; and much of their procedure they adopt in common. An attempt will be made to describe their valuation process and to suggest certain means whereby this process may, in due course, be changed for the better. These suggestions, let it be noted, are not based, proximately at least, upon any theory of value, but upon a theory of valuation. A theory of value may be conceptual only—most theories of value are. But theories of valuation are statistical. They do not go beyond the bounds set by the data that are, or that may become, available. A theory of valuation treats of selecting a set of procedures appropriate for discriminating data in the form of money-valuations. It is but an elementary and specialized kind of statistical theory. Statistical theory is a theory of measurements that are subject to error.

Certain elementary propositions drawn from the general theory of measurement have especially weighty significance in this special field. These propositions are assembled in the list below. The list does not purport to be complete; for while, in a sense, all general propositions about measuring are applicable to valuation, many of them find their chief significance only in fields in which analyses become mathematically complex or in which errors can be reduced to small ranges. Only those thought to be most significant in the present stage of accounting development are listed. Both the existing procedures discussed and changes proposed will be referred to these propositions.

Propositions about Populations that Are Not Classified

1. **Nature of a Statistical Population.**—If individual measures are to be merged by summation or otherwise, the individual things measured should belong to a common population. That is to say, these things must all be sensibly alike with respect to the property (or set of properties) or the variable character (or set of characters) under investigation. All persons resident in a defined community at a specified time constitute a statistical population if the property under investigation is density per square mile. They do not constitute a statistical population if one is investigating age at which first marriage occurs.

2. **The Unit of Measure.**—If measures are to be merged, the unit of measure must have a sensibly common significance throughout the measuring. Tons of fresh fruit hauled over a specified railroad division may have a sensibly like significance with respect to the operating of refrigerator car lines. But the tons of this fruit have a different significance with respect to food value.

3. **Stability of the Unit.**—If measures are to be merged, the unit of measure must either be uniform in magnitude throughout the measuring, or all units employed must be convertible into the unit in terms of which the measures are merged. Measures to the nearest yard are not convertible into measures to the nearest inch, but measures to the nearest inch are convertible into measures to the nearest yard. Statures of mature men expressed correct to the nearest yard, converted to

inches by multiplying by 36, would find most men to be 72 inches tall!

4. Method and Circumstances of Measuring.—If measures are to be merged, the method and circumstances of measuring should be as nearly as possible common to all measures. Statures measured when the subject is prone cannot be properly added to those measured when the subject is erect.

5. Degree of Error.—If measures are to be merged, the degree of error (error per unit of measure likely to occur) should not significantly vary as between one variate and another. Measures with instruments of precision should not be added to measures made with instruments of approximation or estimate.

It will be noted that these propositions are not a counsel of perfection. Statistical theory forbids no measuring, however crude or fantastic; it declares against the merging of significantly unlike data. To express these notions in the imperative mood would be to forbid all accounting. What the propositions do prescribe is this: if the condition cannot be fulfilled, either limit the summations to a sample of the population, or classify the population and deal separately with the classes; and if a sample is dealt with, this may or may not require to be classified. In accounting valuations it is necessary to depend upon samples and it is always necessary to classify if the valuation summations are to be convenient for those who employ them. Not all those separable elements of service having the economic essentials of assets are called assets; and no accountant is content to express a mere undifferentiated summation of assets; he presents a classified list.

Propositions about Classes and Sub-Classes

1. When to Classify.—If the significance of one or more variates is materially different from that of any other variate or variates, classification should be resorted to. Material differences of significance, as between one unit and another, should not be permitted to exist in any undifferentiated summation. This is true no matter whether the disparity arises from doubt of the eligibility of the thing measured to be considered a member of the population, or from lack of a common significance of the unit of measure, or from instability of the unit, or from the differences in degree of error in measuring, or from any combination of these. It is one thing to write:

| Total liabilities | $100,000 |

It is quite another to write:

Overdue notes, bills, and accounts payable	$ 90,000
Other liabilities	10,000
Total liabilities	$100,000

It is still a different thing to write:

Accounts and notes payable not due	$ 50,000
Bonds payable (due in 10 years)	50,000
Total liabilities	$100,000

2. **Relations of Classes and Populations.**—All the propositions made above about populations that are not classified hold equally for classes and sub-classes. This is true though it should result in setting into a balance sheet a class that consisted of one indivisible item only.

Propositions about Samples

1. **When to Employ a Sample.**—If a true population cannot be dealt with as an entirety, a sample may be taken for measurement. This is true not only in the obvious case in which the population is too large but also in the case in which some elements of the population may elude identification or, if identified, are incapable of significantly reliable measurement. Public accountants, in general, do not attempt to verify every unit valuation; they test and scrutinize. Some elements having

the essential economic attributes of assets may escape discovery; presumably some escape notice in every large engagement. Some elements, like the purchasing habits of steady customers, may be too difficult to value.

2. **Samples as Indexes.**—Samples may be employed either as indexes to the total population or as though they constituted a population. If the sample is related in some known way to the entire population or class from which it is taken, it is possible to discuss the larger body in terms of the observations upon the smaller. If the properly sampled items in a test of inventory stock sheets prove reliable, reliability of the entire list may be inferred. But if the relation of the sample available to the total population or class is not ascertainable with significant reliability, the sample may be dealt with as though it constituted the population. Every accountant admits that a true element of goodwill may exist without his being able to place a reliable valuation upon it under the conditions of his engagement. To issue a balance sheet without notice of goodwill at all, that is, to issue one that exhibits all the assets properly valued by listed classes and to exhibit a valuation for the proprietor's net estate that ignores a goodwill believed to exist, is wholly justifiable. Objection to expressing a valuation for a goodwill element that can be established with significant reliability is quite another matter.

3. The propositions made above about populations and classes and sub-classes thereof, hold equally for samples and for classes and sub-classes of these.

Criteria of Superiority

The objects of valuation being agreed upon, one theory of valuation may or may not be better than some other. So, also, may one basis of classification or one method of measuring, or one unit of measure be better than some other. But it is not always possible to justify a choice on any better grounds than arbitrary personal preference. Revenue acts, for example, may possess differing degrees of merit with respect to convenience to the taxpayer, economy of administration, minimizing the likelihood of fraud, and so on. All good citizens will assent to the proposition that the more convenient and economical a tax is and the fewer frauds that become possible, the better the tax. Suppose tax A to be better with respect to frauds than tax B but tax B to be more convenient to honest taxpayers. How much inconvenience, however measured, is equivalent to a given amount of fraud? Unless all fully informed, disinterested persons can agree upon some coefficient of conversion, no general proposition of superiority in one of these taxes can rise above personal preference. Only the somewhat dubious test of the predilections of a majority is available as a test. Money values and ethical values are, in general, not interconvertible. Fortunately the conflict of incommensurable quantities plays no leading part in determining choices in the field of valuation. A mode of valuation may possess differing degrees of merit with respect to timeliness, reliability, etc. But these are capable of defensible money valuations; they are, in essence if not always in statistical fact, commensurable. A mode of valuation, too, may possess different degrees of merit with respect to the legitimate interests of directors, administrative officers, creditors, shareholders, and so on. To a great extent these, too, are measurable in money terms. It is possible, too, as between two modes of valuing, that one may be better on all scores than the other.

"Best" Measure vs. Many Measures.—Fortunately the impossibility of proving one method of valuing to be better than another, when such an impossibility is encountered, is seldom of great moment. The difference of merit in dispute may be agreed to be small, so that no one is seriously harmed by an election. But what is important is the fact that the optional choices are never mutually exclusive. If there are several good methods, each differing materially from the others with respect to one form of merit or another, there is no reason at all why more than one valuation should not be made and expressed. There is nothing whatever to hinder the valuing of an inventory both at cost, at market, at cost or market whichever is lower, at selling price, at selling price less allowances for selling and other expenses, and so on. Cases are plentiful in which more than one figure is enough better than any one to warrant the finding of more than one. No harm is done by an accountant's expressing a choice of one as a best "all-purpose" figure in given circumstances and in furnishing figures of a different meaning for the benefit of those who may differ in opinion, or who may have only special needs for information. As between two good but materially different methods of valuation, the most sensible election is often to choose both. The parallel of this problem of choice is well known in general statistics. No longer do writers in statistics argue furiously about which of indefinitely many averages is "the best." If for any series the arithmetic, geometric, and harmonic means, the median, and the mode are given, more is told about the series than can be told by any one of these or by any set less than all of these.

The interminable argument that has been carried on by the text writers and others about the relative merits of the many formulas for measuring depreciation has failed, not only to produce the real merits of the several methods, but, more significantly, it has failed to produce a rational set of criteria of excellence whereby to test the aptness of any formula for any sub-class of fixed assets. Still more significantly the parties to the controversy, while they may admit that no one is always best, have failed to consider the possibility of simultaneously adopting more than one.

The same kind of controversy has been carried on among economists about the merits of formulas for index numbers. Before Fisher's book, "The Making of Index Numbers," was published, a great many formulas had stout champions. While he may possibly not have settled the question by his "ideal" formula, he has shown beyond doubt the form of argument whereby the relative merits of formulas are to be discriminated —a contribution immensely more valuable than a mere list of the merits possessed by any formula or set of formulas.

Any thoughtful examination of the reports of professional public accountants will quickly disclose some degree of implied recognition of the propositions made above about statistical populations, samples, classification, methods of measuring, and criteria of superiority. Whether or not the degree of implied recognition is adequate and whether or not a formally expressed and applied set of propositions—fuller, of course, than the one set out here—would lead more rapidly to betterments of practice, will be a part of the subject matter under examination in the remainder of this book.

CHAPTER XI

VALUATION PROCEDURE: DIRECT VALUATION

This book is concerned with the statistical nature and meaning of accountants' results rather than with giving instruction in the art of accounting. The discussion of valuation will, therefore, be organized on the basis of modes of valuation and their effect upon the meaning of summations. The usual organization, of course, proceeds first to group and classify the items to be valued and then discusses their valuation piecemeal. There is, of course, a good deal of comment in the literature on the fact that a wide diversity of methods of valuing is exemplified in every balance sheet. Full recognition is given, too, to the fact that for many significant and common balance sheet items there are many markedly differing competing formulas, or techniques of valuing, in the field. Very little attention is given, on the other hand, to the effects of a mixture of methods upon the meaning of statements. Still less is said of the importance of making valuations that are to be summated as nearly homogeneous as possible. Almost nothing at all has been done, in an explicit orderly fashion, to discover to what extent a common, general method might be expected to enhance the usefulness of the principal statements.

Conditions under which Direct Valuation Is Possible

It was noted in the chapter on Financial Position [1] that some valuations must of necessity be indirect in the sense that no separable realized income series, in terms of money receipts, can ever be found for some types of assets. There is no means of determining sales receipts many years in advance.

---
[1] See pp. 183-191.

Nor, even though it were possible to do so, could such receipts ever be analyzed into the component elements to be derived from the several contributing agencies or services of agencies. Nor could any one seriously consider the abandonment of readily applicable direct methods, such as those applied to determinate debts, cash, etc. The meat of the theoretical and practical problem, then, seems to be to find out to what lengths direct valuation should be carried and to discover some system of indirect measuring that will supplement the direct measures with as little statistical error as possible. What things ought to be valued directly? What indirect measure or measures should be adopted? What is the effect of the confusing mixture of methods now in use?

A direct valuation is possible when, and only when, a realized money income exists and is statistically determinable.[2] The increments of such an income may be either positive or negative in sign, and may be distributed in future time in any way. Any direct and separate or separable conversion into money in a future time—no matter whether the conversion gives rise to a coming in, or to a going out of money—gives rise to a realized income. If one could approximate the whole future series of money outgoes and of money receipts of an enterprise, one could find, given a rate of discount, a direct capital value of that enterprise. The degree of reliability of such a valuation would be dependent solely upon the reliability of the estimates of amount and time of receipt and outlay and upon the propriety of the rate or rates of capitalization employed.

But it is rarely, if ever, possible statistically to project either the series of receipts or the series of disbursements far into the future. Both series may be substantially completed with respect to such elements as cash, accounts and notes receivable, the liabilities, evidences of debt (of others) held.

---

[2] "Realized income" is employed throughout this chapter in the sense in which Fisher employs the term. (See "Capital and Income," index citations under "income" and "realized income.") See also, pp. 154-155, *supra*.

Both series may be fairly approximated with respect to finished goods inventories. Certain sales orders for goods under manufacture, certain corporate stocks, e.g., non-participating, cumulative preferred shares in controlled companies that exhibit a stable earning power well in excess of dividend requirements, and many others. In some degree both series may be forecast for materials of manufacture on hand, ore deposits in sight, timber stands, etc., but for these the range of probable error in the estimate becomes great.

In a general manufacturing industry, or in any private enterprise holding long-lived assets not for sale but for use conversion, the series of future receipts, beyond the conclusion of the operating program now in process, becomes indeterminate. Until a decision is reached both as to what will be prepared for sale, how much will be prepared, and when the offering will be made, no series of receipts can be written at all. Even if sales prices could be forecast an operating program must be determined before the products, price times quantity, can be written. With respect to the services of certain long-lived assets not held for sale the future series of outlays to be incurred can often be approximated to a useful degree. Our experience with steam-generating plants, for example, permits a fair approximation of future outlays for certain kinds of maintenance, upkeep, repair, etc. The "natural" service of such an assembly as a steam plant can be more nearly approximated than can future sales receipts. Steam generated may be used for indefinitely many final purposes, i.e., for the manufacture within an establishment of a great variety of ultimately merchantable goods. But until these goods are determined upon, no conversion of the steam-generating service into a money-bringing-in service is possible.[3]

---

[3] The amount and character of equipment installed may compel some plant operation in order to minimize loss, despite unfavorable market conditions. A steel manufacturer may have to continue operations (in some kind or kinds of products) even though he must lose money; for he may lose less by continuing than he would by abandoning his plant or selling it to another, or dismantling it for scrap. In general the "natural" income,

Advantages of Direct Valuation.—The advantages of direct valuations, if they can be made with a fair degree of reliability, over indirect valuations, are obvious. If a merchant has made a sale of goods to a solvent purchaser and has taken in exchange a note for three months the present worth of the note is more useful information to every one interested in the enterprise than is the "cost" of the goods sold or any other index of value, however derived. On the other hand, an attempt to obtain a sales-yield valuation of the raw materials inventory of a watchmaker—no matter how carefully one estimates allowances for manufacturing and other costs or outlays, one is not likely to find a figure more reliable than some more simply determined indirect valuation. "Cost" or "market" or "cost or market whichever is lower" applied to each class of materials in such an inventory may be equally or more reliable; and any of these avoids a spurious appearance of accuracy. Cost of such an inventory may not be very satisfactory information, but if any one treats it as though it were a reliable direct valuation he has himself to blame for any adverse consequences of his adoption of the figure. The valuer has discharged his duty when he has ascertained or closely approximated the cost and has described his mode of ascertaining cost.

Limits of Direct Valuation.—Just where direct valuation should leave off and indirect valuation should begin is a matter that cannot be simply expressed in general terms. To decide, as the accountants formerly did, that only certain kinds of items, e.g., cash, accounts and notes receivable, debt securities held, the concern's own liabilities, etc., can legitimately be valued directly, and that these must always be so valued is needlessly to limit the usefulness of their own reports. Circum-

---

the direct immediate service of a capital instrument, is much more stable and more readily forecast than is a future sales receipts series. Despite the prevailing degree of specialization actually observed in output it is rare that the equipment of any concern is limited in usefulness solely to the production of any one product of given specifications. A machine, even though it can render only truly unique services, may nevertheless be useful in preparing many different kinds and grades of product for the market.

stances may exist in which elements of each of these (except, possibly, cash) may not be appropriately valued directly. But the chief needless limit upon usefulness lay in refusal, in appropriate circumstances, to value certain items directly. If the error in a direct valuation is very likely to be less than the difference between the true value and any index or indirect valuation, it is plainly advantageous, cost of ascertainment aside, to adopt the direct measure.

No great amount of space need be given here to the valuation of those items which accountants habitually value directly. Their direct valuations very closely conform to theoretical requirements. Some few minor inconsistencies need to be pointed out and, in the case of certain items, the form of expressing the valuation requires comment.

Valuation of Financial Items

Accounts Receivable.—If, and to the extent that, direct valuation is undertaken, all valuations should be properly adjusted with respect to time. The prospective receipt of a dollar tomorrow has a different significance from the equally probable prospect of a dollar a year hence. The realized income, in other words, must be discounted. In valuing cash or demand liabilities, since the waiting period is zero or negligible, no discounting operation need be performed. The valuation is completed by multiplying the item to be realized in the (extremely near) future by unity instead of by the reciprocal of one plus the interest on one. When time becomes zero, interest, no matter what the rate, becomes zero. In valuing accounts receivable, accountants make an allowance for excess of customers' balances over the amount that is expected to be collected—the familiar allowance for bad debts—but they rarely discount this adjusted balance for a period corresponding to the accounts receivable turnover period. Granting the propriety of the allowance actually made for bad debts as such, the residual balance is habitually overvalued. Moreover there are other elements of overvaluation in this item. Rarely, except when some extraordinarily expensive difficulty in collecting some account or accounts is anticipated, do the accountants make an estimate of collection costs and deduct this from the amount outstanding. Some accountants, though the number is becoming fewer, do not eliminate from this item the amounts of cash discounts still available to customers. Except to the extent that the allowance for bad debts may be great enough to equal the losses plus discounts to be taken, costs of collection, and interest on the investment, the accounts receivable may be overvalued. That is to say, there is not a probable dollar-for-dollar equivalence between the cash item and the accounts receivable.

It will not do to object that the waiting period is short, that all costs of collection do become charged, and that some available discounts may not be taken. Every one knows that the proportion of available discounts varies, that, at times, collections, though certain, may be slow and expensive, and that the amount of accounts receivable balances fluctuates from year-end to year-end. Nor is it satisfactory to object that generous allowances are usually made for bad debts. The valuation may be conservative but the wrong expense accounts are affected.

Notes Receivable.—Notes receivable are similarly valued. If the notes are "interest bearing" and are shown at "face" value there will appear an "accrued interest receivable" valuation account to express the increase of value since the issue of the notes. Non-interest bearing notes that arise out of loans of money are also expressed at face value, but an "unearned interest receivable" valuation account with a credit balance will offset this special overvaluation. But if non-interest bearing notes arise directly from sales at invoice prices that contemplate a credit under such notes, not all accountants will reduce the face valuation to allow for interest. Nor do all make allowances for expense of collection. This latter item, except on dishonored notes, is relatively small when the debtor makes the note payable at a bank. There is some tendency to overvalue notes receivable but it is a lesser tendency than in the case of open accounts.

Investments.—Investments in bonds and other instruments or contracts that are readily capable of direct valuation are usually properly valued in the sense that appropriate effect is given to waiting periods. In the case of some relatively short-term issues the discount or premium accounts are sometimes scaled down from period to period in amounts determined by dividing the total original balance (of the discount or premium) by the number of periods to run. This practice, as compared with the appropriate effective rate method, undervalues bonds bought at a premium and overvalues those bought at a discount.

Short-Term Debts.—The relatively small errors found above in the short-term receivables have their counterparts in the valuation of short-term debts. A debt of a dollar due a year hence has, numerically, a smaller value than one due in one day. But on commercial obligations, not by their terms interest-bearing, accountants habitually state the future amount to be paid rather than the present worth. Some, too, do not deduct cash discounts available at the date of the balance sheet even though it is the habitual practice of the concern under audit to pay all its commercial accounts within the discount period. Failure to deduct the discounts receivable often results in larger error than is made in neglecting the interest factor on accounts that are to be allowed to run their full term.

Statistically Erratic Procedure.—It will have been noted that the errors just considered tend to cancel one another, as far as their effect upon the net proprietorship is concerned. An overvaluation of a current asset, since it has a positive sign, has the opposite effect from a numerical overvaluation of a liability. The credit or debit balance of errors is usually very small. Neglect of discounts available, either to customers or to the concern under consideration, and neglect of collection costs is believed to be worth remedying. Neglect of the interest factor, on the other hand, is not so serious. Indeed, a very good case can be made out for stating both the current receivables and the current payables (within a limit of, say one year) at their full future value, i.e., at principal *and* interest. If these current financial items are so expressed they would exhibit expected dollar-receipts from the asset sources named, and dollar-disbursements required to be made, as a result of the business done in the late part of the previous period. Such an exhibit is, in some ways, more convenient to use than one in which effect has been given to interest. But one or the other ought certainly to be chosen. Either all current receivables and all current payables should be discounted or none should be. Interest is implied in every contract of deferred payment whether it be expressed or not. Nor does an expressed rate of interest necessarily conform to the real rate implied in the transaction. Thus if the alternative terms available to a buyer are: (a) $100 with 2% discount if paid in 10 days, net $100 due in 30 days, or (b) a note for $100 due in three months with interest at 6%, the real rate for three months is $101.50 — 98/98, or 3.57%, or about 14.29% per year.

It must not be supposed that the remarks just made about the valuation of current items are intended in any serious way as an adverse criticism of accountants. Rather the opposite is true; the smallness of the errors in detail and in resultant aggregate is intended to be depicted in order to exhibit a proper contrast with the much larger errors of estimate that cannot possibly be avoided in certain of the indirect measures. In the following paragraphs the case of inventory valuation is discussed. There is no ground whatever for hope that direct inventory valuations, except in a few scattered cases, can ever become so reliable or so precise as the direct measures now commonly found for current receivables, current liabilities and conservatively secured evidences of debt. But there is ground for hope that direct valuation of inventories may become generally more reliable than the indirect valuations that now prevail.

Valuation of Inventories

Experimenting with Rules.—One does not have to go far back into the literature to find accountants dealing summarily with the subject of inventory valuation. The great handbooks on auditing, notably Dicksee's and the earlier editions of Montgomery's, dismissed the subject with a few sentences or paragraphs. From "cost" as the prevailing rule, a shift, later concurred in by the profession in America, was made to "cost or market, whichever is the lesser." This latter rule was spoken of as "more conservative." But the recent literature shows a marked discontent with both these rules. Close observation of recent practice will disclose the fact that the older rules can no longer be said to prevail. As yet no clearly marked tendencies toward the general adoption of any particular rule can be shown. The profession is, consciously or unconsciously, experimenting with rules.

But is this experimenting a new thing or merely a more striking manifestation of a continuing willingness to alter procedures to fit new conditions? Even in the days when an almost unanimous assent seemed to be given to the rule of "cost or market, whichever is the lesser"[4] both by the writers and the practitioners, there was no real uniformity that went beyond the mere "form of words" used to describe practice. To have a meaning at all, the cost or market rule must have its terms statistically defined. Let us see what they did mean.

[4] For the sake of brevity this rule will hereinafter be referred to by the term "cost or market."

Meaning of "Cost or Market."—In the first place, neither cost nor market referred to the inventory as an entirety but to the severally considered specific commodities entering into it. A crude scheme of the process can be shown as follows:

THE A TRADING COMPANY
MERCHANDISE STOCK SHEETS
December 31, 1927

Commodity	Quantity	Cost	Market	Cost or Market
A............	24 doz.	$ 30.00	$ 28.80	$ 28.80
B............	100 lbs.	50.00	60.00	50.00
C............	10 cases	27.00	25.00	25.00
X............	50 cases	125.00	140.00	125.00
Totals......	....	$27,000.00	$28,000.00	$24,000.00

If for some items "cost" is the lesser and for others "market" is the lesser then the "cost or market" summation is necessarily less than either the "cost" total or the "market" sum. It is well known that even in periods of general change in price level particular commodity prices do not move in parallel lines; some rise while others stand firm and still others fall.[5] Even in a period of rapid, general rise of prices, cost or market will generally show a total less than cost; and during periods of rapid price declines the cost or market figure is less than market. Much has been said about the "conservatism" of this rule. Later we shall inquire into the merits of this kind of conservatism.

Meaning of Cost.—But what is cost? What items enter into the cost summation? Even in the heyday of the rule there

---
[5] To get an adequate notion of the instability of particular prices with respect to an existing price level see Mills, The Behavior of Prices, items indexed under "price dispersions" and "price displacements."

was no agreement. There has never been a general agreement upon any single element of cost! Consider a simple case of a retail merchant. In his closing inventory he finds 12 cases of a given brand of canned asparagus. He had 10 cases on hand at the previous stock-taking. In the interval he has bought 120 cases. He has bought from various persons at fluctuating prices. For simplicity's sake assume that all lots were bought on the same terms, 2/10—net/30, f. o. b. seller.[6]

His last three shipments received, in calendar order of receipt, were 10, 5, and 4 cases at invoice prices of $2.60, $2.50, and $2.55 respectively per case. He took his cash discount on the first of these, he lost it on the second, and, on the inventory date he still has the privilege of a cash discount on the last. What is the *purchase-price cost element* in these 12 cases on hand? Is it the implied cash price available within 10 days of shipment, or the invoice price, or the invoice price less such discounts as the merchant took advantage of? All three of these purchase price elements have been recognized. But which purchase lots determine this cost price: (1) the last one only; or (2) 4 cases (the size of the purchase order) at the last price of $2.55, 5 cases at $2.50, and 3 cases at $2.60; or (3) some average of the whole year's dealing? All three (counting several kinds of averages as one) of these methods found a following. Does freight and cartage inward enter into this cost? If so how much and how determined: (1) some percentage of the year's total inward freight; or (2) the freight actually paid on each shipment? Again there was no agreement.

If for "retail merchant" we substitute "manufacturer" the diversities of meaning attached to "cost" become endlessly numerous. How shall the materials used be priced; how shall "direct labor" be charged; how shall overhead be distributed? What items enter into overhead; how shall "unearned burden" be treated? Does it make any difference whether "process"

---

[6] That is, the buyer pays the freight. He may pay the invoice price in 30 days, or if he elects to pay within 10 days of shipment, he will receive a discount of 2% on the invoice price.

costs or "manufacturing order" costs or no cost accounts at all are kept? In statistical reality "cost" has indefinitely many meanings.

Meaning of Market.—The meaning of "market" was (and is) even more confused than that of "cost." In a loose way it can be said to be equivalent to cost (whatever cost means) of replacing the inventory on the best terms available at the date of the inventory. No difficulty that is encountered in finding "cost" is absent in finding "market"; and there are several additional difficulties. Prices quoted are not necessarily the prices the concern in question would have to pay. Freight charges on carload lots, made up of many kinds of things bought simultaneously from one seller, are less than charges for small shipments of particular commodities, etc. In the case of manufacturers there is often no price quoted except those of competing sellers of like goods. For partly manufactured goods there are no quoted prices at all. For these latter items accountants usually adopted the most recently experienced costs of production.

When it is said that in statistical reality there is not, and never has been, *a rule* of cost or market but a myriad of rules described by *the same form of words*, it is not implied that there ought to be one rule and one only of this type. The writer does not believe that any best "all-purpose" rule for the indirect valuation of inventories is capable of formulation. Even if such a rule be expressed in a formula sufficiently detailed to cover all cases, there is no good reason for supposing that for the greater number of enterprises a better rule special to the enterprise could not readily be found. There is abundant ground for supposing that the diversity of rules found in practice occurs for this very reason; the client and the accountant are simply agreed that both "cost" and "market" need to be defined with reference to the special problems presented in the enterprise under examination.

Choice of Rule.—Nor when the merits of a direct valuation are urged is it intended to be asserted that professional accountants are wholly or even chiefly responsible for failure to adopt the superior method. Accountants do not manage businesses. Even when they direct the taking of an inventory they are not wholly free to take it in any manner they see fit to adopt. After all, it is not the accountant's inventory. The accountant's whole duty to his client and to the public is summed up in this: is the inventory valuation such a valuation as is likely to mislead any legitimately interested person to his serious harm? If it is, the accountant, as an independent, responsible principal, must not certify to the balance sheet setting it forth without some qualifying comment upon the valuation. If it is not he may accept it without comment. That which does not deviate materially from the usual and normal, i.e., that which conforms to established custom, is acceptable without comment.

If accountants have been at fault in inventory valuation the fault lies in not urging upon their clients a more rational and direct mode of valuation. To what extent accountants have urged better methods the present writer does not know, but he does presume a goodly amount of inertia in the matter on the part of both accountants and clients.

Inventory Value and Going Concern Value.—Given favorable conditions, how ought an inventory of merchantable goods to be valued? To answer this requires an answer to the question, what is "going-concern" valuation? That is here taken, ideally, to mean "that valuation which would be most significant and useful to the owner or prospective owner of the valued thing in the conditions and circumstances in which it is held." This amounts to saying that the valuation should be dependent solely upon the contemplated use of the valued thing in the operations of the enterprise. With respect to an inventory of merchantable goods held for sale, this contemplated use is the bringing in of money funds. The present worth of the amount of money that can be got for them in the conditions in which the enterprise is placed, less the present worth of the future outlays and expenses properly referable to such a dollar-volume of trade expresses not merely the chief but the only significance this existing stock of goods can have.

The Proper Rôles of Direct Valuation, of Cost, and of Market.—It is not asserted that cost is without significance. Cost has a very great significance. Cost already incurred plus future costs to be absorbed by the margin between cost and future selling price determine how much net operating revenue will result as a direct or proximate result of having acquired these goods for sale. Cost is needed to determine how much of the outlays and expenses incurred in this year are properly referable to next year's operating reports. The cost of this year's closing inventory is not a cost incurred in obtaining this year's net income. But neither the amount of net revenue to be got from the purchases represented by this inventory nor the cost incurred with the intent to obtain income next year measures the significance of the goods themselves. There may be some numerical relation between the amount of cost and the amount of net yield to be had; cost series and income series may be related, but they are not identities. The importance of the goods, the probable results of having decided to get the goods, and the division of costs between the year that has closed and the year that is opening are not only wholly distinct but wholly independent ideas.

Nor is it asserted that market is without significance. Clearly the spread between the existing market and the available selling price may be of the utmost importance in determining what goods to acquire for sale in the future. The spread between cost of acquiring goods and the selling price of them must provide for both the expenses of selling and general administration and for whatever profit is to be had. But the significance of acquiring *more* goods of a given kind is quite a different thing from the significance of goods that *have been* acquired.

The essence of the situation is this: goods have been acquired and are now on hand; nothing can be done, now, about the costs incurred to acquire them; costs are history. Nor, with respect to the inventory actually held, can anything be done about market. Market has to do with operating cycles not yet begun. Inventory valuation has to do with the unfinished business.

Cost and market figures may, indeed, throw some light upon probable selling prices. If in any particular industry the spread between cost and selling price seems to center about some particular interval, the existing market quotations may help to form an opinion about the stability of an existing selling price. If a high degree of correlation exists between current costs (market) and selling price then any marked deviation of an existing margin from the predominant margin can reasonably be expected not to persist long. But if the degree of correlation between selling prices at one date and selling prices at a date a week or a month later is greater than that between present market (or past cost) and selling price a week or a month later, then present selling price is better evidence of later selling price than is either cost or market. It is, of course, desirable to have all the valid evidence available. Cost must be estimated in any case; market needs to be determined if budgets are to be prepared. But primary valuations based on going selling prices and adjusted to take account of any change of future selling price that has been announced, or any change implied by the status of market costs, may be more reliable valuations than are found by other methods.

Valuation at Selling Price Minus.—The lead in valuing inventories at selling price, less expenses of conducting a volume of business operations corresponding to the amount of the inventory, has been taken by the meat packers, mining concerns, oil-producing and refining enterprises, and concerns dealing in cotton and grain. In a considerable number of local instances retail merchants, particularly department stores, have adopted the practice. It is no longer matter for surprise to find an unqualified certificate attached to a balance sheet in which the inventory has been valued at selling price less estimated expenses allocable to the volume of sales represented by the inventory.[7]

This book is not a proper place in which to set out a fully developed discussion of inventory valuation; the purposes of this book are satisfied by a sketch of conventional practices, mention of what appear to be true recent advances, and the bare outlines of a scheme toward which it seems desirable to work. It will be noted that the scheme proposed below does not abandon cost or market but supplements that rule. It attempts not only to find figures appropriate for carrying value in the balance sheet and for use in determining cost of goods sold but also to find figures that show the position of the concern in the market in which it buys (or manufactures) and in the market in which it sells. It provides, in other words for the three aggregates, viz., cost, market, and net selling value to yield some named rate upon the investment. Each of these figures has a special significance. The simultaneous exhibit of all of them in their proper relations one to another must, of necessity, be more convenient than any one figure to the management, to trade creditors, to bankers, and to shareholders. The proposal is outlined in the paragraphs immediately following.

For finished goods, that is, goods intended to be sold in the form in which they are held, unit prices should be expressed

---

[7] For an index to the recent developments of the professional accountant's views upon this problem of inventory valuation compare the text matter on the subject in the second, third, and fourth editions of Montgomery's Auditing Theory and Practice. See also the Income Tax Regulations on the same subject for the corresponding period.

for cost, for market, and for carrying value. The unit prices for cost and for market may be determined in any way thought to be most suitable to the enterprise. The method of determining unit cost and unit market prices should, of course, become a part of the inventory record and be certified to by the person responsible for pricing. The carrying value price might be determined in a number of ways. The one suggested here is to multiply each unit selling price by a fixed constant, k. This constant is determined as follows. (1) Standard ratios to sales (preferably averages of the concern's own experience) should be found for loss on bad debts, selling expenses, and general expenses including costs of collection (but not interest paid or other distribution items like income taxes). (2) Some normal industrial rate of return converted to an average rate on the concern's own inventories should be found. The constant which is to be multiplied into each selling price then becomes one minus the sum of the rate allowances for subsequent expenses and for a normal profit on the inventory.[8]

The A Trading Company

Stock Sheet, Inventory of Finished Goods, December 31, 1928.

Items	Quantity	Unit Prices			Values			Cost less Carrying value	
		Market	Cost	$k \times$ sales	Market	Cost	Carrying Value	+	−
A.......	100	$1.25	$1.20	$1.27	$ 125	$ 120	$ 127		$ 7
B.......	200	4.00	4.10	4.05	800	820	810	$ 5	
C.......	200	5.00	5.10	4.80	1,000	1,020	960	60	
D.......	1,000	4.50	4.55	4.30	4,500	4,555	4,300	255	
E.......	1,000	5.00	4.90	4.95	5,000	4,900	4,950		50
X.......	500	2.00	1.75	2.15	1,000	875	1,075		200
Totals...					$124,000	$125,000	$118,000	$8,000	$1,000

[8] Thus if the following rates are found: for loss on bad debts, 0.01; for selling expense, 0.24; for general expense, 0.12; and for normal net profit on sales, 0.03, the constant, k, becomes $1-(0.01+0.24+0.12+0.03)$ or 0.6. This figure times the unit selling price gives the unit carrying value or the price per unit upon which a normal profit can be made.

Stock sheets should be devised to provide columns as follows: (1) identification of items; (2) quantities on hand; (3) unit prices at market, at cost, and at k times the selling price; (4) values at market, at cost, and at k times the selling price; and (5) excesses of cost over carrying value and excesses of carrying value over cost. The illustrative sheet above is intended to be schematic only; it is not put forward as a form.

From the summaries of the stock sheets the balance sheet items can be made up directly thus:

Finished goods inventory—cost.......	$125,000
Add excesses of carrying value over cost..........................	1,000
	$126,000
Less excesses of cost over carrying value	8,000
Carrying value estimated to yield x% net on sales	$118,000

A footnote to the inventory item may then be expressed thus:

Inventory at market.......................... $124,000[9]

Advantages of Multiple Valuations.—It is obvious that the carrying value may be higher than the greater of cost or market or lower than cost or market or may occupy any intermediate position. But in no case can the balance sheet exhibit be said to lack conservatism unless *all* of the valuation figures are too high. On the other hand, it should be observed that it gives, in addition to the information that *any one* of the figures could give, the following items of information:

---

[9] It will be noted that provision for any additional analysis that special circumstances suggest may readily be made. Cost or market can be had by inserting a column in which to record the cost valuation or the market valuation, whichever is the lower. Or two columns may be inserted in one of which excesses of cost over market may be recorded; in the other, excesses of market over cost may be entered. Similar analyses of differences between market and carrying value may likewise be made. Whether or not these difference data are worth computing can be determined only by the special circumstances of an enterprise. The writer thinks such data likely to be much more useful to department heads, to sales managers, to budget officers, to bankers and others than much of the current output of "research departments" of many concerns.

1. The trend of the buying market (or of manufacturing cost). Both aggregate cost and aggregate market are shown. The difference between them measures the movement within the carrying period. In the illustration given, $125,000 — $124,000 = $1,000, or a decline of 0.008 on cost.

2. The spread between current cost (market) and net selling value to yield a normal profit. In the illustration given $124,000 — $118,000 = $6,000, or 0.048 on market. This indicates the deficiency below a normal rate of profit that the concern may expect to earn on new business within the near future.

3. The spread between cost and net selling value. In the illustration this comes to $125,000 — $118,000 = $7,000, or 0.053 on cost. This is the expected deficiency below a normal rate that the concern expects to experience on their present inventory.

4. A measure of dispersion of price spreads. In the example shown the concern has a prospect of earning $1,000 more than a profit at the normal rate on some goods and $8,000 less on others.

Not only does the proposed plan give this additional information, but the carrying value extended in the balance sheet has the special merit of being more conservative than any of the prevailing rules when conservatism is most needed, viz., in periods of declining prices in which concerns are forced to sell at a loss and at end-of-season inventory periods when prices are cut to move seasonal goods, and in the case of concerns that are low profit earners.

Much has been said of the conservatism of the cost or market rule. It is not conservative in any sense whatsoever except this: The figure thus found is a lower sum than is the sum of costs or the sum of estimated replacement costs. Not only are there times when both market and cost are so high for a whole trade that a profit cannot be made on either, but there are always some enterprises that cannot possibly earn a profit or break even on such a valuation. In the year 1920, we had the spectacle of many trades unable to move their inventories at prices that would either repay their actual costs or the prices at which they could have replaced their stocks.

If by "conservatism" were meant "a valuation at which there is a reasonable prospect for a fair profit," the cost or market rule is least conservative when conservatism is most needed, viz., (1) in periods of falling prices; (2) in the case of concerns that are generally losers or low profit earners; and (3) at end-of-season periods when stock must either be moved at low prices or at high costs of selling. On the other hand it is most "conservative" when conservatism is least important, viz.: (1) in periods of rising prices; (2) in the case of steadily prosperous concerns; and (3) in the case of beginning-of-season or mid-season inventories. In such cases conservatism may be a dubious merit.

A Shortened Procedure.—The procedure outlined above can be greatly shortened and still be better than either the cost, market, or cost or market rules. If cost is found in the ordinary way and extensions are made at selling prices also, the summation of the selling value column can be multiplied by the constant described on page 222. But the labor saved (admittedly considerable) must be set off against the value of nearly all the special information, mentioned above, that can be had only when several valuations are made and when the differences among them are analyzed.

The shortened process proposed above should be much less difficult and expensive than the cost or market procedure both in the original record and in subsequent verification by public accountants. Certain "market" data, of course, can always be obtained. The great works on auditing recite at considerable lengths the means of "verifying market prices." But the difficulties of "verifying" a price not actually paid or a "cost of replacement" not actually incurred, are obvious. It is the writer's opinion that both "market" pricings in inventory sheets and their verification by auditors are much less reliable than the corresponding "cost" pricings. On the other hand, both costs and selling prices and the elements that enter into the value of the constant to be multiplied into selling prices are all matters of record in the accounts and vouchers of the concern under audit. And the time that must necessarily elapse between the date of the final statements and the date of their certification by public accountants is sufficiently great to disclose the existence of fictitious selling prices and unit costs that may have been taken into the stock sheets whether through inadvertence or with intent. If in following the suggested procedure the "cost" is less than the carrying value and if the accountant feels it to be objectionable to "anticipate profits" to the extent of the difference, an item corresponding to this difference can be shown in the surplus items under some such caption as "deferred profits, excess of inventory over cost," just as is now commonly done in the balance sheets of those who sell on instalment contracts.[10]

In the income statement the cost valuation is obviously the figure to employ in establishing the figure for "cost of goods sold." The difference between cost and carrying value should be given effect as an independent item of gain (or loss).

In some cases it may be possible to treat partly manufactured goods in the same way. Thus if the finished goods to result are definitely known. i.e., if the partly manufactured goods attach to manufacturing orders that specify the finished product completely, an estimated cost to complete can be made at the most recently experienced costs. From the estimated sales prices of the finished goods, the cost to finish, as

---

[10] Whether profits are "anticipated" or not depends upon the answer to the question "where do profits begin?" Certainly profits are not anticipated by the procedure, for valuing at selling price less allowances, described above in any sense in which they are not anticipated in the conventional mode of valuing accounts receivable.

well as other items to be deducted from finished goods, can be subtracted.

Once into the field of unfinished goods and raw materials, it becomes plain that the forecasting is at much longer range and subject to much larger degrees of error than it is in the case of accounts receivable.

Summary of Inventory Valuations.—Whether or not a direct valuation, year after year, can be more reliable than "cost" or "cost or market" is a matter to be decided in the light of all the evidence available in the case of each enterprise Whichever promises to be the more reliable indicator of net funds to be produced by the conversion of the inventories should be chosen. Since an inventory valuation, as such, can have no significance except as an index of funds to be produced, no rational grounds can be assigned for preferring a less reliable to a more reliable index.

If any substantial increase in reliability can be had at reasonable expense by resorting to direct valuation, clearly it is worth getting, and, in any event, the direct valuation gives *additional* information. The inventory is almost always the biggest single current item in merchandising concerns. In mercantile establishments, too, it is often the largest item in the balance sheet. The present writer's belief is that, in proportion to the effort needed to accomplish it, improvement of inventory valuation offers a prospect for a greater gain in usefulness of accounting reports than does any other element of technique in accountancy.

Once more it is emphasized that the theory of inventory valuation is not concerned solely with finding a "conservative" value or a value that most reliably indicates the outcome of the unfinished business represented by inventories. Almost any two valuations can give more reliable information than either taken alone. If several are taken and an analysis of their difference is made, the value of the additional information may be of the utmost importance. This is particularly true of concerns that are compelled by the character of their business to project their operating programs far into the future, and for concerns whose problems of joint costs and of unused capacity are major problems.

CHAPTER XII

INDIRECT VALUATION

"Capital Value" vs. "Prudent Investor Valuation"

In the preceding chapter only those items capable of direct valuation were dealt with. But, as was shown in the chapter on financial condition,[1] there are many items not capable of a direct valuation. Certain assets, for example, are held not for sale or for separate hire, but to be used jointly with many others in bringing forth some final marketable product or products. When it comes to the value or to the valuation of these at intervals of a fiscal period, the economist's pronouncements are not of much assistance. It is a commonplace of economic theory to assert that at the margin of purchases the value of capital instruments is derived from and determined by the value of their expected services. Thus Fisher says:[2]

> No one will dispute that the buyer of any article of capital will value it for its expected services to him, and that "at the margin" of his purchases, the price he will pay is the equivalent to him of those expected services, or, in other words, is their "present worth," their "discounted value" or "capitalized value." But some doubt may be felt regarding the professional seller. As to him, he is simply a speculator as to the possible demand. He sells for what he can get, affixing whatever price he believes will, in the end, profit him most, sometimes making out of the transaction more than his costs of acquisition, sometimes less, usually, or normally, covering those costs plus interest on them for the time elapsing between their occurrence and sale.

Meaning of the Economist's Theory of Capital Value.— Before one can intelligently accept or dispute the proposition

---
[1] See pp. 183-191.
[2] Capital and Income, p. 189.

about the value of an article of capital, one must know what it means. The proposition might mean:

1. Unless he thinks the services of an article will have a money value, no buyer will pay money for the article.
2. From the amount of money a buyer pays, we *may infer something about* the amount of money value he attaches to the future services of the article. If the purchase be "at the margin,"[3] we *may infer that the price is no greater than the present value placed by the buyer upon the services of the article in question.*

On the other hand, the proposition might mean:

1. An article of capital is capable of rendering a series of unit services.
2. These unit services can be foreseen with some degree of accuracy both with respect to number and time of receipt.
3. A money value may rationally be attached to a unit of service.
4. A money value may be placed upon a correspondingly scheduled series of disservices, i.e., repair charges, maintenance, etc.
5. The capital value of the two series of money-valued items (units of service and units of disservice) *determines the price to be paid for an article of capital* in purchases "at the margin."

Propositions about the value of articles of capital substantially like the one quoted from Fisher above abound in economic writings. Careful examination of them and of the context in which they appear shows that either or both of the meanings outlined above are implied in these propositions.

---
[3] Purchase "at the margin" is taken to mean that at the time of the transaction and in the whole of the material circumstances and estimated prospects of the buyer, he will take no more units of the article in question than he actually does take. Assuming ability of the seller (or sellers) to transfer more units of the article than are actually taken, every purchase implies the inclusion of a marginal purchase. If only one article is taken that article is a marginal unit.

If the meanings of the proposition are brought to the accountant's problem of valuation, it can be said that in the first meaning the theorem is very nearly useless, and that in the second the proposition is not true. The first meaning asserts nothing about how the numerical magnitude of the valuation is determined in the first instance; and the second lays down conditions to the assessing of valuations that cannot be fulfilled.

Deficiencies of Capital Value Theory.—Consider the deficiencies of the first meaning. The accountant is faced with the problem of valuing simultaneously many articles of capital. His balance sheet exhibits valuations as at the close of business of a named date. At that point of time no purchases, marginal or otherwise, are being made. Moreover, with respect to the articles of capital held, not for separate sale or for separate rental, no really corresponding articles have been, or will be, purchased. Whatever might have been inferred about the value of the future services of the articles when they were bought can no longer be inferred. Not only is the future series of services now available a different one from that which was available at purchase, but it is available in different present material circumstances, and it is available for a future course of affairs that looks different from the prospect at the time when the article was bought. This meaning offers no real help at all except at the time of the original valuation entry.

Upon the "prudent investor" meaning, whereby the price paid for an article is imputed to (rather than derived from) the value of the services to be rendered, the accountant can and does approve entering an article of capital at cost. This acceptance of cost as an original valuation is founded upon the presumption that the acquiring of the article in the circumstances and prospects was a reasonably prudent act. If acquired by one acting in a representative capacity, there is a further presumption of good faith. But even for a first valuation these are presumptions only; and if at some later time the accountant discovers sufficient evidence to overturn either or both presumptions, he must determine his present valuations in the light of that evidence as well as in the light of changed conditions and prospects. The existence of what is called a "purchaser's surplus" lessens but does not eliminate the desirability of reconsideration.

Consider the deficiencies of the second meaning. In this sense the proposition implies a mode of determining a capital value. In some measure all of the conditions can be fulfilled except the third. Unless an article is thought to be capable of rendering services, it is, by definition, not an article of capital. All our experience shows that, one item with another, we can make a better estimate of the amount and time distribution of services than any mere random or ignorant guess. The physical properties implied in the specifications of the article are, in general, well enough known and are sufficiently stable to enable us rationally to assume with confidence at least some minimum time schedule of technical services. We also know from experience, either with like objects in use or from observation of the behavior in use of the elementary parts of an object, a good deal about what repairing and maintaining operations will have to be performed to get the technical services. And we can form some estimate of the future operating outlays necessary to reduce cost per unit of service to a practicable minimum.

But the condition of independent, or primary, valuing of the service unit *in terms of money* can be fulfilled when, and only when, those services *are separately to be exchanged for money*. To the extent that a price per unit of service, whether for all or part of the service, can be rationally forecast we can value directly. But the items under consideration are those not to be sold or rented but to be used in conjunction with others for the making of a product that is to be sold. In a plant in which tractors are manufactured for sale, how much of the service of bringing in the dollar-receipts from a given sale is attributable to coal burned under the boilers, how much to the service of the boiler, how much to the various devices in foundry, machine shop, assembly floor, how much to the firemen, moulders, machinists, and night watchmen?

Value of Service not Derivable from Cost of Service.— We can, perhaps, approximate the contribution of the purchase or the hire of each of these agents to the total *cost* of the tractors sold in a given lot; and we might divide the sale price up into parts proportional to the elements of cost. *But this assumes the very set of capital values that we set out to determine!* For surely the purchase price paid for the article of capital becomes a part of the cost of the products upon which its services are expended. This kind of service unit valuation can be made to support any set of asset valuations whatsoever.

Capital instruments used jointly with others in turning out goods for sale do not, properly speaking, have separate *capital* values at all. Separate values they have, to be sure, but not values derivable from, and determinable by, any money-valued service series ordered in time. Their values represent a kind of opportunity differentials rather than independent summations. The economist's theory of capital value and of capital valuation has nowhere near so great a capacity for describing the conduct of men in exchanging capital instruments as most economists seem to suppose.

The Professional Buyer-Holder-Seller.—Consider now the adversative proposition quoted above, "But some doubt may be felt regarding the professional seller. As to him, he is simply a speculator as to the possible demand. He sells for what he can get, affixing whatever price he believes will, in the end, profit him most, sometimes making out of the transaction more than his costs of acquisition, sometimes less, usually, or normally, covering those costs plus interest on them for the time elapsing between their occurrence and the sale." It is this antithetical statement that needs development if economic theory is to throw much light upon the valuation of capital goods. Doubt is, indeed, felt as to the professional seller. Perhaps he is simply a speculator, but his speculating is no simple matter. For the professional seller, except of his own labor services, is a professional buyer and a professional holder also. It is this professional buyer, holder, and seller who chiefly feels the need of valuations of his holdings. The professional seller seldom sells exactly what he buys unchanged in form, amount, place of delivery, and so on. There is a professional seller or a professional buyer in nearly all transactions; and in the great preponderance of transactions there are both a professional buyer and a professional seller. Doubt about the positive proposition in the case of the professional seller's valuation turns out to be doubt about most valuations.

Nature of an Enterprise.—The professional buyer-holder-seller, the business man, operates through an organization that we call an enterprise.[4] *The essence of a business enterprise is an ordered selection and integration of controlled services calculated to enable the directing person or persons to bring into the market goods or services that can be sold with advantage.* It is no mere chaotic aggregate of things and persons or of the services of things and persons. It is an ordered, though changing, assembly. Design, selection, integration, alteration, and control characterize it quite as much as aggregation. It can survive change of identity and kind of operative agents, whether men or things; it may survive change of ownership in holdings, change of management, change of goods or services offered to the public. It is a creation of men capable of many changes at their will and capable of use by successors to its organizers.

---

[4] It was said (p. 55) that the personification of the enterprise is a mere figure not in accord with realities. But an enterprise is nevertheless a real thing with a real existence apart from any particular party (or class of parties) in interest. Paton's discussion of the enterprise as an "institution" (Accounting Theory, pp. 472-480) is an admirable one.

The Prudent Investor's Valuations

Services—Not Agents—Are Wanted.—But with respect to any projected operating policy or program, there is one thing not capable of change, viz., the set of services essential to the bringing into existence of the thing or things to be sold. The steel manufacturer wants, not blast furnaces, open-hearth furnaces, and rolling mills, but *separation* of metal from ore, heat *treatment* of metal, and *shaping* of metal. He might get along without a private power plant but not without a power *service*. He does not primarily want men and machines; he wants the events that can be made to occur by means of men and machines. He does not care whether a service is to be performed by a man or by a machine. But if he is to run his enterprise at all he must have the service at *whatever price he has to pay for it*.

How Services Are Obtained.—How do organizers and managers obtain and perpetuate this controllable stream of component services in order to obtain the resultant money income? Given a cross-section of this complex service flow that shows the due proportion and identity of the essential elements, how is that flow to be maintained? So far as the problem of valuation is concerned, the significant element in the answers to these questions is this: this ordered *set* of services cannot be acquired in infinitesimal increments continuously supplied; they must be acquired in stocks. Housing for the internal operations of a machine shop cannot be supplied from moment to moment; nor can it be supplied economically from year to year. Within some relatively brief period provision for most of this service for a long future period can be most economically provided. So also with all the rest of the essential services or elements of these essential services. The only significant difference as among these services is the amount of the stock that can be most economically acquired at one time. The time element may vary from day-to-day purchases of the services of those things of which there is an assured, available and economical supply, to purchase of a site that may be required throughout the existence of the enterprise. A railroad company *can* buy postage stamps from day to day; it *must* acquire a right of way for the duration of its franchise.

There must be an investment for the future. Funds must be applied in the present to acquire services in the future. In a system of private enterprise there must be a giving of hostages to fortune. These investments once made are sunk. To be sure, a direct separate recovery by piecemeal sale can be had in whole or in part if the future prospects indicate that a realization is the best course open. But in modern enterprise a relatively small fraction of the investment is thus directly recapturable. Willy-nilly the natural services of the serving agents acquired must be utilized in making some other, marketable thing if the investment is not to be lost. To be sure, most capital agents are capable of rendering more than one kind of service. But this variety of service is strictly limited by the physical or intrinsic properties of the agent. More than one kind of combination of services, that is, more than one kind of product, can be had. In some cases many of these may be had with profit on the whole investment, past and future. But sometimes no combination can be made of an existing stock of services that will pay a profit on the investment. Sometimes no utilization of the existing stock can be made at all that will even pay a return on the future investment in the necessary supplementary services.

The Accountant Cannot Choose Conditions.—The accountant's valuations have to be made in the conditions that he finds. When he goes to work there is an investment already made, made in part for the very near future only and in part for the long distant future. All kinds of intermediate distributions of service stocks present themselves for his consideration. He may find abundant evidence to support the opinion that there are many optional combinations of present service stocks with future acquisitions that will pay high rates of return upon the whole investment past and future. He may find evidence that the concern is a hopeless loser, that no refinancing, no reorganization, no change of policy promises anything better than does. a complete winding up. He may find an intermediate condition. But no matter whether he has to prepare statements in support of an enormous goodwill valuation upon change of ownership of a prosperous concern, or a statement of affairs and deficiency account for a bankrupt, or the ordinary periodical reports of a going concern, he must make piecemeal valuations of whatever stocks he finds. And only in the case of the bankrupt can he rely wholly upon direct valuations or true capital values. In every other case he must make at least some valuations that are not, and cannot be, true capital values. There is no rational mode of dividing all future money receipts among the component services that, in their organized totality, have this future money income as a resultant.

Opportunity Differences.—What the accountant can do, and what modern practice is tending more and more to accomplish is to estimate *valuation differences*. How can this be done? If the absolute capital values cannot be determined, how can differences be found? The answer is that his valuations are not capital value differences at all; they are *opportunity differences*. In Chapter X[5] certain hypotheses of indirect valuation were expressed. In the light of what has just been said about the business enterprise, let us examine these propositions about indirect or opportunity valuations.

Note first of all that the propositions rule out the case in which no enterprise capital value exists in excess of that represented by the direct or true capital values. Where the accountant comes upon no item that is not either intended directly to be converted into a future money receipt through sale or that

---

[5] See pp. 187-189.

will not result in an outflow of money in the course of enterprise operations, no resort need be had to an index. He can express direct absolute values, though these, except in the case of money in hand, are subject to error of estimate. Thus the case of the concern that is being wound up is outside the propositions; for valuations that contemplate a termination consider only piecemeal receipts and disbursements. It is, of course, possible that the winding-up valuation of the enterprise should be equal to a going-concern valuation that contemplates continued operations. In such a case the *going value* is zero. *Going value* represents only the excess of the enterprise capital value over the winding-up or junk value.

Aside from the winding-up cases and a few trivial cases in which all items are held for direct conversion only, all engagements require a resort to going-concern, or indirect, or opportunity valuation. That is to say, the existing stocks of service available for future use can be so combined with stocks acquired in the future as to yield a rate of return on *future* outlays greater than that necessary to induce the future outlays to be made. Or, put in another way, the excess of the capital value of future receipts *for some given period* over the capital value of the incident future outlays implies a normal rate of return on a present sum greater than the capital value of the future outlays.

To speak of a value of future outlays implies two things: (1) the acquiring of future technical or natural services that are *necessary* to operations and hence to getting the future money receipts; and (2) the existence of an anticipated price at which the services can be had. But observe that though the present worth of the outlays is a true capital value of outlays, it is not a true capital value of the services to be had. These services must be had at *whatever* they cost provided only that the *sum* of the capitalized costs does not exceed the *sum* of the capitalized receipts. If one can afford to pay, and must pay in the conditions of the labor market, $50 for the services of a plumber *and* of a carpenter, it makes no difference whether one has to pay $25 to each or $49 for one and $1 for the other. Indeed, if the plumber cannot be had for less than $60 and the carpenter will pay $10 for the prestige of having worked for this employer, it is all the same to the employer. There is not only no necessary but no discoverable relation between separate service costs of two services and separate service values of the two services, provided both are requisite to the objective in mind.[6]

The Accountant's Indirect Valuations

The Case of a Losing Enterprise.—Suppose, now, the accountant coming to an engagement, finds: (1) that a large investment in future technical services has been made; (2) that there is a prospect of earning more by operations than could be realized by winding up now; but (3) that the total return that has been had and that may be had is less than the total investment that has been, and will have to be, made. How shall he value the technically employed assets of this concern that for want of prudence or want of good fortune was doomed from its foundation to be a losing venture?

Note first that it will pay *now* to continue operations rather than wind up. Heavy losses have been incurred that can never be wholly recouped, but this loss has not been so great as the total investment made less the total receipts thus far. To continue at all will require the acquisition of more services like those now available in stock as represented by the assets on hand. It is possible that some service of each kind now in stock must be acquired. It is further possible that some of each principal kind of service now in hand must be provided in the future. Moreover, it may not be possible to obtain any

---

[6] This does not imply that there is no direct, separate capital value of a service to the seller of the service. On the contrary, all services have a capital value to the seller of them. The buyer's necessities and the possible substitutions of serving agents available at a known price, determine the seller's bargaining position with respect to a particular buyer.

further service on terms in any way preferable to the terms on which the presently held services were obtained.

Suppose the concern to be designed and equipped for general machine manufacture. It has on hand certain metal-cutting tools. Like tools new at prices equal to those paid for the present tools are the most economical means available for continuing the metal-cutting service.

With respect to a particular kind of necessary tool, let the cost per unit of tool service (cost to include purchase price, stockroom and tool-dressing charges, etc.) for a new tool to be $0.05 per hour. Suppose a tool of this kind now on hand is capable of half as many hours' service at an equal cost of service per hour. Neglecting for the moment interest to represent the difference in duration as between a new and used tool, it is obvious that the used tool is worth at least half as much as a new one. This is true not because it is possible to capitalize the money equivalent of the services of the two tools and find that one is twice as great as the other; for that cannot be done. It is true because (1) tool service is necessary to carrying on operations; (2) it will pay to carry on operations; (3) tool service can be had at this price per unit; and (4) no substitute agent is available at a price which will permit getting the service for a lesser cost per unit. With respect to the whole situation it would be foolish conduct to pay more for a like used tool or to accept less for this used tool than half the price of a new one.

The argument made with respect to the used tool can be made for every capital instrument held. It is true even for the longest-lived capital instrument on hand. Consider the case of the building, assuming the site to be a leased site having a direct sublease value equal to the present worth of rentals paid. Suppose that, as a structural entirety, it will outlast any equipment within it. But it may require repairs, that is, replacement of some part or parts before it is abandoned. These parts may be, for all we can surely know, any part or parts. Repairs are paid to get future building service just as original construction was made to that end.

Aggregate of Fixed Tangible Assets a Sum of "Opportunity Differentials."—If the accountant does go through the whole establishment in the way suggested and does value every service stock in relation to what it would cost to get like service now, it is obvious that the sum of the asset valuations would be greater than the true capital value of the enterprise. But that is no adverse criticism of his valuation of assets. It merely illustrates the difference between direct and indirect valuations, or the diversity of "opportunity differential" valuations and capital valuations. Statistically considered, the summation of values of assets held for technical use is a sum of differences. Each item represents the difference to the concern between having a particular stock of services of a particular kind *without future outlay for it* and being wholly without such services in the buying-holding-operating-selling position of the enterprise at the time of valuation. Without altering the selling situation at all any one of the items could, legitimately, be higher if the buying present or future position were *worse*. All of the items could be higher in the like case. The only limit is that when the buying-holding-operating position becomes so bad that the enterprise capital value falls below the winding-up or scrap value *all* technical-use opportunity values vanish.

The Case of the "Excess Profit" Earning Enterprise.—Suppose, now, the accountant comes to an engagement in which there is abundant evidence to support the opinion that the concern can go on operating within a wide range of available choices of program and enjoy a difference between future receipts and future outlays that has a present worth vastly greater than the total outlays that have been made to obtain the present available stock of services. That is to say, the rate of return on outlays past and future that is now in prospect is greater than is necessary to induce *simultaneous present investment* in an amount equal to that made for service stocks or assets now in hand. Will the accountant find a *different* set of piecemeal asset valuations than he would if he found this *same stock* under the conditions previously assumed? Should he find a different set of valuations?

The first question is hard, indeed, to answer. No general answer is ventured here. In some instances the basis of valuation seems to be in inverse relation to the degree of prosperity of the concern. There does seem, on the part of some firms, to be a greater willingness to understate a genuinely great surplus in a very prosperous concern than to insist unconditionally upon the full statement of a large deficit. But it must emphatically be denied that there is conclusive evidence on the point. There are far too many factors like reasonably possible great losses from obsolescence that both the management and the accountant can appreciate. Nor is there even as much evidence to support the belief that accountants incline to accept underestimates of depreciation, etc., in the case of really prosperous concerns with any less reluctance than they would express at like overvaluations in a losing venture.

The second question is relatively easy to answer. There is no sound reason why the piecemeal valuations of assets, so long as the concern can advantageously continue operations, should be affected by the rate of gain or loss on the whole enterprise investment. It is just as irrational for a prosperous concern to value a given stock of technical services at more than it would cost to provide those services as it would be for a losing concern to do so. A prosperous concern could take no less for a diminution of an available stock of services than could a loser. A great diversity between the summation of asset valuations and a proper estimate of the capital value of the enterprise is wholly inescapable. The two valuations are of quite different orders.

Accountants' Valuations and Cost of Replacement.—It must not be supposed from the foregoing paragraphs that accountants have a "cost of replacement less depreciation" theory of valuation or that their practice in any way implies such a theory. "Cost of replacement less depreciation" usually refers to cost of replacing *capital goods* with others of like kind and quality. This is a fundamentally different thing from cost of replacing *stocks of services*. It is only when the cost of obtaining a given service by means of an instrument like the existing capital item is equal to or less than the cost of obtaining the like service by some other means that the two views would find numerically equal valuations.

Suppose A expects to require a great amount of calculating done. Upon that expectation he correctly foresees that he can get the work done at a lesser cost per unit, including interest on his investment, by buying an electrically driven calculator at $1,000, than by any other available means. But after getting only a small fraction of the service anticipated, his prospective requirements become so much less that he can get the work done cheaper by having clerks use their incidental idle time in working out the calculations without machine aid. In the meantime the price of such machines has advanced. Should A's book valuation of the machine reflect the increase in replacement price? Certainly not. It is worth no more to him than a price to yield him calculation service in the required amount at a cost per unit equal to the cost per unit by the most economical alternative means unless that valuation should fall below the resale value of the machine less cost of selling it. That is, if the technical-use differential value is less than the direct sale value the latter should be recognized.

Replacement of Services and Replacement of Agents.—The difference between cost of replacement of *instruments* and cost of replacement of *service* is not only great as an absolute matter of ideas, it is also great as a matter of money-value consequence. Suppose A has bound himself to a single payment lease contract upon a building and site for fifteen years. He has just set up his business on the premises. He now learns of an equally good site and building that might be had at a rental for a like term for $5,000 less than the one he has taken. Does the proper value of his site and building service diminish by $5,000? Not at all. It would cost him something to move his goods and equipment, he would lose some sales in the process, he would have to find a tenant for the rest of his present lease or lose what he paid for it. If all these adverse items amount to $5,000 or more, the other site is no more available to him in any practical sense than if the other site were held at a higher figure than he has paid. If the cost of reinforced concrete construction goes down in relation to the cost of masonry structures of like serviceability, the maximum economical service life of a masonry building may be affected (if late year repair charges are high or if rentals fall) but the whole difference in the change in cost will not be immediately deductible from the value of the masonry structure. Certainly one would not abandon his masonry building. It is a bird in the hand.

The *consequential* difficulties and losses from substituting one instrument for another, whether they are like or unlike in physical character, are in general so great that the actual cost of the unused portion of a stock of services is nearly always a more appropriate value than any other. Even in the case in which the capital item in use can be replaced by another at a price less than was paid for the one in use, it does not follow that this price reduction should necessarily affect the proper valuation of the present instrument. It may not pay actually to replace now. The interference with operations incident to the replacement, the difference between the expense-free resale price of the used asset and its value to yield services at a unit cost equal to that of a new one after it is installed, the risk of getting a faulty machine, etc., may make no benefit of this price decline actually available to the concern.

There is a great deal more to be said for the accountants' reluctance to allow so-called replacement costs of fixed tangibles to affect book valuations than is usually said. Their reluctance to recognize changes in the market price of things not actually to be bought is more fortunate for all concerned, perhaps, than is commonly supposed. Certainly better grounds can be assigned than the text writers commonly assign. Whether they oppose changes that ought rationally to be made when sufficient and proper evidence supports the reality of the proposed revaluation is difficult to say. If one were to rely solely on the arguments that some of them offer in conversation, one must infer that they sometimes do. But far oftener they decline responsibility for revaluations that are without merit. Many statements adopting "sound" values are plainly unsound statements.

The writer anticipates a hesitancy on the part of the economist to accept the views on valuation just expressed. How can it be maintained that a sum of asset valuations vastly greater or vastly less than the true enterprise capital value, may be, in any sense, true valuations of the assets? If that distrust of the dicta here expressed arises from any notion of the possibility of true capital valuations of assets, it can only be reaffirmed here that true capital valuation is statistically impossible. To urge the merits of the theory of capital valuation is useless unless the primary data can be independently estimated by some means better than pure guesswork. To smuggle in, consciously or unconsciously, a preconceived value of the capital instrument, and then capitalize this service series, is worse than guesswork. Confessed guesswork misleads no one. But to express a valuation process in the form of a capital valuation process when the essential data are fictitious or *are derived from the value to be found*, is statistically vicious. It makes a spurious claim to the merits of true capital valuation.

Obviously the capital value of an enterprise, if it can be estimated with sufficient reliability, is a much more significant figure than the summation of the assets. But the annual grist of bankruptcies, of speculators who lose their stakes, the volume of bad debt losses, of frozen bank resources, and of corporate reorganizations, all testify weightily to the unreliability of capital valuations of enterprises. There is just as weighty a line of evidence in the wholly unexpected degree of success that attends other concerns.

To hold the accountants responsible for failing to stake their reputations on expressed capital valuations of enterprises is to pay them a high compliment whether intended or not. When the most skilled business men we know are obviously unable to do so for their own enterprise, concerning which they have vastly more opportunity for intimate detailed knowledge than the public accountants have, by what legitimate right do we ask the accountant to risk an opinion?

Deficiencies in Indirect Valuation Procedure.—So far as the theory of indirect valuation implied by modern practice is concerned, the chief criticisms that can be made are of three kinds:

1. Sometimes—all too often in the writer's opinion—accountants employ indirect valuations when legitimate and reasonably reliable direct capital values can be found. This is the case with finished goods inventory.

2. They omit data from their formal statements that could have very great value to readers. When the same accountants year after year prepare the statements and have access to the full reports and working papers prepared, it would be a very simple matter to attach to the two standard statements a schedule or table of the book value of assets at the end of each of, say, the last five periods together with the enterprise earn-

ings (net income and interest charges being the chief components), and the percentage relation between earnings and book value of assets. Such a table, assuming proper valuations of assets, would inevitably make the segregation of high profit earners from steady losers that the single-year statements fail to make. Such a statement involves no responsibility for predicting future rates; it does suggest the need for wariness to the general reader.

3. The technique of valuing, that is, applying the theory of valuation, can be greatly improved in the direction toward which modern practice seems to be tending. It will be the concern of the next two chapters to point out some of the ways in which this betterment of technique may possibly come about and to show how, with improved technique of valuation, somewhat less erratic judgments of enterprise capital value may be formed.

CHAPTER XIII

REVALUATION TECHNIQUE: SIMPLE MEASURES

This chapter deals chiefly with the technique of revaluing assets that are expected to appear in successive balance sheets and that cannot be directly valued. The category of assets under discussion is not identical with "fixed assets"; for some fixed assets are capable of direct valuation and some fixed assets are not necessarily expected to appear in more than one balance sheet.

Original Valuations

The original book valuation of purchased assets of the kinds dealt with here requires little discussion. The purchase price must, in any event, be recorded as having been paid or agreed to be paid. If an improper price (one paid without due prudence by a principal or in bad faith or abuse of power by a fiduciary) is paid, no harm is done by showing the price paid in the asset account even though a simultaneous adjustment is made to show the true status. There is, on the other hand, no possible excuse for perpetuating a gross blunder or the results of a misdeed in the asset valuations. To do so is gross negligence that may harm innocent persons. To "distribute" the effect of a gross overvaluation or undervaluation, through the depreciation or other expense account over a series of periods, is a gross statistical error for which no valid excuse can be presented.

Assets Acquired by Stock Issue or in Exchange for Treasury Stock.—The case is not greatly different when assets of the kind in question are received as consideration for shares whether originally issued or delivered from true treasury stock.

A grossly overvalued consideration received, if booked at that value, requires adjustment as soon as the erroneous valuation is discovered no matter whether the consideration is legally adequate in the jurisdiction or not. It requires adjustment simply because it is an overvaluation and, as such, will mislead innocent persons to their harm. So long as it is continued in the accounts, it will have the effect of falsifying all future net incomes and all earning rates, unit costs, and all other statistical data in any way dependent upon book valuations. If the consideration does not constitute full legal consideration, another grievous fault results from failure of adjustment. The value of the corporation's remedy, whether on suit instituted by the corporation, or by creditors in case of need, or by a non-assenting shareholder who has been discriminated against, is omitted from the list of assets and may be lost.

No one who has made a study of the history of American capitalistic combinations and who has examined their successive statements can entertain a possible doubt that many huge initial overvaluations have been passed over in silence by public accountants. No plea that it is a commonplace of promotion practice to ignore the public law governing the terms of issue and sale of corporate securities can be heard in extenuation. To certify a balance sheet as correct when as a matter of provable fact it is not correct is, of course, no worse than the deed of the original wrongdoer, but morally it is no better.

Professional Ethics and Valuation.—Let it be understood, however, that no duty of public disclosure is asserted. The accountant's duty in that regard is exactly that of any one else in receipt of a privileged communication. He is bound not to make a willing or wilful disclosure unless ordered by competent authority to do so. He is equally bound in duty to the public not to be a party to a future *consequent* harm to another person. Should the corporate client refuse to permit a proper revaluation, the accountant is bound, in all decency and honor, whether responsible in damages or not, so to express his certificate as to make it *clear* to all that he does not assert the propriety of the valuation in question.

Most public accountants who enjoy professional standing accept the full measure of duty expressed above. But not all have always done so. The commonest form of evading the duty, when it is evaded, is by so phrasing the certificate as to make it difficult to determine whether the accountant does or does not accept the valuation as proper. "Weasel words" is a term of reproach among accountants. Words that suck the essential meaning out of others employed with them receive from the leaders of the profession the scorn they merit.

Let it be further understood that no superhuman judgment of the propriety of valuations is expected either. There is always a wide latitude to be given for honest differences of informed opinion in matters of valuation. It is easy long after the event to see that a valuation has not been borne out by subsequent experience. But business men cannot occupy the easy position of second guessers, nor have the accountants any duty to come after them as second guessers. The first few years after an enterprise is started is a heyday for those chiefly gifted with hindsight. The accountant's duty to his client and to the public is to see to it that a minimum of *future* harm is done to those not responsible for the initial prevision. There is no more sense in *parading* mistakes of the past than there is in enjoining solemn duties that normal human beings cannot discharge.

Adjustment of Original Valuations, or Revaluations

In all that follows in this chapter it is assumed that all initial valuations are proper or that they have been properly rectified.

Given appropriate initial valuations of assets, upon what do their subsequent valuations depend? In view of the theory of valuation expressed in the preceding chapter, the following variables are asserted to be by far the most significant:

1. What amount of services is still to be had from the stock under examination; that is, of what amount of economically available services does the essence of the asset consist?
2. What time-distribution of those services is most reasonable to contemplate in the light of existing policies and the existing conditions?
3. What outlays must still be made in order to get the residual services at the most economical (observe, not necessarily the cheapest) cost per unit of service?
4. What time-distribution of these future outlays, for repairs, etc., may most reasonably be expected in the light of experience?
5. At what price per unit are like services really *available* by some reasonably good alternative means?
6. What scrap or directly recoverable value can be expected?

Consider these variables in order.

Amount of Service Still Available.—The chief significance of this variable is obvious. Assuming the necessity for service of the kind in question or any employment of the service thought to be advantageous, the more of the originally procured service still available the more valuable the stock will be. But note that it must be *economically* available. Only so much is economically available as can be had at a *future outlay cost* per unit not in excess of some available alternative cost per unit. By spending enough for part replacements (repairs), it is possible to keep any machine running for an indefinitely great length of time, but it does not *pay* to do so. Query: How does one know just when a machine is "worn out"?

Time-Distribution of Services.—Given the amount of services economically available, what time-distribution of them may be expected? Clearly, whatever a unit of service may be worth, assuming it to be necessary at all, the quicker one gets the benefit of that unit the better he is off. A young foal may present as good a prospect for a given aggregate of farm service as a newly broken four-year-old. But the farmer must wait longer to get it in the case of the colt. Quite aside from the fact that the idle colt must be maintained until he is broken to work, the mere having to wait is an adverse condition. Horse-hire paid for in full as the work is done can be paid for at a higher outlay per unit of work than is economically advantageous to pay if the paying must begin many years before the work is done. Since it is an opportunity cost of service that forms the foundation of valuations of this kind, time-distributions of service units can be discounted by exactly the same process as that applied in direct capital valuations.

Future Outlay Costs.—Given the amount and time-distribution of services still to be had, it is clear that the less the future outlays necessary, e.g., for maintenance, upkeep, and repairs, the better the owner is off. Given two machines that will render equal and identical services similarly distributed in time, that one which will yield its service with a lesser outlay subsequent to acquisition cost is the more valuable.

Time-Distribution of Future Outlays.—Given two assets identical with respect to economically available future services, time-distribution of those services, and equality with respect to total future outlays, that one which permits the longer delay of future outlays is clearly the more valuable. If for no other reason, the differences in future outlays could be invested to yield some return. But quite independent of the other factors previously considered, the longer the outlay of a dollar can be deferred the better.

Alternative Source of Service.—Clearly no asset can be worth more than the like services could be had for by some alternative means. It is equally clear in considering alternative service agents that all outlays and all sacrifices consequent upon the possible change must be taken into account. That is to say, the services of the alternative agent must be really available and the total sacrifice to get them must be contemplated in determining a unit cost in terms of which a partly-used agent is to be valued.

What Substitutes Are "Available."—But, as was pointed out above,[1] a mere *possible* substitute is not necessarily an available substitute. Unless it will *pay* to make the substitution *now*, the substitute is not available *now* in any real commercial sense. The test of availability can often be put thus: Does the cost of getting rid of the present agent (outlays for dismantling and removal less salvage value) plus the outlays for procuring and installing the substitute, plus the value of plant operating time lost during substitution, imply lower operating cost per unit of service than that implicit in a zero book valuation of the agent now in service?

Future availability is, in general, of much more importance than present availability. A substitute is available now if, and only if, it will pay to scrap now. Future availability raises the present question of when should future scrapping be contemplated. Suppose A has just installed a machine at a cost that includes a purchase price of $5,000. The present quoted price is $4,500. A new machine is not an available substitute now; it may become an available substitute at some future time. But at what price will it become available? The mere fact of a recent price drop is not sufficient evidence that a correspondingly low price will be open to the buyer when the time for scrapping comes. Present costs of replacement have nothing to do with present valuations unless present replacements are contemplated. If there is good evidence, however, that future costs of replacement, when the time comes to make them, will be less or more than those which have been experienced, it is

---

[1] See p. 244.

obviously the part of wisdom to operate the present agent in a manner consistent with the expected change rather than consistent with the actual costs incurred.

If there is good reason to suppose that a machine that cost $5,000 can be replaced when the time of replacement comes, for $2,000, it is obviously bad policy to spend as large amounts for repairs, etc., as it would pay to spend if the prospective replacement price were $5,000 or $8,000. It would pay, in other words, to let the machine "run down" and "wear out" earlier if it could be replaced cheaper. Having bought a machine, the owner is anxious to conserve it not so much because of what he has paid for its services as for what he may expect to be compelled to pay for more services when he has to buy another stock. Accountants are properly skeptical of valuation bases other than original cost. But when the weight of evidence tends to show that some higher or lower basis is *really* more probable they are not unwilling to revise valuations.

Outlay cost is a real thing—a fact. So, too, will replacement cost *become* a real thing when it is incurred. But because prices of equipment fluctuate, because there are always many alternative ways of getting service, that is, many kinds of serving agents that will do a given kind of work, and because the amount and kind of service needed in an enterprise change with its selling, as well as with its buying, opportunities—because of all these extremely elusive matters it requires a good deal of positive evidence to show on which side of experienced cost per unit of service a future unit cost is likely to lie.

Cost Less Depreciation.—It cannot be truly said that the accountant's rule of valuation for assets of this kind is cost less depreciation (however measured) based on cost. It can be said to their credit that they require to be shown cause for departure from it. The objections that they have opposed to other bases are sometimes not wholly creditable, but their reluctance to accept another basis has a perfectly sound ground.

It very seldom will pay to marshall enough evidence to create a presumption that future actual replacements will most probably be made at some particular figure other than past cost. Purely imaginary decisions are not likely to be made with the same degree of caution and prudence as decisions that are to be backed up by money actually spent.

For the reasons given above, the type of alternative considered in the following discussion, unless otherwise specified, will be a new agent like the one in use, available when wanted at a price equal to that paid for the one in use. It must be emphatically repeated, however, that there is no real merit in an original actual cost, as such, to serve as a datum point for revaluations. On the other hand, it must be as emphatically asserted that adequately to consider possible future substitutions is as difficult and expensive a task as a redesigning of all plant and fixed equipment—obviously not a task to be undertaken annually and obviously not a task for accountants. The present writer is even more skeptical of most appraisals, particularly of cost of reproduction (of existing agencies) than accountants appear to be. We do not often see old establishments duplicated in new ones. Cost of reproduction new less an allowance for depreciation may be a good working rule in damage suits; it is absurd as a sole rule of going-concern valuation.

Scrap Value.—By scrap value is meant the amount directly recoverable through sale when it is no longer economical to utilize the technical services for which the asset was intended. This includes the case of serving agents that may still be more valuable in their intended technical use *to some one else* than they are to the person who has them first. Some motor bus companies make it a practice to scrap all tire casings as soon as the first visible break in them occurs. To keep them longer in service may cause deviations from their schedules so great that some competing transportation system will get the patronage. But such tires, in ordinary use, often have more than half their original mileage-life left. They command prices much above rubber junk prices.

The definition includes the case of the agent that, at the time of discarding, will cost more to dismantle, remove, and sell than it will bring in as salvage sales. In other words, scrap value may be negative. Because of this fact book value may be negative even before it will pay to abandon the asset. Cost of getting a used agent out of the way is just as much consequent upon a decision to utilize its services as is any portion of its purchase price. A house condemned and ordered to be torn down within a year may have been rented to produce a rental of $500 before the wrecking starts. But it may cost $1,000 in excess of scrap sales to get it wrecked. Clearly the future series of money services and disservices is worth less than nothing. It is equally clear that it would not pay to wreck the building at once unless the scrap sales would be increased. Nor does it make a real difference whether the building is rented or is being used by the owner until a new one is available.

The definition of scrap value is also intended to cover the case in which the final recovery value is expected to be greater than the initial valuation. Real cases of this kind occur. Urban land is often purchased and improved with some "inadequate" improvement or "taxpayer" structure or other temporary development. Rentals of the structure are not expected to be great enough to procure a normal rate of return on the whole investment, land and building, during the service-life of the building. These rentals are merely expected to produce something in excess of a normal rate upon the investment in the structure only. Increase in the conversion value of the land is looked to as a supplement to rentals. In California some men have made a paying business of buying land tracts, planting them as orchards, and bringing the orchards into commercial bearing with the full intention of subdividing the orchards for sale to those who wish to operate them commercially. Breeding of fancy dairy stock, poultry, etc., presents many instances of this kind.

Interdependence of Variables.—It is obvious from what has been said of the six variables listed above that they are not independent one from another. No one can foretell the amount of service that a used agent will render unless he knows what repair and maintenance policies will be pursued. To run an internal combustion engine for a short time with unlubricated pistons and uncooled cylinder walls will make junk of the best engine block ever made. Cost of repairs is not unrelated to original cost. We could goldplate ship hulls and so avoid all painting and repainting costs, but it wouldn't pay. Long service-life is desirable as such but it may not pay. A lamp manufacturer recently said in his advertising, "We know how to make light bulbs that would burn continuously for a thousand years, but you wouldn't want them. Their efficiency would be too low. You would have to buy too much current. We also know how to make technically more efficient bulbs than we sell, but you wouldn't want them. They wouldn't last long enough."

No pretense is made here of showing all of the indefinitely great variety of relations that can, and generally do, exist among these six variables. The writer freely confesses that to do so is far beyond the range of his mathematical powers. It will be pointed out, however, that some of the extremely important interrelations that do exist seem to have escaped the attention of those whose mathematical proficiencies seem adequate to deal with them.[2] This book is content with show-

---

[2] It is often asserted by public accountants that accountants have no need for training in the higher mathematics. If they mean by that that modern accounting practice involves no conventional procedures that go beyond elementary algebra, it is true. But the problems with which accountants deal daily, fairly bristle with questions that cannot be resolved without resort to mathematics far beyond the scope of preparatory school algebra. In an examination set in Accounting, on May 16, 1923, by the American Institute of Accountants there appeared a problem that could be most con-

ing the techniques now commonly used, with exhibiting their major merits and shortcomings, and with suggesting certain other techniques little used and, apparently, little known, which are often within the range of practicable applicability. Certain rough but simple tests of superiority of one technique over another will be shown.

From what has been said about indirect valuation in this book it should be apparent that the following discussion of valuation technique with respect to particular assets does not consider true capital values at all except to the extent that scrap or conversion values may enter. Nevertheless a mode of approximating the capital value of the enterprise is the chief objective in mind. It must be remembered that any writing down of an asset has the concomitant result of diminishing the net income and the net enterprise revenue from operations.[3] If, therefore, an overcharge is made for depreciation, both the book value of the assets and the book figure for net operating revenue are expressed at figures less than the real condition of the enterprise implies. The rate of return, net revenue divided by book value of operating assets, is therefore expressed at a figure lower than the true ratio; for, while both numerator and denominator of the ratio are reduced by the same absolute amount, the numerator is always smaller than the denominator. Thus, if the true book value of assets be $100,000 and the true net revenue be $10,000, a rate of revenue of 10% is implied. But if, arbitrarily or negligently, there is

---

veniently solved by writing a set of simultaneous equations in three variables. Out of nearly one hundred applicants for state licenses, whose papers the present writer read, only two even saw the nature of the problem involved. Of these only one wrote the equations and he confessed inability to solve them. The competent public accountant of the future, unless the profession is to fall out of line with modern business training, must have a sufficient competence in mathematics to open modern statistical writings to him.

[3] Net enterprise revenue for any one period is to mean hereinafter "the sum of net income and of those financial charges (chiefly interest charges) that have been deducted from gross income to find net income." The term ought, ideally, to be made somewhat more inclusive, but the sum of net income and of contractual interest charges has the double advantage of simplicity and of including the great preponderance of the significant amount.

written off $10,000 too much depreciation, the rate of return is 0. On the other hand, if $10,000 too little is written off, the rate is over 18%. In either case a gross misstatement is made about *the most important matter that the accountant has to deal with in a year's reports.*

Revaluation Errors and Income Rates.—For it is upon the successive rates of net revenue that all opinions about the net earning power of the enterprise must be based. A mode of valuation that exhibits, for the enterprise, a definite statistical bias, creates the appearance of a purely fictitious trend of earning power. An erratic mode may create the appearance of unstable earning power. A mode of valuing that is invariant to real earning power, on the other hand, may create a spurious appearance of stability.

Moreover, to the extent that the management act in accordance with the conditions implied in erroneous valuations, they may be worse off than they would have been with no valuations at all. Thus, if the valuations for a particular year imply a cost per unit of service for a particular machine of $0.05, when as a matter of fact it was $0.15, the products upon which that machine has worked will appear to have been a more profitable line than they really are. If, to exploit the apparent advantage, they attempt specially to increase the sales of this product, they are courting future losses. And, what is quite as important, they are withdrawing funds from the output of other lines, which may, as a matter of fact, have been more profitable.

If the management base their policies upon the cost accountant's figures at all, then any error in valuation, *no matter in which direction,* misleads the management to their harm. All too often the effect of bad balance sheet valuation upon business policy is left out of consideration. The question of "adequate" rates of depreciation, in the sense that they will ultimately adjust the valuations to the realities, is often discussed as though it had no effect upon ultimate profit at all. Of some modes of valuing it is said that they tend to overvalue some assets and to undervalue others, but the aggregate of book values found is nearly right. If the management pay no attention at all to the unit costs implied in such valuations no harm is done. But if the cost accountant gives effect to these individually bad valuations through a machine-rate burden charge, and if the selling policy has regard for apparent unit profits, the valuation may lead to the worst rather than to the best possible policy.

In the discussion of the various formulas to be taken up, regard will be had principally for three properties of the formula: (1) its effect on book valuations of assets; (2) its effect on the net operating revenue shown on the books year by year; and (3) the implied effect upon unit costs. To effect this showing, an attempt must be made to find two quantities: (1) What cost per unit of service is implied in the acquisition and operation of an operating agency? (2) How much of this cost, with respect to a used machine, is a cost of future services? The difference between the two is made up of costs of past service and of losses not expected to be repetitive.

Illustrative Revaluation Data

But before any formulas are introduced it is desirable to exhibit schematically the conditions under which the several formulas may have to be employed. For the sake of simplicity in comparison, all types of assets will be assumed to have equal initial costs installed new. V_o in each case equals $100. For a like reason equal salvage or scrap values will be assumed. V_n in each case equals $5. That is, the asset is expected to yield $5 in excess of the cost of removing it at the end of n periods. n, throughout the exhibits, will be taken as 10. The scheme of asset types employed will, therefore, vary only in these particulars: Amount and time-distribution of direct outlays necessary for their operation. These amounts will be designated by the symbols,

$$O_1, \ldots O_2, \ldots O_a, \ldots O_n,$$

meaning operating outlays in the period indicated by the subscript. Thus O_1 means operating outlays in the first period of use. The subscript a means any given period of use. The second particular in which assets will vary is in the measured amount, and time-distribution, of the use to be made of the asset. The symbols,

$$S_1, \ldots S_2, \ldots S_a, \ldots S_n,$$

mean units of service expected, on the average, in each year indicated by the subscript.

Range of Asset Types.—Inspection of the schedule on page 262 shows that for some types, A, D, and G, an annually increasing outlay charge for operations is contemplated. For others, B, E, and H, a constant charge, except for one extraordinary repair, is presupposed. For the other three a declining charge is assumed. The like variation in expected service distributions is also indicated. The arrangement provides for all nine possible combinations of increasing, constant, and declining outlays and service schedules.

No pretense is made, of course, that these types represent any particular actual set of assets. It is, however, easy to show that any or all of them may be found in any establishment in any possible combination and in any possible relative frequency of occurrence.

Many representatives of type A are to be found. A machine bought in the full knowledge that less than full-time employment for it can be contemplated much before it is worn out, may be nevertheless the most economical way of getting particular work done. In the early periods, both because all parts are in good order and because it will be little used, the charges for maintenance, upkeep, and repair are expected to

SCHEDULES OF REVALUATION DATA FOR A SCHEMATIC SET OF ASSETS

Time-Distributions of O_a for Assets of Types

Period	A	B	C	D	E	F	G	H	I
1	$5	$1	$15	$5	$1	$15	$5	$1	$15
2	7	1	13	7	1	13	7	1	13
3	9	1	11	9	1	11	9	1	11
4	11	1	9	11	1	9	11	1	9
5	13	1	7	13	1	7	13	1	7
6	35	21	25	35	1	25	35	21	25
7	17	1	3	17	1	3	17	1	3
8	19	1	3	19	1	3	19	1	3
9	21	1	1	21	1	1	21	1	1
10	25	1	6	25	1	6	25	1	6

Time-Distributions of S_a for Assets of Types

Period	A	B	C	D	E	F	G	H	I
1	10	10	10	1	1	1	50	50	50
2	15	15	15	1	1	1	50	50	50
3	20	20	20	1	1	1	45	45	45
4	25	25	25	1	1	1	40	40	40
5	30	30	30	1	1	1	35	35	35
6	35	35	35	1	1	1	30	30	30
7	40	40	40	1	1	1	25	25	25
8	45	45	45	1	1	1	20	20	20
9	50	50	50	1	1	1	15	15	15
10	50	50	50	1	1	1	10	10	10

Other Data

$n = 10$ for all types.
$V_o = \$100$ for all types.
$V_n = \$5$ for all types.
In the 6th period an "extraordinary" or "major" repair at a cost of $20 is contemplated in all but Type E.

be less than in the later periods. Indeed, in some enterprises fixed assets of this type predominate. A waterworks and distributing system installed in a growing town is a case in point. It doesn't *pay* to construct with regard to present market demands only. A great proportion of American railway lines were built under such conditions. As will be noted later, it almost never *pays* to make the cost of unit service a minimum.

Type B differs from type A only with respect to the future operating charges. It makes little difference in the upkeep of telephone poles whether they carry two lines or ten. Except for a resetting charge, there is little reason to expect one year's outlays to exceed another's.

Type C has many important representatives. Earthworks, such as the roadbeds of railways and of mountain highways, require a "seasoning" process. During the early periods of railway operations over earthwork fills, the costs of releveling and realigning tracks are much heavier than in later years despite the lesser volume of traffic.

Type D is a commonplace type in modern continuous process manufacturing. A machine performing some one operation in the chain must take the pace of the plant as a whole or be replaced. Shutdowns during operating hours cannot be tolerated. It will nevertheless pay, especially if replacement cost is high, to spend more for repairs, etc., in the later years to keep up the efficiency of the machine rather than to scrap it early. It may well happen that more or less service, one year with another, will be obtained, but there may be no reason to anticipate any particular fluctuation or any trend other than a constant amount of use.

Type E is likewise frequently found. Many types of equipment like desks, show-cases, sprinkler systems, require a fairly constant expense and render a constant service. Except for the difference between original cost and resale value, which may be reversed without affecting the major argument, land adequately improved for a specialized purpose is, perhaps, the commonest case.

Type F is, perhaps, less common than any other, but approximations to it are sometimes of importance. Full use of an earthwork may be required from the time it is first made.

Type G finds a host of representatives in machines that are not required to take the pace of an enterprise. Characteristically the repair, maintenance, and upkeep curves go up; the service actually rendered goes down. Buildings held for rent exhibit this character in almost every class. Not only does deterioration affect them to increase repair charges, but obsolescence (particularly the inadequacy factor due to changes in building styles, shifts of population, etc.) cut down the rentals, and changes of site values require earlier or later rebuilding than may have been contemplated. Very few office buildings are allowed to stand in American cities for the full term contemplated by the architect.

The critical student will note that n with respect to this assumed asset is obviously wrongly determined. Except under the most unusual conditions, it would not pay to operate asset G ten years before replacement. Reference to Appendix A will show that all the really good revaluation formulas detect this error and serve notice of it by finding negative valuations long before the nth period. But *none* of the formulas in current use will ever show a negative value unless the best scrap value available is negative. No formula, without revaluation of the constants, will show exactly when an asset is "worn out," but the good ones will nearly all show that a wrong estimate of n has been made before any substantial real loss has been incurred.

Type H often finds its counterparts in assets not subject to great variations in operating charges that are undergoing obsolescence with respect to the requirements of the particular enterprise. Some service continues to be needed but at increasing intervals. Contrary to the supposition of some writers [4] obsolescence is not, characteristically, a surprise factor. It may not be specifically foreseen when an asset is procured, but relatively seldom does it suddenly and unexpectedly terminate the use-life of an asset. Some shortening occurs, but even then, it is a common experience that no damage or loss, with respect to the future, is involved. No user of a machine is harmed by the bringing upon the market of a better machine, unless he foolishly keeps the obsolete device in service.

Type I likewise is often met in the case of assets that have an outlay schedule that varies directly with volume of use but that is becoming obsolete.

This scheme, of course, does not provide for all types of assets. But all types at some time or other during their service lives, do approximate these types. Orchard trees, for example, begin somewhat like type A; and at mid-bearing begin to resemble type I, though in general the decline in physical productivity is somewhat more abrupt than the rise. But the matter that is of the utmost consequence is this: that during the phase of service-life corresponding to one of these types the problem of revaluation corresponds with that of the types shown here.

Straight Line Formula

The straight line formula can be expressed in the general form,

$$V_a = \frac{(V_o - V_n)(n-a)}{n} + V_n$$

The decline in value may be expressed for any period by

$$D_a = \frac{V_o - V_n}{n}$$

Since D is a constant, the book values in successive periods constitute an arithmetic series. In general, only two primary

---

[4] See, for example, Hotelling's article, "A Mathematical Theory of Depreciation," *Journal of the American Statistical Association*, Vol. 20, p. 342.

estimates require to be made, viz., scrap value at the end of n periods and the numerical value of n. In general, nothing of great consequence is involved in fixing upon scrap value. It is usually, except in the case of land, numerically small in relation to value new. But the case is quite different with respect to n. Obviously the number of periods of contemplated use of an asset can seldom be intelligently estimated without reference to the anticipated conditions of use. If the formula is to be respectable at all, the value of n must be the most probable number of periods that will yield the most economical use. For how many periods, in the use contemplated, will it pay to keep the asset going, i.e., how long will it be before it will pay to scrap the asset?

This question can never be answered rationally without considering costs of operating, other than first costs, and without considering the amount of service that will be required and that can be made available. Most types of artifact assets can be kept in good operating condition for an indefinitely long period provided enough money is spent for the needed repairs. Any and all portions of a steel rail can be built up by blowtorch methods to overcome wear and deterioration, but it does not ordinarily pay to do so except at the ends where the battering causes most rapid wear. Obviously, this battering wear is a function of traffic volume, of train speed, etc. But neither the amount of future repairs, etc., nor the amount of service that will pay best, can be determined independently of the probable time-distribution of these two series. For both maximum tolerable expense and maximum economical use are functions of time of use, and quite apart from their independent relations to time, they are intimately related to one another. Neither the total actual cost of service nor the most economical service program are in any way dependent upon the distribution of expense shown on the books, though, of course, a distribution that does not accord with the realities may be mistaken for the real thing.

Book Values and the Straight Line Formula.—But, to make out the best possible case for the method, suppose n is properly determined and suppose the contemplated operating policy and use schedule is correctly estimated. Under what conditions will the method yield book values that approximately conform either to an original valuation or to a replacement valuation? Must these same conditions prevail if the net income figures are to record the real experience year by year? Must these same conditions likewise be found if the implied unit costs of the asset services are to be a reliable guide to policy?

Assume that in every one of the types sketched above both V_n and n have been accurately forecast, that is, that the most economical service-life possible is ten years, that V_n is $5, and that the schedules of operating outlay and of services correctly show the program actually to be realized. The formula will then show exactly the same book values for each of the assets at the end of any given period during the ten years! But do any two succeeding book values for any one asset have a common dollar-for-dollar meaning? Are the book values for any two assets at the end of any period, though shown at equal amounts, equal in any useful sense, i.e., equal in any but a pure numerical sense?

Service Unit Cost and the Straight Line Formula.—Consider an asset of type A. During the first year the total charge against gross income is $9.50 for depreciation and $5 for operating outlays—a total of $14.50. This implies a cost per unit of service for the year of $1.45. During the last year the corresponding deduction from gross income is $34.50, and the corresponding unit cost is $0.69. Can it be said in any useful sense that of the total spent and to be spent a total outlay of $14.50 has been incurred to get this first year's service or to get this asset's contribution toward this year's net income? Is $90.50 the amount spent, or agreed to be spent, to get services after the first year? Did the concern really incur a cost of $1.45 per unit of service? Of course, if what is really meant by depreciation, by net income, and by unit cost is something that is written in a book or published in statements, the answer to all these questions will be in the affirmative. But if these terms are to correspond to the real status of the enterprise during the period, the real change of status during the period, and the real position at the end of the period, we shall have to enter a very emphatic negative.

Nor is the result in type A the worst of the lot. In type H, for example, the figures for the first year are: (1) depreciation $9.50; (2) operating cost $10.50, including depreciation; and (3) unit cost $0.21. In the last period the corresponding figures are $9.50, $10.50, and $1.05. Depreciation and total operating costs are the same on the books, for the two periods, but cost per unit of service in the last period is made to appear to be five times as great as that in the first. The only general conditions under which the successive book values, depreciation charges, deductions from gross income and unit costs produced by this method approximate the real state of affairs is when O and S are constants.[5] When these are constants the only error, which is important only with respect to relatively long-lived assets as compared to short-lived ones that will do the same kind of work, is the neglect of the differences of length of time for which investments must be made and during which service must be waited for. The competition of alternative investment opportunities does not permit even this element to be ignored.

Effect of Error in the Estimates.—So far we have considered only conditions in which the primary estimates, upon which subsequent statistics are to depend, have been made upon accurate forecasts of future operating conditions. What happens when the forecasts are not accurate? This, of course, must always be the really characteristic case. There is no

---
[5] See Appendix B.

a priori reason for supposing, nor so far as the present writer has been able to observe, is there any factual experience-reason for supposing that errors of judgment about proper operating policy and about service to be expected are more likely to occur in one direction than in the other.

Take the case of an asset like type A. We may have a perfectly rational ground for assuming that some increasing schedule of future outlays and some increasing schedule of service will be experienced, but we are as likely to err in one direction as in another. The rate of increase may be either greater or less than that estimated. The series of ratios

$$\frac{D_a + O_a}{S_a}$$

actually experienced later, as contrasted with those shown by the books, are as likely to deviate from the estimated ratios in one direction as in the other. We are as likely to overguess as to underguess the unit cost for the whole experience. Errors of estimate actually acted upon consistently do not cancel one another. Both make the real situation worse.

It makes a very real difference, too, what types of assets preponderate in an enterprise. For industry in general, and particularly in a rapidly changing industrial age, the types of asset for which depreciation is a serious problem consist largely of types A, D, and G. None of these is really "fitted" by the straight line formula. Where any or all of these prevail the formula is not only erratic but biased.[6]

---

[6] In Appendix A an exhibit is made for each of the types of asset of all the successive book valuations, yearly operating charges, and unit costs that would be found by each of several of the formulas to be discussed herein.

No formula is "biased" with respect to the service-life of an asset as a whole. All charge exactly the same outlays in exactly the same total time. But a formula may be biased with respect to the constitution of assets existing at any one time. And for a series of years less than n a formula may have a bias, but this latter bias is later followed, of necessity, by a bias in the opposite direction. There are a number of formulas, however, that, by reason of the error in the estimate of n, may cumulate an error so great that only a charge (or a credit) to surplus can be resorted to for adjustment. The net income in the income statements, therefore, can never be adjusted. The straight line method is a bad offender in this regard—particularly in the

It is often said of the straight line formula that "on the average" it approximates accuracy. Seldom, however, does any one who says this tell what he means by "on the average." If this statement means that for assets of any given type it approximates accuracy, the statement is absurd except for asset types in which O and S are nearly constant. If it means that, one asset with another, it will write off the total depreciation in about the right number of periods, or that it is as likely to write off the wearing value too soon as too late, the same can be said of any formula ever proposed. But in some formulas this error nearly vanishes. If it means that the totality of book values for an enterprise will be nearly right, that is, that the implied overestimates will about cancel the underestimates, the assertion can be true only when the constitution of assets permits this to occur. This meaning could never apply to concerns that build and equip structures in anticipation of increased demands to be made upon them, nor of concerns that built and equipped for a trade that is running down.

Service Unit Cost and Unit Product Cost.—In general the latter meaning, approximately correct total book value, seems to be the one most often intended. Suppose that it is really true of a particular enterprise. Is this a very important merit? The real financial position of a concern depends upon what it can and will do in its future operations—not upon what has happened in the past except to the extent to which unexpended services have been made available. Consider what may very well happen, and presumably does happen to a considerable extent in a manufacturing enterprise that can make many optional kinds of goods and that does make several. Let the straight line method be assumed to find a "correct" *total* of asset valuations. Assume, now, that the resident cost accountant accepts the depreciation figure not merely in total but in detail and that he distributes the depreciation and other operat-

---

case of assets whose term of service depends more upon wear than upon mere exposure.

ing charges through a system of machine rates. Obviously the erratic total unit cost charges that result from this method will affect the apparent unit profit of each particular product. And unless for all types of product the proportions of service required conform to the proportions for the plant as an entirety, which is an absurd assumption in most kinds of multiple-product manufacturing,[7] the cost accounts can be expected to show a set of differential advantages, as among classes and types of goods, that does not conform at all with the real differentials. If the management takes its cost figures seriously, the lines that they attempt to push may turn out badly and the ones they minimize may have been the preferable. As between really good valuations and the erratic figures produced by this method, every action based on an error of valuation will be a relatively losing action. They will attempt to exploit their *spurious* book value advantages and to diminish the effect of *spurious* book value disadvantages.

The cost accountants, to be sure, do certain things that diminish the effect of bad piecemeal valuation by diffusing them. The adoption of "standard" costs as an index of operating efficiency does this to some extent.[8] Various modes of distributing overhead, other than the machine rate, do diffuse the bad individual valuations and so make it less likely that these will be responsible for bad policies. In the interminable discussion of modes of distributing overhead or burden, however, no one seems to have pointed out with respect to any of them that they prevent reliance upon bad valuations or place a premium on good ones. Little attention seems to be given

---

[7] Suppose, for example the manufacture in one enterprise of various classes of firearms, building hardware, tools, and cutlery. No correspondence, one specified product with another, between the relative proportions of kinds of asset-service can very well be imagined.

[8] The term "standard cost" is a grievous misnomer. Whatever may be the true character of the things called by that name, they are certainly not "costs." Let any one who doubts this write the statistical formula for one of these costs, either with respect to a unit of product, a production process, or a "department's" activity. If he does so and still thinks the expression describes a cost, then cost has to bear so many meanings that it has ceased to be useful as a word sign for any idea.

to just what is to be distributed and *when* it is to be distributed through burden charges.

To What Extent Is Simplicity a Merit?—A great many unite in declaring the very great advantage of the straight line method on the score of simplicity. There is no denying its simplicity—it *is* simple. But it is also ridiculously erratic and often biased. So long as it continues to be the prevailing method, it is to be hoped that cost accountants will avoid the extremely plausible machine rate,[9] a mode of distributing overhead that is excellent provided the *right amounts are distributed,* but an extremely dangerous mode if wrong amounts are involved.

It must not be supposed, though, that any proposal to throw out this method altogether is made here. For, as we have seen above, there are conditions under which it is sound well within the limits of probable error in the original estimates upon which all formulas must be based. Certain other formulas approximate the true going-concern values under other conditions. A combination of formulas having proper regard for the types of asset to which they are applied may well turn out to be preferable to any one mode, and this despite the high authority that stands behind some of the more complex and more general formulas.

It must not be supposed that simplicity is not a great merit. The cost of making the primary estimates and of doing the clerical work of calculating must never be forgotten. One may suppose the invention of a formula that would give perfect valuations within the limits of error in the primary estimates, but one cannot entertain a hope that that formula will be simple. It might cost more to value the assets than the assets are worth. Put more exactly, if the value of the assets is to depend upon all of the charges incident to their ownership and operation,

---

[9] By machine rate is here meant what Scovell calls the "new machine rate." See his "Cost Accounting and Burden Application," items indexed under the quoted term. Note also his discussion of depreciation, repairs, etc.

including the charges necessary to their revaluations by a perfect formula, many assets might turn out to have negative valuations, that used without revaluations at all, could produce a real profit in enterprise.

Hotelling [10] solves an integral equation to determine the mutual effects upon one another of charges like capital value taxes, etc., and value of the asset subject to taxation. If this has to be done, then both the tax and the book value are dependent upon the cost of solving integral equations to find them. And the amount of the tax and book value, in turn again, will have to depend upon cost of solving integral equations in the assessor's office. Persons who combine in themselves the requisite mathematical training and the knowledge of facts necessary to make the primary valuations of the constants are scarce and can, in general, be more adequately employed. The cost of performing the operations implied by a formula is a property of that formula.

Sinking Fund Formula

After the straight line formula the one perhaps most widely used is the sinking fund formula and the modifications of this method. The general formula for book value at the end of any specified period is written

$$V_a = V_o - \frac{AW(I^a - 1)}{i},$$

wherein A is the rent of an end-of-the-period annuity that, at i rate of interest, compounded periodically will amount to 1 at the end of n periods, $I = 1 + i$ and $W = V_o - V_n$. The amount of depreciation for any given period is $D_a = AWI^{(a-1)}$

It will be noted that the annual charges, instead of being constant, as in the case of the straight line method, constitute a geometric series of which the common ratio is I. When $I = 1$, i.e., when $i = 0$, or when $n = 1$, it is identical with the straight

---

[10] *Journal of the American Statistical Association,* Vol. 20, pp. 345-346. See p. 351 also for his comment on a simple (?) formula.

line method. But when $i>0$ and $n>1$, which are the only conditions that concern us here, it will be observed that book value, at any time after first valuation and before date of scrapping any asset, will be given a higher figure by this method than by the straight line rule. Between these time limits the sinking fund curve has the greater ordinates and so implies a greater aggregate dollar-year investment.

"Rate of Depreciation" and "Rate of Interest."—There are some who seem to suppose that the accumulated depreciation for any given number of periods is equal to an annuity sinking fund—by that time—which has actually (or in imagination) been established to accumulate the difference between cost and scrap value during the use-life of the asset. There is, of course, no such equality. The rate of exploitation of a stock of services that promises to be most economical seldom has any correspondence to any specified rate of interest. The rates of change of exploitation rates do not conform to rates of change in the earning power of any simple form of investment.

Depreciation Expense and Depreciation Funds.—There is a much larger number who in some way try to identify the deposits to a sinking fund or the deposits and earnings thereon with "depreciation expense." The only source of an "expense" of depreciation is the outlay or outlays made or agreed to be made for the asset in order to have the enjoyment of the service. The real or realized expense occurs when the outlays are made for the service. For convenience, the outlay or outlays are *referred to* the years on behalf of which they were made. The necessary deposits to create a fund equal to the difference $V_o - V_n$ are always, unless interest is zero or less, less than depreciation expense. If one could meet his depreciation expense so simply, he could for $760, interest being 5%, get rid once for all of a difference $V_o - V_n = \$100,000$ in 100 years. This may be a form of independent investment, but it is not depreciation expense.

Deficiencies of the Formula.—The deficiencies of this method, aside from its apparent tendency to mislead people into believing that there is some connection between a mode of accumulating free funds and an appropriate mode of exploiting the asset, are very like those of the straight line method. For, given the value of n and $V_o - V_n$ (and a value of i which relates to rate of return on some *other* investment than that in the asset), all subsequent book values, all annual charges for depreciation, and all implied unit costs are determined. For the set of assets sketched above exactly the same set of book values is found for each. Neglecting interest on the changing investment in the asset, this formula fits, when and only when,

$$\frac{AWI^{(a-1)} + O_a}{S_a}$$

is a constant.

There is neither an *a priori* reason nor one drawn from experience to lead one to suppose that a curve like the sinking fund valuation curve will fit the real facts any better than the straight line determined by the other formula. Both formulas are invariant to the time-distributions of O and S except to the extent that these determine n. But the same value of n is found in either case. The value of i *referred to its proper base*, as will be shown later, does influence the value of n but does not influence n when i is referred to some *other* investment. But even if i be the proper rate to contemplate on the investment in the asset, it should be referred to *all* outlays—not to a part only.

When the condition that

$$\frac{AWI^{(a-1)} + O_a}{S_a}$$

be a constant is more nearly fulfilled than the condition that O_a/S_a be a constant, the sinking fund method is better than the straight line rule, but not otherwise. The two judiciously applied may be better than either alone. But cost of calculation should not be forgotten.

Fixed Percentage on Declining Balance Formula

This formula is described in all the general texts, but, fortunately for all concerned, is little used in practice. It may be given the general expression,

$$V_a = V_o \cdot r^a, \text{ when } r = V_a/V_{a-1}, \text{ a constant.}$$

The general expression of the decline in value in any given year can be written

$$D_a = V_o(1 - r)r^{(a-1)}$$

Having found n by the considerations mentioned in discussing the straight line formula, the problem here is to find a rate, r, such that $V_o r^n = V_n$. This, of course, means that r is 0 if n is positive, and $V_n = 0$. But if both n and V_n are positive, r is found by the equation

$$n \log r = \log V_n - \log V_o$$

From the general expressions it can be seen directly that the series of book values, V_a, is a geometric series of which r is the common ratio. It will be recalled that under the sinking fund formula the D_a series was a geometric series.

Deficiencies of the Method.—This method can be summarily rejected for a reason quite independent of the deficiencies of formulas 1 and 2 above. Overwhelming weight is given to V_n in determining book values. If V_n is zero, then r is zero, and rigorously applied, the book value at the instant after acquisition becomes zero. Applied to any asset in the schedule given above, the difference in value at the end of the first period that depends upon a difference between $V_n = 0$ and $V_n = \$5$, is $74.11. Thus the least important constant in reality is given the greatest effect in the formula.

There may be cases in which the formula fits the facts, but aside from the case in which the asset becomes instantly an item to be scrapped, or $V_o = V_n$ so that $r = 1$, the chance of its being a formula of close fit is remote indeed. Its chief usefulness seems to be to furnish drill in the use of logarithms for students in accounting.

Sum-of-the-Year-Digits Formula

This rule is known under many names, none of which seems to suggest the nature of the method. The general book value expression is

$$V_a = \frac{W(n-a)(n-a+1)}{n(n+1)} + V_a$$

and the annual depreciation charge is

$$D_a = \frac{2W(n-a+1)}{n(n+1)}$$

The series of values D_a is a declining arithmetic series of which the first term is $\frac{2nW}{n(n+1)}$ and the common difference is $\frac{2W}{n(n+1)}$. Having determined n, as in the straight line formula, the procedure is to take the sum of the successive residual life periods as a rate base. Thus, if $n = 10$, this rate base is $10 + 9 + 8 + \ldots + 1 = 55$. The first year's depreciation becomes $\frac{\$10\,W}{55}$ the second year's is $\frac{\$9\,W}{55}$ and so on to the nth period when it becomes $\frac{\$W}{55}$.

Special Defect of the Formula.—This rule is free of the special faults of the rule previously discussed in that it gives no excessive weight to the scrap value estimate. It does, however, give a peculiar weight to the mere *numerical* value of n itself. Thus if we assume a five-year service-life and apply this formula first on the basis of five one-year periods and then on the basis of ten six-month periods, we shall have different book values at end of the year periods. If $V_o = \$100$ and V_n is $5, we should get book values for the four intermediate year-endings as follows:

BOOK VALUATIONS AT THE END OF:

Length of Period	First Year	Second Year	Third Year	Fourth Year
One Year........	$68.33	$43.00	$24.00	$11.33
Six Months......	67.18	41.27	22.27	10.18
Difference.......	1.15	1.73	1.73	1.15

This particular property, while not one to be looked upon as desirable, is not of great practical consequence since n is almost always determined in whole years. When interim statements are prepared, it is common practice, no matter what formula is used, to interpolate the semi-annual, quarterly, or monthly allowances for depreciation.

Special Case of Usefulness.—The conditions under which this formula gives results correct but for errors in the primary estimates and for neglect of interest upon the investment, are easily shown. If $\dfrac{D_a + O_a}{S_a}$ is a constant, the formula is satisfactory. When this condition is more nearly approximated than are the conditions expressed for formulas 1 and 2 above, it should be preferred to them. Such conditions are met, for example, in the write-off of a bond premium or discount on a serial issue in which a like par amount is retired annually beginning with the first year, or if a like amount is to be retired after the maturities begin. Thus, if the issue, consisting of $100,000 par value, sold at a discount $1,500, is to be paid off in five $20,000 annual blocks beginning one year from date of issue, the first year's credit to the valuation account will be $500, the second year's $400, and so on to the final year when $100 will be credited. The year's credit is strictly proportional to the par of the bonds outstanding during that year. The corresponding charge is made to interest or discount expense. The charge to interest expense under the so-called "scientific" compound interest method, will, for short-term serial issues, be nearly the same as that by the rule under consideration.

As a sole rule it is, one class of assets with another, a poorer one by reason of systematic bias than either the straight line or the sinking fund method. But as one of a set of rules judiciously applied it may be accorded a place.

Service Unit Formula

This method, which has been making considerable headway in recent years for some types of asset and in certain classes of enterprise, does not necessarily require an estimate of service-life in terms of fiscal periods at all. Service-life is estimated in terms of some function of service rendered that is more nearly proportional to amount of service enjoyed than is mere lapse of time. If we set

$$\frac{V_o - V_n}{\sum_{t=0}^{t=n} S} = U = \frac{V_a - V_n}{\sum_{t=a}^{t=n} S}$$

in which the denominator summation signs mean, respectively, "the sum of all units of service to be had between time of installation $(t = o)$ and time of scrapping $(t = n)$ whatever the value of n may be" and "the sum of all units of service to be had between the time of revaluation $(t = a)$ and the time of scrapping $(t = n)$ whatever the value of n may be," it is evident that U is an average cost per unit of service. But it is only an average of that part of total cost of service represented by the difference between first installed cost and scrap value.

280   THE ECONOMICS OF ACCOUNTANCY

Given the estimate of amount of service to be had economically from a new asset and the amount still to be had economically, from the one now in service, we can solve for the book value, V_a. This relation can be expressed

$$V_a = U \sum_{t=a}^{t=n} S + V_n$$

and the general formula for the year's depreciation is US_a.

Meaning of a Unit of Service.—There is little difficulty in assigning some appropriate measure of service, though it is sometimes inconvenient to obtain the record of service. But automobiles, trucks, and busses are equipped to show a record of miles run; rolling stock statistics show like records for cars and locomotives; job records show machine hours under assigned operations, and so on. In all concerns in which any but the most sketchy cost accounting scheme is in use, the requisite data are found for other purposes in any event. General contractors' records show earth removed by various devices, yards of concrete mixed, hoisted, and poured, and so on.

In the case of many types of asset, to be sure, useful life is more nearly controlled by mere lapse of time than by service output. Thus, under light traffic, railway ties "wear out" because of rotting. A building site, so long as it is used for that purpose only, renders a continuous service. In these cases the formula evidently becomes identical with the straight line rule; for the denominators of the two fractions equated to U vary in direct proportion to calender time so that the annual charge is a constant.

In a sense, this formula offers no new idea for consideration as compared with the three previously discussed. All these latter differ one from another in their explicit suppositions concerning the way in which an element of cost is, or ought to be, divided among the years to which the cost attaches. But they all agree impliedly that the "year-in-service" is the appropriate measure of service-use. This one merely amends the unit measure of service-use. It merely asserts that under certain circumstances certain other measures or functions of service can be more significant and convenient. But having adopted a unit measure of service or index of unit service, the element of cost is to be distributed among the unit measures of service in direct proportion to their quantity just as in the straight line method. For a motor bus it merely substitutes miles run for years of service.

Special Merits of the Formula.—Whether or not this method presents anything novel for consideration—the others being before us—is of little consequence. What is of vast consequence is the introduction of a system of service measures in lieu of a single arbitrary measure. There is no more reason why we should struggle along with one common service measure, the year of use, than that we should try to get along with one unit of physical measure for objects. Every one can see the inconvenience of speaking of tons of houses, of lumber, of cloth, of pianos, and of gravel walks. Exactly the same kind of rigidity and inconvenience results from attempts to value services of houses, of lumber, of textiles, of pianos, and of gravel walks in terms of a common non-monetary unit which is to be converted into monetary units by an arbitrary system of multipliers.

It takes no great insight to see that one year's use of a truck may vastly differ from another year's uses in everything that is really significant. But if a ton-mile-under-useful-load has a stabler significance, and if the ratio of miles run to ton-miles-under-useful-load for periods as long as a year is relatively constant, then miles run is a better (that is, more convenient and, hence, more significant) measure than is a year of use.

In Appendix B of this book a proof is given of certain conditions under which this method will give superior book valuations, year's deductions from gross income, and unit costs of service, as compared with the straight line method. The treatment given there does not purport to be a complete or comprehensive comparison, even as between these two methods. It is inserted merely to indicate the character of investigation likely to lead to really useful results in valuation theory. It can be noted here that under any general set of conditions in which the straight line method will give correct figures, the service unit formula will give identical results. But the latter rule will give correct results throughout the use-life of some assets for which the former rule will give wrong results—wrong, too, by indefinitely great amounts.

Aside from the one great merit noted, substitution of a better service measure, this rule has another great merit. It disregards n altogether except to the extent that the rate of exploitation *must* be constant or that mere exposure rather than exploitation fixes the amount of service to be had. These exceptional cases are not the ones in which n is difficult to estimate. On the contrary, it is for the exposure-limited and the constant-service types that n can be most nearly estimated. Where wear, which is always a function of exploitation rate, is the effective or predominant cause of operating outlay, n is very difficult to estimate. Errors in the estimate of n are one of the most serious kinds.

Any one who drives an automobile and watches his expenses knows that gasoline cost, tire costs, valve grinding, greasing, bearing adjustments, reboring of cylinders, etc., are much more closely related to miles run, under given road and use conditions, than they are to months or years in service. Certain other charges for repainting, registration fees, and the like are dependent on time also, but the preponderant charges for all power consumers and producers are geared to rate of exploitation rather than to fiscal years. Any textbook on machine design will show why this is true. Any testing laboratory and any well-kept machine register will show that it is true.

At the risk of tedious repetition it must be repeated that no primary estimate whatever is needful in the case of this formula that is not equally needed in any other. n cannot be intelligently determined for *any* formula without regard for the amounts of O and of S that may be anticipated. Nor can the most economical combination of these with V_o and V_n ever be determined without thought of the parallel time distributions of O and S. Neglect to consider these at all will bring its penalty in any case. If a trend of either or both of these will most probably be some trend other than that of a line parallel to the base of the time coordinate, this method does better than the straight line method on the same estimates and in every case. It is not legitimate to argue that O and S cannot be accurately forecast or forecast at all; for the straight line method and every other involving n as an effective symbol implies willy-nilly that some particular trend is expected.

Within the limits of our ability to forecast at all, this method has much more to recommend it than any other simple method yet proposed. Nevertheless, if simple methods only are to be used, there is no good reason why this should be the sole method. It will be the concern of the next chapter to discuss some of the variants upon these simple methods that have been proposed.

CHAPTER XIV

REVALUATION TECHNIQUE: ADJUSTED MEASURES

In the previous chapter several simple techniques of revaluation were considered in some detail. There remain for examination a number of modifications of these simple methods that have been or may be proposed. Variants upon the straight line rule, upon the sinking fund rule, and upon the service unit rule are to be noted, but only the latter have merit enough to warrant careful consideration. The writer has made a test of every formula proposed in the literature and has invented some hundreds of modifications upon these. But every one of these can be demonstrated to be inferior in the conditions that prevail in use to the modifications of the service unit rule proposed here. Nearly all can be rejected on the ground of being seriously and adversely variant to the characteristic errors of primary estimates, some on the ground that they imply a conduct of men contrary to real conduct based on accurate information, and the rest, though mathematically sound, are too expensive to operate. Many of the latter type give results so nearly identical with those given approval here that they cannot become practically preferable.

Modified Straight Line Rule

Many text writers discuss the case of the "major repair" or "extraordinary charge." If in the course of use-life some very large item or items recurring at intervals much longer than one fiscal period are to be expected, it will be seen, from what was said of the simple rule, that the occurrence of such an item will seriously falsify the net income and the cost statistics. Obviously one does not reshingle a house merely to get service out of the house for the rest of the year in which the work is done. The job is done in order to get service from the house as long as the new roof lasts. One does not repaint a house every year in most climates. But the fact that such a job must be done, and be paid for, certainly affects the value of the house. If the house is worth repairing at all at the cost of repairing, the difference in value between the house just before and just after repairing is not less than the cost of the repair itself.

Extraordinary Outlays.—To provide for such large and infrequent amounts of outlay the following formula is often employed:

$$V_a = (n-a)U - \sum_{t=a}^{t=n} E + V_n \text{ and } D_a = U - E_a,$$

wherein U is defined by the equation:

$$\frac{V_o + \sum_{t=0}^{t=n} E - V_n}{n} = U = \frac{V_a + \sum_{t=a}^{t=n} E - V_n}{n-a},$$

in which E means "extraordinary charges not amounting to additions." The effect of this modification is to spread these extraordinary repair costs equally over all the years of use. U becomes the amount debited to depreciation and credited to the reserve for depreciation. In the years in which an item of this unusual kind happens, its cost, E_a, is debited to the reserve for depreciation and credited to cash, or to some liability account, if unpaid. It will readily be seen that the balance, or net entry, to the depreciation reserve account in any particular year may be a debit balance. This means that as between the beginning and closing book valuations the latter is the greater. Only in the years in which no extraordinary item occurs will the valuation curve be a straight line.

What Outlays are "Extraordinary?"

But what is an extraordinary outlay? How large must it be or how infrequent in recurrence? Does the simultaneous occurrence, or the occurrence in any one period, of an unusually large number of small charges constitute an extraordinary item? If we neglect for the moment the relation between amount of service and the amount of concurrent outlays, it can readily be seen that non-uniformity of periodic charges is the only really significant matter. For it is mere non-uniformity that disrupts the statistics of income and of unit costs. Absence of any charge for repairs at all in a specified period is quite as extraordinary as the occurrence of a large one, and has the same kind of effect upon the income and cost figures, though of course, of opposite sign. Can a concern increase its *real* net income during a period by failing to make repairs, or to repaint a building? Suppose one buys a machine on an understanding that the seller will "service" it for a year without further charge. Does the buyer escape an implied charge? Or does the seller see to it that the purchase price is big enough to reimburse him for his inconvenience if the buyer should hold him to the agreement?

What shall be done with the case of asset types that exhibit a characteristically increasing series of outlay charges, or one that usually declines, or that departs from uniformity in any specified way? The lazy way to deal with this nasty problem is to assume that, one year with another, these operating outlays will come to about the same figure, or that they will vary with sales volume. But the range of variation on either of these bases, one enterprise with another, is great both absolutely and relatively, and the dispersion within the range is characteristically broad. It is often, very often, not the part of wisdom to try to force uniformity. A well-financed and well-managed railroad spends more for repairs to rolling stock, tie replacements, etc., in the off-season periods and in light traffic years following a year of heavy duty than it does in the busy season or year. There is a great deal of business wisdom in the parable of the wise and the foolish virgins. Instead of saying "if the operating outlays *are* uniform," one should say, "if only they *could sensibly be made* uniform." Investment in repairs is made in advance of resulting services in exactly the same sense as investment in purchases of equipment is made in advance of service. The decision to buy carries with it an economically inevitable decision to make further outlays to conserve. A dollar of a purchase price has exactly the same consequences as a dollar of repair bill except for the fact that the latter lags behind the former.

While there are some cases in which the modification of the straight line rule under discussion makes that rule as good as any modification of it can be (see assets of types B and H in the preceding chapter), these cases are far from representative. To stop with "extraordinary items" is merely to nibble at the root of the difficulty. In a vastly larger number of cases more can be done by taking account of the whole schedule of charges. To do this it is necessary, so far as the formulas given above are concerned, only to substitute O for E.

But even this is only a palliative at best except in those cases in which the service to be rendered period after period can be counted on to remain approximately constant. For it is only in these that one can sensibly wish to make the total charges uniform. If we were indiscriminately to apply this modified rule, it is doubtful that we should benefit at all. The very uniformity in the annual charge may be absurd and may result in unit cost statistics even more fantastic than those produced by the simple rule.

Cost of a Unit of Service.—Applied to assets of types B and H (see page 266), the rule gives the unit costs on page 288 as contrasted with those produced by the unmodified rule.

The average outlay per unit of service on these types of asset is the same, viz., $0.39+. On assets of types D and F, on

UNIT COST OF SERVICE BY TWO RULES FOR SPECIFIED PERIODS ON ASSETS OF:

	Type B		Type H	
Period	Simple Rule	Modified Rule	Simple Rule	Modified Rule
1	$1.05	$1.25	$0.21	$1.05
10	.21	.25	.25	1.25

the other hand, the modified rule is quite satisfactory and is much better than the straight line rule. On the assets of type E only do they agree and here they are both correct.

Relative Deficiencies of the Method.—But in no case—and this is the important matter—does either rule give any better results and in most cases neither gives anything like so good results as a rule to be proposed below (see page 290). No modification of the straight line rule that stops short of eliminating the very essence of it can become a generally applicable method if one really cares to achieve anything more than mere numerical accuracy of arithmetical operations. The straight line rule in all its forms seems to be merely a special case of the popular fallacy that the arithmetic mean, by divine or natural ordinance, is *the* average and that any other average is an evil to be avoided if possible. As in all other cases, too, it makes a difference what quantities are taken into the total and what divisor is employed. Statistically considered, an average is something more than the numerical result of a dividing operation. In valuation procedure the arithmetic mean can be a useful and convenient measure provided the right things are averaged with respect to the right variable and in the right circumstances, but all these conditions must be fulfilled. In the present instance, total cost of service should be averaged over all units of service.

Modified Sinking Fund Rule

There are many variants upon this rule to be found both in the texts and in practice.[1] They are mentioned here merely because, unfortunately, they are sometimes used. There is no denying that conditions can exist under which any of them will approximate really significant figures. But cases of this kind are rare. And in *every* case it is possible to find a rule that is equally or more reliable that requires no more difficult estimates or operations than do the sinking fund variants.

The sinking fund principle may be a good one as a basis for bargaining about the administration of an investment or of a debt retirement fund, but its prominence in valuation is one of the best pieces of evidence that the common technique of revaluation is a very crude device.[2]

Modification of Fixed Percentage and of the Sum-of-the-Year-Digits Rules

Any rule is capable of modification in indefinitely many arbitrary ways. From any beginning formula any other may be derived if one is sufficiently ruthless. But having made a bad beginning, it is often easier to make a fresh start than to tinker with the faulty first product. Burning down houses is one way of roasting pigs, but is an expensive mode of cooking and probably does not prepare the most appetizing barbecue. So far as the writer is aware, no modifications of either of the rules under discussion is in current use, except in rare instances of setting a purely arbitrary positive value for V_n in the fixed percentage rule. It is not algebraically difficult to make either

---

[1] See Saliers. Depreciation: Principles and Application, for a list of these. Saliers disapproves of the principle underlying all of them, but does not by any means indicate the whole of the special shortcomings attaching to the principle and to the modified rules that make use of that principle.

[2] Two rules that involve very considerable modifications of the sinking fund rule will be discussed later (see pp. 305-306). But in both of these the modifications are so very great that the sinking fund principle is largely overborne. These rules will be discussed not because they are good but because they have been given the approval of highly trained technicians.

of these rules fit any real set of successive values if one makes the right modifications every time an asset is to be revalued. But to make either mode generally reliable is a task suitable only, perhaps, for class drill in manipulating statistical formulas.

Modification of the Service Unit Rule

Not only is the simple form of this rule more generally reliable than any other yet proposed, but it is easily capable of modifications that do not require the employment of any variables that do not also have to be considered in assigning values to the symbols in any simple rule. Nor do the additional data requisite for the operation of the modified rules require information that is not furnished by any well-kept set of accounts. In discussing that rule it was noted in the last chapter that no effect is given by it to departures of O/S from its mean expected value. That is to say, if period by period $O \neq KS$, where K is a constant, the unit cost of services, $\dfrac{D_a + O_a}{S_a}$, is not a constant. Departure from this relation is a defect.

Postulates Underlying the First Modification.—This last statement is too broad to be left without substantiation. The foundation for it, in the present writer's mind, can be described by the following postulates:

I. When a machine is bought it is acquired because:

(a) The service it can render is necessary to a program of operations in which other serving agents are to be employed jointly with it; and

(b) It is expected to render the essential service at a more *economical* outlay per unit than that service could be obtained for from any alternative agency available to the buyer.

II. A machine cannot be intelligently chosen from among alternative devices capable of rendering essentially like services unless estimates better than pure guesses can be made of:

(a) The amount of service that it will most probably pay to get from the machine; and

(b) The amount of outlays, other than the purchase price less salvage value, that will most probably have to be incurred as a direct and immediate consequence of its ownership and operation if the machine's service is to be had most economically.

III. The technical service of the machine is capable of measurement in terms of a unit such that there is no reason *assignable in advance* for preferring any one unit of the service to any other like-measured unit except that of preference for early as against deferred services.

IV. The number of fiscal periods within which the service is to be exploited and in which the outlays subsequent to purchase are to occur is not reliably determinable unless:

(a) Within the limits, time equals zero and time equals n, $S_a/S_{a\pm1} = 1$; or

(b) The service requirements, $S_1, S_2, \ldots S_a, \ldots S_n$, can be forecast.

V. The time-distribution of O is more nearly determined by the time-distribution of S than it is by mere lapse of time unless the time-distribution of S can be forecast. Elements of O that are time-functions, $O(t)$, (such as annual license fees, repainting, etc.) must be allowed for on a basis of a most probable value of n.

VI. Optional purposes of employment, i.e., the making of one or more kinds of goods or services for sale at different selling prices and in varying amounts, are expected to be open to the management. That is, the purchase of the machine commits the enterprise to no rigidly limited operating policy unless the results of that operating policy can be reliably forecast. This excepted case is the case of a concern that contracts for the sale of its entire output for a long term of years.

VII. The rate of time-preference (the rate of interest on

additional investment necessary to induce the enterprise management to *continue operations*) is either:

(a) Ignored in the valuations, that is, set impliedly at zero; or, more often,
(b) The rate is omitted because the time of investment involved for V_o, V_n, O, and hence for S, is capable of prediction to such a small extent that a proper rate taken into the calculations is unlikely to better the valuations sufficiently to pay for the additional calculating cost.

These postulates, while they do not purport to be a wholly comprehensive set, are nevertheless thought to be reasonably complete and reasonably necessary to one another. They are not mutually inconsistent nor do they depart widely in their assumptions from the conditions under which most assets of the kind under discussion are required and employed.

First Modification—Interest Ignored

Under these postulates the most probable outlay referable to a unit of service is denoted by U when, the primary estimates having been made, we set

$$\frac{V_o + \sum_{t=0}^{t=n} O - V_n}{\sum_{t=0}^{t=n} S} = U = \frac{V_a + \sum_{t=a}^{t=n} O - V_n}{\sum_{t=a}^{t=n} S}$$

Book value at the end of the ath period then becomes:

$$V_a = U \sum_{t=a}^{t=n} S - \sum_{t=a}^{t=n} O + V_n = V_{a-1} + O_a - US_a$$

The annual charge against gross income with respect to the cost of this asset's operating service is US_a. And the decline in book value (increase if D_a is negative) is given by

$$D_a = U \cdot S_a - O_a.[3]$$

---

[3] Formulas very like the set just given and very like the set next to be given were first published by J. S. Taylor in "A Statistical Theory of Depreciation Based on Unit Cost," *Journal of The American Statistical*

"Minimum Cost" and "Most Economical Cost" of a Unit of Service.—The problem of the business man who has already bought a machine, is not how to get the cheapest possible technical service out of it. That latter problem seldom if ever arises in the real world of affairs. It can present itself to a business man when, and only when, the *maximum profit to him* is contingent upon the operation at the optimum capacity of each and every device, either in his present possession or at his present disposal through purchase. The flour-milling industry has a plant capacity sufficient to turn out flour faster than two populations could eat it, if by plant capacity is meant the rate of commodity output that, continued indefinitely long, would permit flour to be milled at the lowest milling cost per hundredweight. Neither the industry nor any unit enterprise in it has ever occupied that position for any considerable length of time. Both maximum profit and minimum loss characteristically entail operating some or all devices at other than this optimum capacity. The overwhelming fact about business is that the business man does not rule the world in which he does business. His buying market for all things is determined for, rather than by, him. So also is his selling market. His job is to prepare for opportunities that may present themselves, to see them and seize them when they do, and be ready to shift when adversity threatens.

Association, p. 1010 (December, 1923), and were commented upon and modified by Harold Hotelling in the same journal, Vol. 20, p. 340 (September, 1925) in an article entitled, "A General Mathematical Theory of Depreciation." Quite independently of these writers the writer had invented the two sets of formulas to be given here in March, 1922. A few manuscript copies were privately circulated in that year and both have been continuously employed by him in instruction since that time. Both Taylor's article (see pp. 1010-1012, *loc. cit.*) and the writer's own work were prompted by the work of Gillette, "Cost Data," 1910, p. 36, and the "Final Report of the Special Committee to Formulate Principles and Methods for the Valuation of Railroad Property and Other Public Utilities," *Trans. of the American Society of Civil Engineers*, Vol. 81, 1917, pp. 1448-1501, in both of which a somewhat extended comment is to be found on the "unit cost" formula. The writer quite agrees with Taylor that the "unit cost" formula has little merit in comparison with certain others. But the postulates expressed or implied in Taylor's article are very different from the writer's, and, as will be made to appear, the formulas have a superficial resemblance only.

The problem of enterprise valuations is to answer the question, how well is the enterprise prepared to seize opportunities that may present themselves and to stave off adversities that may impose themselves in the real world. Just what favorable or adverse conditions are in prospect is the business man's own problem that he cannot shift. The accountant undertakes to say how well he is prepared for whatever *may* happen.

Merits of the Formula.—The formula under discussion possesses none of the demerits urged against those previously considered and possesses not only all of the merits of all of them but many more. If the postulates laid down for its support approximate the truth, the formula produces useful answers to the questions:

1. Of that which has been paid or must be paid for services of long-lived devices, how much expense was impliedly incurred on behalf of services already realized and how much for services that are still to be had?
2. Of those services paid for or to be paid for how much is applicable to the services used this year?
3. How much has been or will have to be paid out per unit of service realized?

The answer to the first question assists the business man to know his financial position with respect to the control of such technical services as the future may make it to his advantage to use. The answer to the second shows to what extent the receipts of the year are freed of concomitant outlays, past and future. The two together answer the further question, what ratio or other relation does this net income (or loss) bear to the investment made to get it. Successive answers to this further question, in time, will establish a trend or a base line to which to refer subsequent experience. These answers also measure the money-getting efficiency of the past management.

From all the answers to the third question a sense of what differential advantages are really open is made possible. The best evidence of what costs in the future will be that we really know anything about is: (1) what the costs of like operations have been; and (2) what changes in cost conditions have taken place since those costs were experienced. Cost figures that are produced by formulas that are not in accord with the characteristic conditions in which the enterprise works are not merely useless. To the extent that they are relied on they are baneful. But good cost statistics are half of the answer to the question, what are the most favorable and least favorable opportunities. The other half, viz., what receipts can be had, is the business man's own burden, not the accountant's. This set of answers, among them, determines: (1) profit-earning efficiency of the past; (2) present readiness for what the future may bring forth; and (3) prospects for the immediate future in relation to apparent strategic advantages. No information can ever become more important to the business man or to the public with which business men deal than reliable information on the three scores just mentioned. No worse pilot could be imagined than unreliable information about these things if the unreliable information is acted upon.

Effect of Errors in the Estimates.—Theoretical proof of the extent to which the estimates implied in this formula may be in error without making the statistics resulting from it worse than those that result from the like errors, when any of the formulas previously discussed are used, goes beyond the scope of this book. In Appendix A, the figures that result from all of them when the estimates are correct are given. The student who really wishes to see what these formulas will do when the estimates are in error is recommended to make a few arbitrary tests. Let him assume estimates for an asset of type C, for example, then successively suppose that n is unexpectedly prolonged to equal 15 or shortened to 5, merely stretching out or telescoping the schedules of O and S. Then try introducing errors into O and S, such as might readily occur, and see how large these errors would have to be before the average error (any average of error) by this method would be greater than that with like *mistakes of estimate* under the other rules discussed.

Service Unit Rule Further Modified—Interest Included

Where, if ever, conditions are encountered that warrant further refinement in technique than those of the rule just discussed, it is suggested that the rule be modified to allow for some rate of time preference. The doubt about whether or not "interest on the investment" should be considered, except when the investment implies a separate income to be separately capitalized, does not arise from any question of its theoretical propriety. Where genuine cases of capital valuation present themselves, that is, where there really *is* an ascertainable income series to be capitalized, the accountant's valuations always, except for very brief periods, imply some rate of capitalization greater than zero. Otherwise a bond for $1,000 upon which the debtor is to pay a twenty-year annuity of $50 would be exhibited at $2,000.

There is just as much theoretical propriety in valuing the services of a machine as though they were worth enough per unit to have a present worth equal to that of the whole schedule of anticipatory outlay costs necessary to obtain those services. It is perfectly possible *arbitrarily* to value the services of a machine at such a price per unit of service as would make the whole outlay for them yield some stipulated rate of net income. And it is no more arbitrary to do so than it is to assign any other money value to them—even outlay cost. Money values of services not themselves consisting of money incomes, are all arbitrary. There is nothing rational about them as individual values. As between valuing a unit of technical service, not exchanged immediately for a separate money income, at the outlay made for it, or at the square or the nth root of it, or at its cost improved at i rate per cent, there can be no possible choice except that of expediency and convenience.

Limitations upon Charging Interest.—In the muddy pool of controversy over the question of "interest on the investment," one finds all kinds of slippery arguments about what rate is to be employed. Most who discuss the question seem to think that, given a correct rate, there is little to object to except the arbitrariness of the rate chosen and of the valuations that result, and the clerical labor involved in the calculating and recording. Some assert that it "inflates inventories." And so it might if one is naïve enough to mistake the cost of a thing directly to be sold, for evidence of its direct capital value at prices prevailing in a current selling market.

But the present writer wishes to urge a somewhat different objection. If interest is to be charged at some agreed rate, into what quantity shall that rate be multiplied? Into book value of the assets? But look at these book values. Consider how they are themselves determined and consider how far they are likely, under any valuation rule yet discovered, to miss the ideally useful and convenient figure. To go through the book valuations found by the simple formulas in Appendix A, where exact prevision of events is supposed, and begin charging interest upon them, is as absurd as trying to correct for the earth's rotation in a snowball fight. To attempt a 5% alteration of an amount which may be 50% in error in a direction unknown to us, is what the kindergarten teachers call "busy work."

The writer has never had the pleasure of examining a set of accounts, and never expects to have it, in which the internal statistical evidence did not create a strong presumption of an indeterminate error, asset by asset, much greater than any proposed rate could be counted on to correct even if we knew the direction of the error. Fancy charging interest on an investment represented by properties exchanged for some of our stock issues! A rate of interest can be usefully applied only to valuing something capable of capitalization, that is, future receipts and disbursements, or to a glorified second guessing long after most of the facts have passed into experience. What is there to capitalize but sales receipts of the future and future outlays on the one hand, or a long series of past outlays and receipts in an attempt to establish a trend, on the other?

Excessive Claims for the Method.—It is legitimate business for the writer on the theory of valuation to consider many ideas that can seldom be employed in the world of affairs. The articles by Taylor and Hotelling, cited above, are easily among the best theory writing in this subject. But Taylor's assumption that unit cost is to be made a minimum presents an interesting problem in algebra that cannot cease to be algebra and become accountancy. Enterprises such as we now know about are not free to make this cost a minimum. Hotelling doubts the applicability of making this unit cost a minimum, in any useful sense, except by doing something to the machine rather than to the books.[4] In this he is quite correct. But on the same page he raises the question of estimating outlays for taxes, insurance and the like, which depend on *value* and hence neither can be found without finding both. The integral equation proposed for this will work only if the assessor and the insurer find their figures by a corresponding method. The real problem of forecasting these items involves knowing how the assessor and the insurance actuary are going to forecast the future.

He further adopts, apparently without reservation, cost as the first value.[5] His subsequent operations, therefore, never produce a valuation better than the original pricing. Through-

---
[4] Article cited, p. 341.
[5] *Ibid.*, p. 343.

out the article it seems to be implied that a value can sometimes be found for the unit of service output that is not itself determined by the cost of that unit.[6]

But this is the very kernel of valuation of this class of assets. If this could be accomplished at all, we should be able to get true capital values of enterprises without resort to forecasting sales. If, however, he means, as he may, that this output unit value is to be derived from selling price of product, then there is no real need for piecemeal asset valuation. If we could find some really reliable future sales series the capital values of this series and of the future outlay series could replace the whole balance sheet for many of its major uses.

Conditions Under Which Method Is Appropriate.—Instances may arise, however, in which future operating conditions can be forecast with sufficient reliability to warrant an attempt to improve on figures found by the set of formulas last proposed. There may be, for example, public utilities for which some rate of return on actual investment fixes the maximum profit not subject to governmental recapture or reduction. And the rate base, once fixed arbitrarily or otherwise at some assessed valuation of all tangibles, may allow addition of subsequent outlays valued to yield i rate on the cost of services.

It may also happen that a long period of operations is to be reviewed so that earlier estimates are subject to check in large measure by subsequent facts of experience. This case often arises when proposals are made to merge a number of concerns all of which have long operating histories. Such conditions warrant a valuation investigation and an estimate of goodwill, whether positive or negative, much more searching than is necessary on ordinary year-endings. For, in such cases, a complete shift of interest of all parties is contemplated. Waiting for any past errors to eliminate themselves is useless.

When conditions like the foregoing prevail, it *may* be pos-

---

[6] But on pp. 343, 344 he indicates that only a shaky foundation can be laid for it.

sible and *may* be worth while to attempt more precise valuations than those given by the formulas last discussed. If it should seem worth while to do so, the following additional modification of the service unit formula may prove useful.

Formula Modified to Charge Interest.—For the numerator of the ratio *determining U* set:

$$V_o + \frac{O_1}{I} + \frac{O_2}{I^2} + \ldots + \frac{O_a}{I^a} + \ldots + \frac{O_n - V_n}{I^n} = V_o + \sum_{t=0}^{t=n} C$$

and for the denominator set:

$$\frac{S_1}{I} + \frac{S_2}{I^2} + \ldots + \frac{S_a}{I^a} + \ldots + \frac{S_n}{I^n} = \sum_{t=0}^{t=n} P$$

For the numerator of the *ratio determined by U* set:

$$V_a + \frac{O_{a+1}}{I} + \frac{O_{a+2}}{I^2} + \ldots + \frac{O_n - V_n}{I^{(n-a)}} = V_a + \sum_{t=a}^{t=n} C$$

and for the denominator set:

$$\frac{S_{a+1}}{I} + \frac{S_{a+2}}{I^2} + \ldots + \frac{'S_n}{I^{(n-a)}} = \sum_{t=a}^{t=n} P$$

The fundamental equation may then be written:

$$\frac{V_o + \sum_{t=0}^{t=n} C}{\sum_{t=0}^{t=n} P} = \frac{V_a + \sum_{t=a}^{t=n} C}{\sum_{t=a}^{t=n} P} = U$$

Book value at the end of any period may be written:

$$V_a = U \sum_{t=a}^{t=n} P - \sum_{t=a}^{t=n} C$$

From this by simple algebra may be derived:

$$V_a = IV_{a-1} + O_a - US_a$$

and the amount of any year's depreciation, D_a, is

$$V_{a-1} - V_a = D_a = US_a - (iV_{a-1} + O_a)$$

That is, when once U is determined, usually by the aid of any standard set of interest tables, no subsequent interest calculations are required except the following: (1) The next preceding book value is multiplied by i in determining D_a; and/or (2) the next preceding book value is multiplied by I in determining its successor. But only one of these need be employed, since we have by definition, $V_{a-1} - V_a = D_a$.

Properties of the Formula.—The formula has a number of interesting properties. It should first be noted perhaps, that it can be employed in valuing any and all determinate real money incomes that consist of one or more discrete receipts, and/or one or more discrete outlays. The formula can be used, n being defined, no matter whether the receipts and/or disbursements are uniform or consist of varying amounts. Or given the first or any other book value, the time-distribution of the outlays and receipts, and an arbitrary rate i', one can determine by it the excess or deficiency of earnings over or under i'. That is to say, any set of receipts and/or disbursements, including purchase price, can be valued to yield any rate whatsoever. If i be the rate implied in the purchase price but is not determined and a rate, i', $(i' \neq i)$ is employed in the formula, the resulting value of U will show $U \neq 1$.

U, as defined by the formula, is the *price* per unit of S that must be realized if i rate is to be earned on the investment, or the cost per unit of S if funds are worth i compounding annually.

If any item O or S turns out to be numerically different from the anticipated value, D_a and V_a will show the effect of the error of estimate. If there is a shift from any period to another period of any unit of O or of S the effect of the shifting is shown.

These properties afford several useful checks upon the precision of estimates. Suppose that on the cards of a machine register *all* of the primary estimates are entered when the machine is new. Suppose also that the schedules of D_a and V_a based wholly upon estimates are filled up at once. Then, as the machine is used from year to year, let the experienced values of O and S be substituted in the formulas for D_a and V_a and let the resulting depreciation and book value figures be entered in parallel columns beside the anticipated corresponding amounts. Discrepancies between the anticipated and the subsequent figures immediately give notice of the book value effect of error.

Excesses of book value over the estimates may result either from a slower rate of use than was expected, or from a higher rate of outlay charges or both. The reverse results can arise from opposite changes. Marked deviations of the resulting figures from those anticipated invite inspection of the machine, reappraisal of the prospective residual values of O and S, and redetermination of the operating policy with respect to the machine. Of course, the like schedules and comparisons can be made in the employment of the formula expressed without interest, but the deviations of anticipated from experienced results have a less simple meaning since neither valuation series evaluates differences in waiting periods by a weight other than unity. Knowledge of the fact of deviations of experience from estimate is always suggestive of the importance of error, but unless the deviations are evaluated, it may be difficult to do anything useful in correcting the error or preventing its recurrence.

A still more valuable check on earning power may be afforded. For if all assets are valued to yield some rate thought to be the minimum that would invite competitive capital into the industry in the competitive market area, then interest on the investment at that rate is in effect charged in the annual series US_a, which become the annual operating charges. Neglecting for the moment deviations of D_a and V_a from the anticipated corresponding values, the balance of the operating revenue account will be zero if i rate has been earned exactly. The balance will be credit if more than i has been earned and debit if less than i has been earned. Whatever balance there is, will show the earning in excess (or defect) of i on enterprise investment valued to yield i.

If, on the other hand, the service unit method that takes account of outlay and service, without discounting either, is employed, a different meaning is to be inferred from the operating revenue account balance. The balance, then, is an excess or deficiency of earning over zero rate on assets valued to yield zero rate. If this zero-rate-on-investment method is used and a credit balance equal to 8% on the book value of assets is found, this does not by any means indicate that the assets valued to yield 8% would have shown a zero balance in the operating account. Differences in the relative time-scheduling of receipts and disbursements and the operation of discounting combine to effect this apparent anomaly. If, therefore, we wish to test for an excess or deficiency of earning against some standard rate with any degree of simplicity, we must value the assets to yield that rate on their cost at the beginning of the period.

Effect of Error in the Estimates.—But—and this is the important matter—we have been neglecting the discrepancy between the anticipated book valuations, those scheduled from the installation of the asset, and the subsequent revisions of these values obtained by inserting the experienced values S and O in the formulas for D_a and V_a. Suppose the machine stands idle for the year. We neither use it nor spend money on it. The non-interest formula does not in any way affect the income account for the year. The values S_a and O_a are zero. But by the interest formula the value V_a becomes IV_{a-1} despite the fact that S_a and O_a are zero. The machine has increased in value at I rate. And the accounts will show an earning at i rate with respect to it. This is, indeed, a matter for concern. Unless we revised our estimates, all we should have to do to earn i rate forever would be to abandon the plant. It must not be supposed that there is anything necessarily wrong with showing a valuation at the end of an idle year higher than that at the beginning. The real state of facts may be that the true *relative* values stand thus. Confronted unexpectedly with an idle year, the *beginning* value of that year should be written down. Unless in the beginning of an idle year an asset is a total loss, it will, unless it disintegrates during the year, be worth more a year later merely because it is nearer to a period of useful employment.

This bias in the interest form of the formula is one that seems not to have been anticipated by Hotelling and Taylor; for their formulas possess it also. Neither of them, in the articles cited, seems to have had in mind the interrelation between the revenue account, the cost accounts, and the valuations. They seem to look upon revaluation as an *end* to be gained rather than as a *means* to determining trends of earning power of business opportunities. Had either of them completed his tests, the bias would have been noted.[7]

It is this bias and the very great difficulty and expense of avoiding the effects of it that impels the writer to qualify approval of this formula, which, to descend to the personal, was for some years his special pet. The non-interest formula, on the other hand, may in some instances carry an error forward, but it never increases it by virtue of its own properties. Misjudgments of n, when the service expected is ordered merely in relation to concomitant outlays and not with respect to calendar time-periods, do not affect its results at all except to the extent that a "telescoping" of services may increase or decrease aggregate cost. To a very considerable degree, it is self-rectifying. Mere relative *displacements* of either S or O work themselves out of the valuations and, thereafter, do not affect the income account. But a displacement of either S or

---

[7] The writer has never been able to get anything but a figurative meaning out of the common expression "the *force* of interest." There does seem, however, to be a real meaning for "the force of interest-*figuring*." The blasting of many hopes, sustained by interest figuring only, is one of the accountant's tasks.

O or of both of them in any direction are never cleared from the interest-form valuations. The interest form is for experts of good character only.

The "Unit Cost" Formula

This method is said to be based upon the principle that the value of an asset should be such as to enable its user to produce all subsequent units of product at as low a cost as the average cost of production would be for the whole use-life of the asset.[8] But, as noted by Taylor, the formula does not produce that result. The wrong averages are taken, the wrong interest charge is made, and the wholly arbitrary and useless sinking fund principle is introduced. Even if the formula would do what its advocates claim for it, it seems incapable of formulation in an expression that avoids tedious calculations.

The Equal Profit Ratios Formula

This formula was devised by Professor J. C. L. Fish.[9] It is based on a proposition about "fair price." Its author says: "A fair price for a second-hand structure is such as will cause the ratio of equivalent uniform yearly profit to investment to be the same for the seller as for the buyer." [10] The formula is much too long to be reproduced here. This formula also employs the sinking fund principle, but, for solution, requires independent, money-valued, service series. All primary data, therefore, are assumed to be real money outgoes and incomes. Really to accomplish the object of this formula requires only the parallel time-scheduling of the receipt and disbursement series for the assumed use-life or income-bearing-life, and solving for the effective rate. The familiar process of interest-

---

[8] For the general formula, see Gillette, Cost Data, 2nd ed., p. 36. For a full, but uncritical, development of the formula see Fish, Engineering Economics, 2nd ed., pp. 183-186. For a satisfactory critical comment by Taylor, see Vol. 18, Journal of the American Statistical Association, pp. 1010-1012.
[9] Engineering Economics, 2nd ed., pp. 186-191.
[10] Ibid., p. 187.

table bracketing to find i will accomplish this. Having found i, one has only to capitalize the residual series after a periods to find the price.

One may raise the question, though, of why such a valuation should ever be wanted unless a contract on that basis has been entered into and has to be adjudicated. Willing buyers at a price to yield low returns are hard to find, and willing sellers of an enterprise to yield more to the buyer than the going investment rate are equally scarce.

Summary of Chapters XIII and XIV

From what has been said in the last two chapters, it must be indicated that the statistical task of finding an enterprise capital value that, in any reliable sense, reflects its most probable value to yield a going rate of return upon the investment, is an extremely difficult task. Not only is it impossible to do so directly, but as has been shown, the attempt even to discriminate between that which has been paid, or is payable, for asset service already utilized, and that which has been paid for future services hoped for, is an extremely difficult task.

No one has yet suggested any more workable scheme for valuing the goodwill, whether positive or negative, of an enterprise than that of capitalizing excess or deficiency of earnings over some nominal rate. But no sound basis for such a valuation can be had without appropriate antecedent piecemeal valuation of the assets. For overvaluation of these implies high book figures for earning power, and low valuations imply the reverse. And, really to measure the excess or deficiency of earnings over some agreed rate, requires valuation of all assets for the successive periods under review at a price to yield that rate. This in turn involves adjustments between anticipations of service and outlay, and the realizations thereof. The formal niceties of the various interest-including formulas proposed require a degree of skill in treatment that few possess in sufficient degree to attain precision. Valuation of assets employed as technical agents only is the most difficult problem with which accountants have to deal if anything like the degree of reliability attaching to their other balance sheet items is to be attained.

So far as the accounting profession is concerned it must be admitted that they have not given this subject the careful thought its importance warrants. On the other hand, it must be emphatically asserted that few concerns are willing to pay for good valuations. If accountants are themselves satisfied, due regard being had for what may reasonably be expected, with their successive balance sheet valuations and income statements, they might afford *some* additional help with little additional expense. A comparative statement of asset book value and of net operating revenue covering five or ten years might be exhibited as a major exhibit of each audit. The rates of revenue to book value shown would at least disclose large and long continued deviations of rates from usual rates.

Finally, a word should be said about the professional responsibility for valuation. Many accountants assert that valuation of fixed tangible assets is a job for appraisal engineers. Others say that it is the job of the management themselves and that accountants have discharged their whole duty when they avoid certifying statements in which the assets have been negligently or fraudulently valued.

The engineers are not too happy with the burden thrust upon them. They say, at least many of them do, that it is impossible to make valuations unless the operating policy, particularly that of maintenance, upkeep, and repairs, is foreknown.

Business men are the ones who really act on valuations. Any one of them is willing to admit the difficulty of the task, and few of them are convinced that either the engineers or the accountants know very much about it.

The writer is convinced that no professional training now conventionally advocated or offered in any recognized professional art is adequate to the job. Valuation is a problem that exists in the real world of affairs, whether it lies in any profession's field or not. Either it is the subject matter of a special art for which no one is yet adequately trained, or it really belongs to those who practice some recognized art but who have not prepared wholly to undertake the task.

With respect to most artifact assets, the roots of the problem lie in machine specifications and machine design, and in structural specifications and design. Power to resist wear and exposure and specification with respect to minimizing upkeep and repairs without unduly increasing first costs, are obviously of the most vital importance.

Plant layout and equipment specification play no small part. The nice putting together of even the best tried standard machines and fixtures in new combinations, cannot but influence the valuation results.

Technical knowledge of how existing equipment can be used to best advantage in the ever-changing production requirements and financial difficulties that confront the production manager clearly is involved. It is idle to speak of reducing unit cost of service to a minimum. Work has to be done when the chance for profit is offered. Equipment must be worked to death in a few days or weeks, if it is the "bottle-neck" in a rush schedule of production.

A better knowledge of mathematics, particularly of probability and of statistics, if the relations between costs, valuations, selling prices of products, and income trends are to be worked out in the light of experience, is required than that possessed by the professions working at valuations. And, finally, that indefinable but none the less real thing called business sense or judgment must be looked to for help.

The valuation problem is a great and a difficult one worthy of the intellectual attention of the most able and best trained minds that can be interested in it. It is also one of the most important for the welfare of society that we have to face.

There can be no possible doubt that bad valuations result in a tremendous volume of waste energy. Nor can there be any doubt that our financial structure could be used to much greater social advantage as well as individual profit if better valuations were the rule. The problem is so important and the reasonably possible improvements in valuation practice are so great, indeed, as to justify a hope that the very near future will see great advances made. Those advances, in fact, are in progress now.

CHAPTER XV

SUMMARY AND FORECAST

Considered historically, the professions of economics and accountancy have independent origins. Within their early common period neither calling took serious notice of the other's literature; and neither foresaw, or indeed, could readily have foreseen, the possibilities for mutual helpfulness that all thoughtful students in the two fields now recognize. Not only are the professional origins different, but also, from the beginning the two groups have had important diverse interests. At no time can either's field of learning be looked upon as including the other's; nor is either calling an offshoot of the other. We can see now, to be sure, that from the beginning the professions were vitally interested in much subject matter in common. But the still prevailing differences of point of view taken toward this common ground and the resulting differences in mode of procedure combine to make the work of each calling difficult of access to the other.

Professional Differences between Accountancy and Economics

All able statisticians appreciate the great difficulties of using data taken from a statistical summary of one study in the analysis of a problem significantly different from the one for which the original data were collected and classified. Unless the statistician is thoroughly familiar with the whole of the procedure underlying the summary from which he excerpts, he runs a very great risk of deceiving himself as to the significance of the summary that can be carried over to the analysis of the problem in hand. He also runs the still greater risk of conveying a false or distorted conclusion to the mind of the unwary or uncritical reader of his own reports.

There can be no doubt that the vast accumulation of accountants' reports available to the economist constitute, for him, a most important body of source data. Equally, there can be no doubt either that these data are really available to few economists or that many who have made large use of the data have done so undiscriminatingly and even naïvely.

Accountants' Reports Specialized.—The accountants' reports are end-products of a highly specialized and intricately developed statistical procedure. To be sure, there is a very considerable degree of approximation to uniformity in this procedure *at any given time,* but this uniformity is a changing uniformity. Any one who has attempted to obtain comparative statistics, ordered in time, even for one enterprise, must have realized this. Whether he is interested in elements or classes of income, of expense, of asset constitution, of funded debt, or of proprietary net estate, he will usually find evidence of reclassification at relatively frequent intervals. When stub descriptions within the statements are changed, the statistical inquirer resorting to the reports is chargeable with notice of a change in procedure. Mere change of descriptive caption raises the presumption of change in procedure, but is not conclusive that a material change, or indeed, any change at all, has been made.[1]

---

[1] Many phrases like "deferred charges to operations" and "prepaid expenses" are used interchangeably by some accountants others employ only one of them, and still others, by their use of both in the same statement, imply that a distinction is to be made. Among those whose reports imply a distinction there is not the least semblance of uniformity in the basis of the distinction. There is to be found in modern procedure, however, a large number of accounts the balances of which imply that expenditures have been made in the past for benefits which are still to be received in whole or in part which the accountant *expects* will be received and will be worth what was paid for them. These benefits may be of indefinitely great variety but they possess certain attributes in common: they are not capable of separate realization in money, so long as the enterprise continues, without a simultaneous expense for like benefits or without incurrence of a risk; and they all report a disposition of funds or the incurrence of liabilities not specifically

Still more insidious are the changes in actual procedure to which the finished reports do not call attention by changes of stub description. All enterprises may simultaneously be confronted with like changes of material conditions.[2]

The Rôle of "Judgments."—To a very considerable degree, too, the summary report data are, and must always be, affected by "judgments" that are not capable of statistical proof. Disagreements of judgment, even among those who are rightly regarded as experts, are notorious.

Add to the foregoing the undoubted fact that every enterprise is, in many respects, unique, and that the set of interested classes to whom the reports are to go varies from concern to concern and changes from year to year in the same enterprise. Since the primary duty of the accountant is to report information in the forms thought to be most useful to the persons who have legitimate interests in the enterprise affairs, the form and classification of reports must frequently be altered. There seems to be, in general, a greater degree of stability in the elementary classes of data, the ledger accounts, than there is in the mode of summarizing these data.

---

represented by either any tangible object acquired or by any distribution to persons having financial holdings in the concern. When the common attributes are those really significant for the economist, he can safely ignore changes of stub caption, or combine items that appear under the two heads. When the diversities are significant, he must either go back to the books of original entry, or break the continuity of his series.

[2] Our somewhat arbitrary federal revenue acts present many cases in point. They permit, for example, a taxpayer corporation to deduct an allowance for depreciation from its gross income in determining net taxable income. But to have the benefit of this provision *as a matter of right* the corporation must: (1) claim the allowance in the year in which the depreciation occurs; and (2) record the depreciation upon their books of account. Such a measure imposes a duty upon directors to their shareholders to assert annually as large a depreciation as can at all reasonably be supposed to have occurred. They must err, if at all, on the side of undervaluation of assets, or else risk a tedious and expensive proceeding to convince an administrative officer of the state that a subsequently ascertained underestimate of some earlier year was an honest mistake of informed judgment and not a mere matter of negligence. The accountants, taking cognizance of the changed condition, continue to report "depreciation" by the *same title*, but the *basis of the estimate* may have changed from a "safe average" or a "most probable" allowance to one that is *almost certainly not too small*.

The Obstacle of Terminology.—Perhaps the greatest difficulty confronting the economist is that of terminology. Certain it is that most of the blunders made in the use of accounting data may well have had such an origin. Such terms as capital, capital stock, income, expense, assets, cost, value, etc., are notorious for their multiple meanings in economic literature. There is an equally great diversity, though not equally notorious, in the meaning of these same terms in the texts and treatises in accounting. These text writers pay less attention than their economist brethren to formal definitions of their terms; and they are, perhaps, more often guilty of failure to observe their own definitions. In such a condition of terminology the possibilities of innocent error are boundless. On the other hand, the likelihood of avoiding errors in adaptation are very small indeed, unless the economist has, first of all, spent years in familiarizing himself with accounting procedure.

The task of gaining such a first-hand knowledge of accounting procedure as will enable an economist reliably to translate accounting generalizations into economic generalizations, is a difficult one indeed. In the present state of accounting literature the task is so great that few economists can afford the requisite time for study. If one may judge by the frequency with which blunders are encountered or by the character of criticism of accountants that economists frequently make, one must conclude both that very few really have learned much about accounting procedure and that very few have any realizing sense of how difficult it is to acquire a serviceable familiarity with the subject.

Those economists who wish to acquire such a knowledge of accounting procedure as will permit the use of accounting data with a maximum accuracy and reliability, must not hope to succeed merely by reading to remember and to believe. The text literature on accounting and auditing procedure abounds with assertions about the objects of elements of procedure and about the intentions of the accountant in performing particular operations. Among this plethora of assertions about intention, there is an abundance of pure conjecture. The self-inconsistencies and the mutual inconsistencies of these assertions are legion. It is not intended to assert here that there is not also a very great deal of sound statement to be found. But the true cannot be reliably separated from the merely speculative except by the extremely difficult test of reference to actual procedure.

Moreover, neither the accountant in devising the elements of his procedure and in generalizing about them, nor the text writer in his attempts to shorten the learning time of the prospective accountant, have had the professional economist's problem of using accounting data in mind. They have been addressing a quite different audience. The economist, therefore, must largely ignore the statements of purpose and of intention that he reads and consider the statistical effects of the procedure he finds. Even if one knew as a matter of indisputable fact just what the intentions of the accountants are, one could not safely rest upon that knowledge. In accountancy, just as in other arts, the things that it is hoped will result from a particular measure are not necessarily identical with the most probable results. The economist who wishes to employ accountants' data must do his own generalizing. A little knowledge is a dangerous thing only when one is unaware of the littleness or when one mistakenly supposes he has knowledge.

Theory of Income.—Looked at from the economist's point of view, the chief preoccupations of the accountant are with income and its concomitant outgo and with methods and techniques of measuring and valuing income and outgo. They are concerned with money-valued income and money-valued outgo in their most general sense, that of a series of events each of which gives rise to an element of service and an element of disservice. With relatively few and unimportant exceptions they restrict their attention to the events of enterprise, chiefly gainful enterprise. Their methods and techniques readily lend themselves to the treatment of individual money-valued income. With considerably more alteration, they might be applied to the problems of social income. But the practice of accountants lies outside the domain of domestic establishments and outside the field of social economy.

In a régime in which the institution of private property and private enterprise and the money and credit economy prevail, a money-valued accounting only may be expected. Values not conveniently and reliably convertible into money equivalents are excluded from modern accounting. Accountants, no doubt, will admit that important standards and values other than money values, even a multitude of them, manifest themselves in enterprise as well as in modes of living. Services and disservices to be weighed and measured by standards other than money may be of great importance both to individuals and to society, but these incomes and outgoes cannot be brought within the same statistical accounting as that employed for money-valued events. At the very outset, then, it appears that the scope within which the phenomena of income concern the accountant excludes much with which the economist undertakes to deal.

The economist, on the other hand, seldom has occasion to consider the money-getting and spending activities of particular persons or the like activities in particular enterprises. Only when these activities of individuals may be regarded as samples representing a class or a population is the economist interested. He has a like indifference to the doings of an enterprise except as a representative of an industry, or of enterprise in general, or, as in the case of a few establishments, when the concern operates on so great a scale as to give rise to problems of public interest.

A proper understanding of the possibilities for mutual assistance of the professions cannot, therefore, be had without realizing that within this common subject matter of income each profession relegates to incidental consideration or excludes altogether much that the other calling looks upon as matter of prime importance.

Theory of Production.—Arising from the difference of interest of the two professions in income, there are differences of interest in sources of income. Whether the economist divides his "factors of production" into "land, labor, and capital," or, as some do, into "land, labor, capital, and organization," or considers them all under the head of "capital," he is chiefly concerned with the *whole of the services* that these agents can be expected to render to society in general. The accountant, on the other hand, has to consider only the services of these agents that are *available in the operations of a particular enterprise.* He weighs the significance of even these, not by their importance to society, but by the extent to which their money value *can be appropriated* by the proprietor of the enterprise. The economist is concerned with these agents both as servants to society and as the means of acquiring a livelihood for their owners. The accountant, on the other hand, considers them only as agents of acquisition within the enterprise for the beneficial interest of the proprietor. The capacity to render technological services, which is determined by the properties inherent in the agent, does not interest the accountant professionally. He is interested only in the appropriable benefits of service.

The two professions have diverse regard, too, for certain disservices or potential disservices of operating agents. The economist does not disregard the deleterious effects upon a population of a smoke pall from factory chimneys, nor the nuisances of stockyard smells and of traffic obstruction. Since the burden of such disservices falls only to a very small degree upon proprietors, as such, the accountant, quite properly, is not professionally interested either in these disservices or in the properties of the agents that give rise to these undesirable elements of industrial events.

Theory of Value and of Valuation.—The economist can be said quite properly to be interested in the value of items of wealth in the most general sense of that term. The value of items of wealth, as the economist views them, can be said to depend upon their capacities to render services and the concomitant, inevitable disservices, though only to a limited extent can such a value be numerically determined from the service-disservice series. But the value of tangible objects, in the economist's sense of the concept, is not a matter of concern to accountants in all cases. Indeed, it is only by an accidental coincidence that his valuation of tangible things is identical in scope with that of the economist in any instance. The accountant values only residual service series that are available to, and appropriable by, the proprietor in the operation of the enterprise in which the object is used. Accountants do not profess that these valuations are all capital valuations in the economist's sense of the term. True capital valuations are, in many important instances, difficult to obtain with reliability; in many other important instances, e.g., in the case of fixed tangible assets not held for separate sale or rental, the object, from the accountant's point of view, cannot have a capital value. For there is no rational way of finding the requisite money valuations of the estimated series of future technological services. The accountant's valuations of the future services of this class of objects is of an order very different from any for which the economist has professional regard.

Neither the valuation of the income and expense in a particular period, nor the valuation of future available services is, in the first instance, the business of the professional accountant. It is the affair, rather, of the proprietor acting through the managers of the enterprise. The accountant comes in as an expert, disinterested, responsible principal to express a judgment of the validity and reliability of the manager's valuations. The valuation figures to which the accountant certifies are, therefore, no sure index to what accountants, as a group of skilled men, might find if they were determining valuations in the first instance. Their certificates say, in effect, that the valuations set forth conform to the honest judgment of informed and skilled business men acting in their own interests.

Theory of Distribution.—With the whole subject of distribution, in the classical economist's sense of the term, the accountant has no professional concern. He does not inquire why wages of one trade are higher or lower than those of another, nor what it is, in general, that determines wage rates. The rent of land, the earnings of invested funds, the profits of the entrepreneur, just as the wages of employees, concern him only to the extent to which he finds existing contracts involving them. He attempts to show the effects thus far of the contracts that have been entered into and to exhibit the present state of affairs with respect to those contracts in force.[3]

Thus in all the fields, production, exchange, distribution

---

[3] It should be noted, however, that in some cases the accountant has regard for matters that look, at least superficially, like the economist's distributive shares. Thus if the businesses of a co-partnership and of a corporation are to be consolidated under the control of a new corporation, no skilled accountant, called upon for advice, would ignore the characteristic differences in mode of dividing enterprise gains. In partnerships generally the proprietors are active in management and in operations. Their shares in the fruits of the enterprise are usually expressed in ratios to total net gains. And even when the partners, by agreement, are paid fixed "salaries" plus some ratio participation in the excesses of profits over salaries, these "salaries," as between the firm and those who do business with the firm, do not give rise to firm debts; they are but modes of inter-partner participation in enterprise gains. If the goodwill of both the firm and the corporation are to be separately valued upon consolidation, the accountant, whether nominal "salaries" are paid or not, will advise placing some valuation upon the services rendered by the partners and the deduction of the amounts of these salaries from the net firm income in order that comparable rates of earning on the investment in the firm business and in the corporation's business can be found.

But even in these cases the accountant merely recognizes the *existence* of the distributive shares. He professes no theory of his own about how the several services of the partners and of the invested capital should be valued. The amounts to be agreed upon are matters for the bargainers to determine for themselves.

and consumption, into which most economists habitually divide their subject, the viewpoint of the accountant is seen to be materially different from that of the economist. The accountants as a profession have hardly entered the field of consumption at all—though their methods and techniques are as applicable to domestic establishments as they are to gainful enterprise. Into distribution they do not go at all. They have regard for only the acquisitive concomitants of production. Their valuations are but judgments upon the valuations of business men.

Statistical Theory.—Many economists are grieved to find that the balance sheet valuations of accountants are of mongrel origin (from the economist's point of view). They find that cash has been counted (a present valuation); that accounts, bills, and notes receivable have been valued at the number of dollars expected to come in (a future valuation); that interim receivable interest accruals are valued separately from the principals to which they attach (an earning); that inventories are valued at cost or market (a purely arbitrary index); that items like organization expense, purchased goodwill, etc., having no attributes in common with the assets grouped with them are included (valuation account balances); that fixed assets are valued at an approximation to the cost of the future services expected to become available provided that cost does not exceed the cost of available substitute services (a division of costs into past and future charges). They find, moreover, that these diverse valuations of diverse things are added to find an asset total that, dollar for dollar, cannot possibly have a common significance.

In the other branch of the balance sheet they find a group of current liabilities valued at the amount to become payable (a future valuation); that fixed liabilities are valued to yield the effective rate implicit in their net issue price (a present valuation); and that a more or less arbitrary distribution of the difference between asset and liability totals is made among capital stock and elements of surplus or deficit (the total thus divided being merely the resultant of the diverse measures of assets and of liabilities). They find that this net proprietary interest figure bears no stable relation to the true capital value (if the latter could be found) of the enterprise as a whole.

No less are they distressed by the figures they find in the income statement for a specified period. They find a mixture of realized income positive and negative, of many negative earnings, of some positive earnings; and of a figure like that resulting from the difference between (1) the sum of purchase costs and beginning inventory valued at cost or market, and (2) the closing inventory valued at cost or market—a difference figure that is neither a realized (negative) income nor a (negative) earning.

The statistical state of affairs complained of does exist. No competent student of the joint field of economics and accounting can doubt that the measurements in accountants' reports are of diverse statistical orders. But that is a very different matter from charging professional accountants with responsibility for statistical absurdities. To such a charge the accountants could make the perfect rejoinder, "Show us a better way of doing this work that is both practicable and that clients would pay to have done."

It is possible, but not very useful, to prepare all income statistics of the past on the basis of realized income and cost valuations. This would be a cash receipts and disbursements accounting only. No accruals or earnings, positive or negative, would be included. That is to say, no depreciation and no appreciation could find a place, no costs of assets like manufactured inventories other than the cost of materials embodied in the goods and of direct labor services, could be shown.[4]

---

[4] Many instances, indeed, will occur to the professional student of cost accounts in which not even these elements of cost can be apportioned among the several varieties of goods and lots of the several kinds. Consider the case of a manufacturing concern that has advance orders in sufficient volume to require overtime operation. Suppose that wage agreements provide for "time and a half" for overtime hours. To what goods shall the wage pre-

SUMMARY AND FORECAST

Such an accounting can show very little that is significant with respect either to a present financial and operating position or to performance during a period that is closed.

Statistics of realized income that are confined to past series are of little significance unless they can be coupled with like series projected into the future. To suggest the difficulties of doing this, it is only necessary to raise a few questions. By what means shall one estimate the character of goods to be offered for sale in the distant future? How shall one estimate the unit selling prices? What will be the sales volume period by period? What market areas will be exploited?

The non-availability of the future series of data, except for certain fragmentary items attaching to the near future, not only prevents the systematic development of realized income statistics to the point of large usefulness but prevents also a full development of capital valuation. For without reliable estimates of all future series to be discounted, reliable present valuations are impossible. Without reliable capital valuations in the form of present worths, it is impossible to prepare statistics of earnings; for statistics of the latter sort are derived jointly from past realized income, past worths, and present worths.

Some compromises, some admixture of realized income and cost (of the past), of present worths (when reliably determinable), of future worths (when conversion to present worths is not significant or will not pay), of earnings (when the requisite present worths can be had), and of indexes of value (past, present, and future), must be resorted to if the accountant is to provide as much useful information as the conditions of his

---

mium be charged, the goods actually worked on during overtime hours, all the goods in process during the calendar period within which overtime operations prevail, these latter goods and some of those in process before overtime operations begin? The decision in any case must be an arbitrary one, and the statistics contingent upon that decision will be of an order different from those which go no farther than to show the number of dollars paid to workmen. This latter is a statement of fact. It is a true (negative) realized income. But the partly offsetting positive element, the cost valuation of the goods on hand, would be but an index of realized income.

engagements will permit. There is no reason to suppose that those to whom the accountant is immediately and chiefly responsible will ever be best served by accounting statistics of a single order. The prevailing form of compromise may change, but compromise is both inevitable and indispensable in the real world of affairs in which the accountant works. Betterments are possible; and it is not presumptuous for the economist to propose them; but the critic who limits his complaint to the mere diversity of order of statistics will waste his words.

Economists Must Make Their Own "Translations."—The foregoing sketch of the difficulties to be encountered by the economist in employing data drawn from accountants' reports is not intended to discourage resort to accounting data. Quite the contrary is true. The economists of the past have relied too much upon hypothesis and conjecture about human behavior in enterprise relationships. If they are to test the adequacy of their hypotheses about human nature for supporting not merely the *validity* but the *truth* of their conclusions about human conduct, some resort to the records of behavior must be made. Progressive refinements of speculation about the nature of an imaginary race of beings and about the conduct of members of that race in imaginary market situations is, for some, a fascinating exercise, but it is not science. The time seems to be coming when it will no longer be economics.

To the extent that the economist deals with the behavior of men in enterprise relations, with the effect of forms of organization upon public interest, with the merits of problems of controlling enterprise activity, large resort *must* be made to accounting data. There are little or no other data available. Certainly there is no other comparable body of data prepared by skilled, disinterested principals who charge themselves both with responsibility to those whom they serve in the first instance and to the public. The nearest rival of this body of data is, perhaps, to be found in the reports of our courts of record.

But these deal only with elements of conduct that have led to dispute between men or that have caused men to fall foul of the criminal laws. Upon the enormously greater body of conduct that goes on peaceably, the law and equity records throw little light.

Even those great collections of data, the census reports, are founded to a very great extent upon accounting statistics. These can be no better than their foundation. Indeed, the accounting foundation of public statistics is much less reliable, and must remain less reliable, than the kind of data with which this book is concerned. For herein little or nothing is said of the product of the private accountant who is a mere employee of the proprietor of the enterprise he works for. Without wishing to deny the excellence of the work of many private accountants, it can be pointed out that there is among them no announced and jealously guarded and enforced body of professional ethics. They are not a self-disciplining profession. To public statistical collections like the census, based upon accountants' findings, the private accountants have contributed more in the first instance than the public accountants have.

The influence of accountants' findings upon statistical data that may seem to be of other origin is incalculably great. One needs to read but little in any of the great financial journals and trade organs to see this. Even the advertising matter in these journals and the circulars and press releases of commercial bankers, investment bankers, and stock and bond brokers, show the great extent to which accounting data influence other statistical series.

There is little reason to suppose that any great body of statistical data about the conduct of enterprise affairs that is independent of the work of the accountant will become available in the near future. Much as the economist might like to have statistical information collected and compiled with special regard for his professional use, there is little prospect of his being able to induce either private persons or the state to undertake either the duty or the expense. If economists are to carry forward their professional investigations upon their present broad basis and with their present point of view, they must choose among a too great reliance upon intuition, an uninformed use of accounting data, and the serious and arduous study of accounting procedure that will enable them to resort to the best available statistical material on enterprise relations.

Prospective Betterments of Accounting Data

There are abundant grounds for hope that the existing barriers to mutual helpfulness may be materially diminished. In many institutions in which professional economists are being trained, not only is a familiarity with the elementary structure of modern accounts required of candidates for higher degrees but special courses of instruction are offered that have for their constituencies not prospective accountants and business men, but prospective economists who wish to achieve competence in the joint fields. An increasing proportion of those who offer instruction in accounting in the universities are men who have studied economics beyond the scope usual to ordinary undergraduate instruction. In courses of study prepared for the training of professional accountants, a larger and larger content of general economics is becoming customary. Not merely do the two fields of endeavor impinge upon one another, they have begun to coalesce.

There is a broad ground for supposition that the data supplied by the accountants in the future will not only be more useful to those served in the first instance, but also that it will be more useful to the economist. The apparently increasing stability of enterprise operations, the often asserted improvement in business ethics, the rising public interest in accounts, the giving of larger scope by business men to the investigations made by accountants, improvement in the technique of accounting, the fuller and broader training now afforded those entering professional accounting practice, the attention to instruction in accountancy given by schools that train economists and, perhaps most important of all, the change of mind on the part of economists as to just what constitutes modern economics, all seem to give grounds for a hope that is more than a wish.

A brief review only of the items in the forecast of the previous paragraph is undertaken here. Prophetic vision is not attempted. Recent apparent trends only are considered. To the extent that these may prove to be true trends we may look for help.

The Apparently Increasing Stability of Enterprise Operations.—Inspection of balance sheets over a term of years confirms the frequently noted observation in trade journals that inventories are becoming a smaller proportion of total assets and of current assets. The ratio of inventories to purchases is declining. Many trades report that a larger and larger proportion of raw materials and of manufactured goods is being ordered for future delivery. So-called productive loans by commercial banks to enterprises, though increasing in aggregate, seem to be subject to less violent fluctuation from year to year and from season to season. All these things seem consistent with the belief that the industrial establishment of the country is becoming more closely geared to consumption requirements.

Many have expressed apprehension at the phenomenal rise of instalment selling—particularly of consumption goods. Possibly the institution is loaded with an unstable high explosive; it is equally possible that its rise is ground for inferring a general stabilizing of realized income. For instalment selling is no new thing. It seems now to be succeeding, whereas earlier attempts to expand its scope were met either by reluctance to invest funds in instalment paper, or by disaster to those who did invest.

If it is true that business is becoming more stable, one of the chief bugbears of the accountant, the idle or inadequately employed establishment, will become less troublesome. The best thinkable methods of accounting produce unreliable results if the enterprise operates spasmodically. Relatively crude methods, however, may bring forth fairly reliable figures for income if the volume of business is stable.

Good Faith in Business Affairs.—Our modern organization of business presents for our consideration the economist's view that men tend to act in their own self-interest and the legalistic view that the utmost good faith can be required and expected of those who act in a representative capacity. How far from being wholly consistent these views are is indeterminate. Our court records and the reports of investigations made by administrative officers prove the existence of much bad faith and abuse of power by those who hold fiduciary positions or control corporate voting. There is good ground for inferring from financial and other presses that the great mass of offenses go unreproved by the state.

There is nevertheless a prevailing opinion among many who are looked to as leaders, and who ought to know, that business ethics are changing for the public good. There is a good deal of evidence to support the view. Witness, for example, the codes of practice drawn up by trade representatives for their own government which the Federal Trade Commission is asked to approve and to enforce.

It cannot be undertaken here to say whether or not the public accountants have always been as skeptical as they ought to have been of the good faith and judgment implied in sale valuations in which there is not a clear separation of interests between buyers and sellers. But the degree of self-government now reposed in the profession, and the zeal with which the governing boards press the matter of ethical conduct upon the notice of practitioners, and their zeal in exposing fraudulent practice and in bringing about the forfeiture of the licenses of those who do not conform to expressed codes, is a hopeful sign.

Such an assertion and expression of professional dignity brought to bear upon the too optimistic views of interested persons and upon the motives often underlying the too "conservative" valuations of concerns earning large profits, can have only a beneficial effect upon the reliability of accountants' reports.

The Rising Interest in Public Accounting.—There can be no doubt of the too great apathy of the financially interested public in the past in procuring disinterested expert reviews of corporate affairs. There can be no doubt, however, that bankers, in the interest of their depositors and shareholders, that investment houses, in the interest of their customers, and that governing boards of the stock exchanges, in the interest of their members and their members' clients, have in recent years done much to press the protective services of public accountants upon corporate business. The comment excited both in the popular press and in financial and trade journals by Professor Ripley's "Stop, Look, Listen," article,[5] in which among other measures, he urged an annual accounting by public accountants acting in the interests of shareholders other than directors and officers, could hardly have followed the publication of such an article fifteen years ago. Pressure for better service by those entitled to receive it can be counted on both to extend and to better the service.

The Scope of Accountants' Investigations.—While the great bulk of the work done by public accountants still consists of "balance sheet audits" and of "detailed audits" covering the activities of a fiscal year, many more important and far-reaching investigations have been required of them in recent years. "Financial and industrial surveys" are often asked for. In these, something more than the history of the concern under examination is brought in. The prospect for the industry as a whole, the form and magnitude of the enterprise most likely

---

[5] *Atlantic Monthly*, September, 1926.

to succeed in the industry, the appropriate capital "set-up," the most advantageous mode of market development, and so on, are considered. Such tasks give scope for the best service of broadly trained, experienced professional men, men whose competence and vision go far beyond that requisite for the conventional procedures of account keeping.

Improved Technique of Accounting.—No one with a wide acquaintance among accountants and with accounting procedure can doubt that the public accountants are competent to render a fuller and a technically better and more valuable service than their clients, in general, are willing to pay for. Neither can there be a doubt that the service clients now wish is a fuller and better one, in general, than that formerly thought sufficient. There are, however, recent signs of changes in technique for the better that can hardly be thought to have been delayed so long by want of a clientele ready to accept them. There has been much avoidable substituting of indirect for direct valuation, and of mere arbitrary and customary indexes for significant primary measures. Particularly are these changes to be noted in the subject of inventory valuation. They mark not merely advances in the acceptance of further service, but also advances made by accountants in their own thought. In a calling that has been of professional grade for so brief a time, there is every reason to suppose that the practitioners have still much to learn about their own art. It is still too early to give the name of "principles" to more than a few elements of accountancy. It is misleading, to say the least, to attach that name to statistical procedures that, on their face, are compromise measures. "Working rules" more aptly describe the great bulk of procedure.

The Training of Public Accountants.—In American practice the period within which any great proportion of prospective public accountants will receive their sole professional training in the offices of practitioners promises to be a brief one.

Not only are office staffs now largely recruited from college or university graduates, but many of these have received a very considerable technical training in school. The shift of the training to the universities is coming about much earlier in the profession's history, for example, than did the corresponding shift in law.

But the universities are new in the field. The present stage of university training for accountancy, though obviously fuller and better than that achieved by them a few years ago, is still far from satisfactory. To judge by published curricula, relatively too much emphasis is given to routine accounting procedure and too little to the substantive problems with which the student will have to deal as a principal when he is ten years out of school. Too little attention seems to be given also to training in those fundamental subjects that, in the academic world at least, are often supposed to lie quite outside the subject of accountancy.

Professional curricula that include as required work enough mathematics to enable the student to read critically the best of modern statistical publications are seldom found. Very few appreciate the fact that the subject matter with which the accountant deals bristles with unsolved, and largely undiscerned, problems that require for their solution a better foundation in mathematics than any but few accountants possess.

Some attention is given to "business law" or "commercial law." But the amount of work that is apparently thought to be sufficient is but a mere smattering beside that which is necessary to a real competence. In such branches of law as bills and notes, bankruptcy, partnerships, and private corporations, the professional public accountant has more need for a comprehensive grasp of both principles and case rules than has the general run of lawyers. To judge both by the writings and by the procedure of accountants, one must conclude that a fuller knowledge of law would often lead to material betterments in their classifications and valuations, and would also cause them to be more cautious about unqualified certification.

An adequate training for the accountant requires as difficult and as long study as does the training for law or medicine. Those who have devised courses of study seem to have had regard chiefly for the conventional procedures that constitute the bulk of work that accountants undertake. They seem to have paid too little attention to problems in the accountant's field that the leading practitioners of twenty years hence may be called upon to deal with if they prove to be competent to do so.

Nevertheless the beginnings of professional instruction that have been made compare favorably with the corresponding beginnings of collegiate instruction in the older professions. It is not unreasonable to hope that the men sent to the offices from the schools in the future will be more adequately prepared to take leadership when their years of experience qualify them for it.

The Economist's Study of Accountancy

The increasing usefulness of accounting data to economists will not all be due to betterments in enterprise and in accounting practice. Even greater possibilities exist that only the economists themselves can convert to actualities. The notion, still too commonly held, that an elementary course, corresponding in content to most university first year courses in accounting, will confer upon the young economist a competence to use accounting data in his economic studies, must be abandoned. A sufficiently intimate knowledge is not so easily to be obtained. Once economists see accurately the complete scope of accountancy, once they see the intricate and intimate mingling of accountancy and economics—both with respect to diversities of interest and point of view and with regard to common views about common subject matter—their ideas of an adequate preparation will change. They will see that an "introduction to accounting" confers no more competence in that subject than does an "introduction to economics" in their own field.

It is recognized, of course, that the difficulties of the task, in the present state of the literatures, are too great to be overcome successfully by more than a few economists. The requisite time for study can be ill afforded. Until those who have a competence in the two fields address themselves to the task of the interpreter, accountancy must remain a closed book, or a book in an unfamiliar language, to the greater number of economists. This book attempts a formal beginning only of that task of interpretation. The present writer has no reason to suppose that others will not better his work. But this book limits itself to the consideration of the larger and more general topics that require translation to the language of economics. Until much that is discussed here in general statement only is supported by published specialized *de facto* studies that substantiate and illustrate the differences in the general theory of the two professions, the young economist will have difficulty in making use of the theoretical work attempted herein. To descend to the personal, the writer makes no apology for this first attempt; and it is from no spurious modesty that its incompleteness is declared; for, to give one illustration only, there is hardly more than bare reference in this book to the problems of cost analysis. The task of describing and generalizing the procedures of the cost accountant from the point of view of the economist, and of showing the effect of specific procedures on the statistics of the public accountant's reports, is at least as great as the task attempted here.

Whether or not the better accounting statistics of the future that seem to be promised are really to become accessible is for economists to determine. It is their task, not the accountant's, to make the translation, just as it is the task of the accountants to interpret for their own professional use whatever of value for them may be found in the literature of economics.

The Shift of Method in Economics.—In one of the most challenging of his many excellent professional papers Professor Wesley C. Mitchell says:[6]

> Eighteen years have passed since Dr. Alfred Marshall, addressing the Royal Economic Society, said that "qualitative analysis has done the greater part of its work" in economic science, and that the "higher and more difficult task" of quantitative analysis "must wait upon the slow growth of thorough realistic statistics."
>
> ... I shall say little of qualitative analysis beyond the obvious remark that it cannot be dispensed with, if for no other reason, because quantitative work itself involves distinctions of kind, and distinctions of kind start with distinctions of quality.
>
> ... The economist of today has at his disposal a wider array of "thorough realistic statistics" than had the economist of yesterday, a more powerful technique, and more opportunities to get assistance. ... But the crucial question remains: What use can we make of these data, this refined technique and these research assistants in solving the fundamental problems of economic science? Are not these the problems qualitative analysis has posed? When a theorist puts any one of his problems to a statistician does the answer he gets ever quite meet his questions? And when a statistician attempts to test an economic theory, is his test ever conclusive? ...
>
> One view is that, despite all the gains it has made, quantitative analysis shows no more promise of providing a statistical complement of pure theory than it showed when Dr. Marshall pronounced his dicta. I think this view is correct, if the pure theory we have in mind is theory of the type cultivated by Jevons, or by Dr. Marshall himself. Indeed, I incline to go further and say there is slight prospect that quantitative analysis will ever be able to solve the problems which qualitative analysis has framed, in their present form. What we must expect is a recasting of the old problems into new forms amenable to statistical attack. In the course of this reformulation of its problems, economic theory will change not merely its complexion but also its content.

After enumerating a number of problems under statistical investigation he continues:

[6] "Quantitative Analysis in Economic Theory," *The American Economic Review*, Vol. XV, p. 1. This paper was Mitchell's presidential address at the Thirty-seventh Annual Meeting of the American Economic Association, held in Chicago, December 29, 1924.

SUMMARY AND FORECAST 333

With all these fascinating problems and numberless others before them in shape for attack, it seems unlikely that the quantitative workers will retain a keen interest in imaginary individuals coming to imaginary markets with ready-made scales of bid and offer prices. Their theories will probably be theories about the relationships among the variables which measure objective processes. There is little likelihood that the old explanations will be refuted by these investigators, but much likelihood that they will be disregarded.

With the forecast of Professor Mitchell just quoted and, indeed, with most of the views expressed in the paper quoted from, the present writer is in substantial accord. In fact, the four years that have passed since Mitchell's paper was read have seen the appearance of more of the kind of work forecast than any previous period of twice the length.

Doubt is felt, though, that the quantitative studies so far undertaken, considered as a group, constitute the best group with which to found a new economics. Doubt is felt, too, that the departure from qualitative theory, at least for the transition stage, need or ought to be so great as that which Mitchell implies. Classical theory, neo-classical theory and the work of the eclectics is, however, headed for the scrap heap. These can no longer offer adequate employment for more than a few whose efforts are devoted to their betterment. But there is a quite different and well developed body of theory represented best by Irving Fisher's "The Nature of Capital and Income," and "The Rate of Interest," that, with a minimum of reformulation, cannot only serve to bridge the gap between the old and the new economics but also be made amenable to statistical treatment.

It might be a serious loss, indeed, if we were to cling to an unpromising, though fascinating, brand of theory that could never become clothed in a statistical dress while the statistical inquirers broke away from an ordered, systematic plan, and developed a multitude of more or less independent specialties.

For there is a great, unified problem of economics corresponding in scope to that which the older economists have had in mind. And this problem, if systematically attacked by any method whatever, is likely to yield more useful results than can be had by working at isolated elements of it only by a corresponding method. If the separate specialties do not have dominant regard for some common fundamental concept, there is little likelihood that a general science can ever be made from an aggregate or assembly of the specialties.

Nothing done or proposed by any statistical worker, or for that part, by any purely qualitative worker, shows possibilities of becoming a simpler or more fundamental concept in economic science than income in its most general sense. No other concepts that disregard the concept of income show promise of a development that will permit their assemblage into an ordered whole. No other concept lends itself so readily to statistical treatment as does income.

There is a great deal of merit in the often repeated dictum that "consumption is the most important branch of economics." But few seem to have been aware that the failure of the older economists to make very notable contributions to the theory of consumption lay largely in these two errors: (1) that the theory of consumption should be the end-product rather than the beginning of economic analysis; and (2) that income, which is the subject matter of consumption, requires more certainly than any other concept, a quantitative rather than a purely qualitative analysis.

Mitchell's expectation that, under the newer method, "books will pass out of date more rapidly," will undoubtedly be realized if statistical workers begin with concepts that are only of ephemeral interest or that are complex rather than simple. In the field of economics that which is most stable, that which survives through successive civilizations, is the group of primary incomes, the rendering of nutrition service, shelter service, etc. The next most stable elements consist of the agents that render these primary services. For how long a period has the bulk of the world population's food consisted of a few cereal crops and the products of animal husbandry from a few kinds of domestic animals? Beside the stability of these the most striking characteristic of systems of property laws, the constituent items of material goods that do not render direct immediate services, and the pecuniary organization of society to which economists devote so much attention is that they are too ephemeral to permit the founding of a lasting science upon even the most complete analysis of them.

It is not, of course, to be hoped that the statistical economists will drop all their investigations of business cycles, all their attempts to forecast the courses of corporate stock prices and of rates of interest, etc., and set to work upon the analysis of income. It is not even to be desired that they should do so. No one regrets that research is simultaneously carried on in the chemical behavior of the human liver, the chemistry of colloids, and the chemical and physical phenomena that occur when a simple salt is dissolved in water or in some other reagent. While the results of the last type of investigation are likely to prove of more lasting usefulness, human lives may be prolonged more immediately by the results of the first. What is to be hoped is that some economists will choose to work at fundamental problems and that others who work at the problems of the current decade will have a proper regard for whatever is fundamental to all economic problems.

Most statistical economists will work to some extent with data supplied by the accountants, and nearly all, if not all, will employ data that are affected to a marked degree by the work of accountants. But those who work at the problems of income can look to the accountants both for a great body of rapidly improving data and for a technique that, with relatively few and simple modifications, can be extended to many income problems with which the accountant has little present professional concern. But this resource of both data and technique can never be most fruitfully exploited by a body of economists who cling to the prevailing organization of economic theory that begins with production and ends with consumption.

APPENDIX A

REVALUATIONS AND SERVICE UNIT COSTS: A COMPARISON OF THE RESULTS YIELDED BY SEVERAL FORMULAS

In Chapters XIII and XIV, certain revaluation formulas were discussed in relation to their statistical effects when applied to assets of different types. (See pages 260-265 for a discussion of these asset types.) For the convenience of the reader who, having the text discussion of the formulas and the asset types well in hand, wishes to see in concrete detail some of the statistical effects of the several formulas, sets of tables are exhibited below in this Appendix. For each type of asset two tables are prepared. The first of each pair of tables describes the asset type. That is, it shows: (1) the cost new; (2) the scrap value and service life estimated; and (3) the time-schedules of estimated operating outlays and of expected service yields. Together with these data are shown the successive end-of-the-period book valuations that would be found by each of eight revaluation formulas.

From the data in the first table of the pair the second table is prepared. This second table shows for each period the cost per unit of asset service that is implied by each of the eight formulas. The cost per unit of service for the first seven formulas is found as follows: To the outlay cost, (O), add the depreciation or deduct the appreciation, as the case may be, and divide this algebraic sum by the number of units of service rendered. In finding the cost per unit of service under formula 8 the same procedure is followed except that interest, at 5% on the book value shown one period earlier is added to the numerator of the unit cost ratio. Formula 8 is the only one employed in this Appendix in which interest on the investment is involved.

The formulas employed are the following:

1. The (unmodified) straight line formula. (See pages 265-273.)
2. The sinking fund formula (interest at 5% compounding periodically). (See pages 273-276.)
3. The fixed-rate-on-declining-book-value formula. (See pages 276-277.)
4. The sum-of-the-year-digits formula. (See pages 277-278.)
5. The (unmodified) service unit formula. (See pages 279-283.)
6. The straight line formula modified to provide for "extraordinary" outlay charges. (See pages 284-288.)
7. The unit outlay cost formula or the service unit formula modified to provide for all direct outlay costs. (See pages 290-296.)
8. This is formula 7 modified to include interest on the investment at 5% compounding periodically. (See pages 296-305.)

The reader who makes careful comparisons will note that the first four formulas are entirely unresponsive to material differences of asset type. Each of these formulas, though finding a set of end-of-the-period book valuations different from that found by the others, finds the same set of book valuations for each of the nine types of assets. But when the unit costs of service implied by these uniform asset valuations are scrutinized, it will be seen at once that this uniformity is spurious; for the unit cost figures behave in an erratic—almost a chaotic—manner.

The service unit formula (5) gives results of a different kind. To the extent that the asset types differ from one another in the characteristic time-distribution of services, this formula, unlike the first four, gives effect to this component in the book valuations. But, again, the unit costs, as between one period and another for any given type of asset, will be seen to fluctuate within wide limits. This is because this formula, like the four preceding ones, ignores the time-distribution of outlays made to obtain the service. Service unit costs are uniform only to the extent that "wearing-value," or the difference between the initial cost item and the ultimate scrap value, is an element of unit cost. Impliedly the formula, like the first four, asserts that there is a substantive difference, with respect to the major problems of valuation, between the sum of money spent initially and the sums of money spent subsequently, to obtain a given set of services.

Formula 6, the first of the modified formulas to be considered, differs from the unmodified straight line rule only to the extent that it charges not only the "wearing-value" but also the "extraordinary" items in uniform annual amounts. Superficially the formula has a good deal to recommend it as against the unmodified rule. But when examination is made of the effect of this formula on unit costs, the modification will be seen to be one of dubious merit. If its use is restricted to those asset types (B and H) in which, but for "extraordinary" cost items, the outlay charges subsequent to the initial item of cost are uniform, it produces better valuations and better unit costs than does the simple rule. For certain other types the fluctuation of unit costs from year to year is much greater than those produced by the commoner method.

Formula 7 takes account not merely of the "wearing-value," but also of all outlay costs and all services expected. It produces for any type of asset a uniform total direct cost per unit of service. Because of this no set of end-of-period book valuations found for any type of asset is identical with that found for any other type. These book valuations have a common meaning. They assert that the used asset is valued to yield its residual services at a cost per unit equal to the unit cost of like services implicit in an economically purchased and used new (or substitute) asset.

Formula 8 differs from formula 7, *as applied in the illustrative tables,* only to the extent that interest on the investment (at 5%) is charged. It does not really produce, therefore, an enterprise outlay cost per unit of service but rather a price per unit of service that, if the services were separately sold, would have to be realized if the outlay costs were to be returned with an earning of the rate employed in capitalization. But the phrase "as applied in the illustrative tables" was italicized advisedly, for the formula requires for its operation a definite estimate of the time within which the economical use of the asset will be completed. The inclusion of the interest charge requires this. Formula 7, on the other hand, does not necessarily involve the estimated time-length of service life at all. Errors in the estimated time-length of service that are not associated with errors in the aggregate outlay and/or aggregate amount of service affect neither the correctness or the uniformity of the unit cost figures nor the validity of the concurrent book valuations. But this is obviously not true of formula 8 nor, for that matter, of any of the others given. The conditions assumed in the comparative calculations are those most favorable to the other methods.

Formulas 7 and 8 are the only ones shown that, given positive cost figures and scrap value, can ever find negative book valuations. There are instances in which true negative book valuations exist, but more often the appearance of negative valuations in the figures resulting from these two formulas merely shows that the asset is already "worn out." None of the other formulas calls attention to such a state of affairs, nor will a set of accounts organized about the other formulas automatically disclose the existence of "worn out" assets. Asset G is deliberately described in a way to illustrate this point (see page 349).

Notice is again served that the writer does not suppose that such a uniformity in unit costs as that shown for formulas 7 and 8 can ever be achieved in practice. All that is intended to be asserted is that, by the use of the better formulas based upon the estimates implied in reasonably prudent asset purchases and operation, a more significant set of book valuations and a less erratically fluctuating set of annual unit costs can be had than those now prevailing. No primary estimate for formula 7 needs to be made that does not equally need to be made no matter what formula is employed. By substituting a more rational and significant measure of service for the usual measure, viz., a year-in-use, the formula eliminates one of the chief sources of valuation error; for the rate-of-exploitation of an asset subject to wear is a function of *time in operation* not of *time within which operation is completed.*

Finally, a word is needed concerning the often asserted automatic compensations of error in the use of certain methods. It is said that while a given formula may find an erroneous depreciation in a given service-life-year of an asset that there may be many assets of like kind in all the stages of service-life from brand new to approximate scrapping time. It is said that the length of life of some will be overestimated and the service life of others will be underestimated. It is said that mixed types of assets will be found in any enterprise. Granted that compensations of these kinds and of others do exist, their existence does not theoretically justify the use of crude statistical methods unless it can be shown that the whole set of compensations makes it a matter of indifference whether one method or another is used.

Such a set of compensations is conceivable, but no study has ever been made on a scale big enough to prove its existence in fact in any industry. There are, however, the firmest of *a priori* grounds for doubting the existence of such a state of affairs. So long as new enterprises, or for that matter, old ones, build and equip in anticipation of an increased volume of business, so long as enterprises continue to be short-lived, so long as enterprises are subject to changing physical volumes of business and to shifts from one line of products to another, just so long will there be preponderances of one type of asset or another. Just so long, too, will the so-called simple methods continue to grind out valuations and costs that are invariant to the conditions upon which ultimate profit and loss depend.

While there is no balance of sound theoretical argument in favor of using the prevailing simple methods, there is a sound practical ground for exonerating the professional accountant for not abandoning these statistically crude rules. Until business men can be educated to the point of discriminating good and bad accounting service and to the point of being willing to pay for good service, the public accountant is helpless. The reform must begin in the account keeping before it can be given effect in the account auditing. Until that reform begins in an enterprise, the public accountant's chief duty is to minimize the effect of errors in the methods in use. Whether or not public accountants are as urgent as they should be in advising their clients about the improvement of their valuation work is a matter about which the present writer has no informed opinion.

REVALUATIONS AND SERVICE UNIT COSTS 343

Schedule of Operating Outlays Made and of Services Obtained in Each Period and Book Value at the End of Each Period as Found by the Several Formulas

Period	Services Obtained S_a	Operating Outlays O_a	Book Value by Formula:							
			1	2	3	4	5	6	7	8
0	0	$0	$100.00	$100.00	$100.00	$100.00	$100.00	$100.50	$100.00	$100.00
1	10	5	90.50	92.45	74.11	82.73	97.03	88.50	90.97	100.75
2	15	7	81.00	84.52	54.93	67.18	92.58	77.00	91.92	98.91
3	20	9	71.50	76.19	40.72	53.36	86.04	65.50	84.86	94.36
4	25	11	62.00	67.45	30.18	41.27	79.22	54.00	75.78	86.95
5	30	13	52.50	58.27	22.36	30.91	70.31	42.50	64.69	76.55
6	35	15	43.00	48.63	16.57	22.36	59.95	51.00	71.58	83.00
7	40	17	33.50	38.50	12.28	15.36	48.05	39.50	56.46	67.14
8	45	19	24.00	27.88	9.10	10.18	34.69	28.00	39.32	47.87
9	50	21	14.50	16.72	6.75	6.73	19.84	16.50	20.16	25.00
10	50	25	5.00	5.00	5.00	5.00	5.00	5.00	5.00	5.00

Schedule of Total Operating Costs per Unit of Service in Each Period as Found if Each of the Indicated Formulas Is Used

Period	1	2	3	4	5	6	7	8
1	$1.450	$1.255	$3.080	$2.227	$0.797	$1.650	$0.803	$0.925
2	1.100	.905	1.745	1.503	.763	1.233	.803	.925
3	.925	.807	1.100	1.141	.747	1.025	.803	.925
4	.802	.799	.862	.924	.737	.900	.803	.925
5	.750	.773	.694	.778	.730	.817	.803	.925
6	1.271	1.275	1.165	1.247	1.207	.757	.803	.925
7	.662	.678	.532	.598	.722	.712	.803	.925
8	.633	.658	.493	.537	.719	.678	.803	.925
9	.610	.643	.407	.489	.717	.650	.803	.925
10	.690	.734	.535	.535	.707	.730	.803	.925

With respect to range of error in unit costs, the first six formulas rank from best to worst as follows: 5, 2, 1, 6, 4, and 3.

APPENDIX

TABLE 2

Schedule of Operating Outlays Made and of Services Obtained in Each Period and Book Value at the End of Each Period as Found by the Several Formulas

Period	Services Obtained S_a	Operating Outlays O_a	Book Value by Formula:							
			1	2	3	4	5	6	7	8
0	0	$0	$100.00	$100.00	$100.00	$100.00	$100.00	$100.00	$100.00	$100.00
1	10	1	90.50	92.45	74.11	82.73	97.03	88.50	97.09	100.85
2	15	1	81.50	84.52	54.93	67.18	92.58	77.00	92.23	99.18
3	20	1	71.50	76.19	40.72	53.36	86.64	65.50	85.42	94.85
4	25	1	62.50	67.45	30.18	41.27	79.22	54.00	76.66	87.73
5	30	1	52.50	58.27	22.36	30.91	70.31	42.50	65.94	77.68
6	35	2½	43.50	48.63	16.57	22.27	59.92	51.00	73.27	84.56
7	40	1	33.50	38.50	12.28	15.36	48.05	39.50	58.64	69.20
8	45	1	24.00	27.88	9.10	10.18	34.69	28.00	42.06	50.51
9	50	1	14.50	16.72	6.75	6.73	19.84	16.50	23.53	28.31
10	50	1	5.00	5.00	5.00	5.00	5.00	5.00	5.00	5.00

Schedule of Total Operating Costs per Unit of Service in Each Period as Found if Each of the Indicated Formula Is Used

Period	1	2	3	4	5	6	7	8
1	$1.050	$0.855	$2.600	$1.827	$0.397	$1.250	$0.391	$0.515
2	.700	.595	1.345	1.103	.363	.833	.391	.515
3	.525	.467	.760	.741	.347	.625	.391	.515
4	.420	.390	.462	.524	.337	.500	.391	.515
5	.350	.339	.294	.379	.330	.417	.391	.515
6	.871	.875	.765	.847	.897	.357	.391	.515
7	.262	.278	.132	.198	.322	.312	.391	.515
8	.233	.258	.093	.137	.319	.278	.391	.515
9	.210	.243	.067	.089	.317	.250	.391	.515
10	.210	.254	.055	.055	.317	.250	.391	.515

With respect to range of error in unit costs, the first six formulas rank from best to worst as follows: 5, 2, 1, 6, 4, and 3.

ASSET C

Schedule of Operating Outlays Made and of Services Obtained in Each Period and Book Value at the End of Each Period as Found by the Several Formulas

Period	Services Obtained S_a	Operating Outlays O_a	Book Value by Formula:							
			1	2	3	4	5	6	7	8
0	0	$0	$100.00	$100.00	$100.00	$100.00	$100.00	$100.00	$100.00	$100.00
1	10	15	90.50	92.45	74.11	82.73	97.03	88.50	109.13	112.58
2	15	13	81.50	84.52	54.93	67.18	92.58	77.00	113.31	120.07
3	20	11	71.50	76.19	40.72	53.36	86.64	65.50	112.56	122.22
4	25	9	62.00	67.45	30.18	41.27	79.22	54.00	106.88	118.77
5	30	7	52.50	58.27	22.36	30.91	70.31	42.50	96.25	109.44
6	35	25	43.00	48.63	16.57	22.27	59.92	51.00	100.69	113.93
7	40	3	33.50	38.50	12.28	15.36	48.05	39.50	80.10	92.93
8	45	3	24.00	27.88	9.10	10.18	34.69	28.00	56.75	67.16
9	50	1	14.50	16.72	6.75	6.73	19.84	16.50	28.38	34.40
10	50	6	5.00	5.00	5.00	5.00	5.00	5.00	5.00	5.00

Schedule of Total Operating Costs per Unit of Service in Each Period as Found if Each of the Indicated Formulas Is Used

Period	1	2	3	4	5	6	7	8
1	$2.450	$2.255	$4.089	$3.227	$1.797	$2.650	$0.588	$0.742
2	1.500	1.395	2.145	1.903	1.163	1.633	.588	.742
3	1.025	.978	1.261	1.241	.847	1.125	.588	.742
4	.740	.710	.782	.844	.657	.820	.588	.742
5	.550	.539	.494	.579	.530	.617	.588	.742
6	.986	.990	.880	.961	1.011	.471	.588	.742
7	.312	.328	.182	.248	.372	.303	.588	.742
8	.278	.303	.137	.182	.304	.322	.588	.742
9	.210	.243	.067	.089	.317	.250	.588	.742
10	.310	.354	.135	.135	.417	.350	.588	.742

With respect to range of error in unit costs, the first six formulas rank from best to worst as follows: 5, 2, 1, 6, 4, and 3.

APPENDIX

ASSET D

Schedule of Operating Outlays Made and of Services Obtained in Each Period and Book Value at the End of Each Period as Found by the Several Formulas

| Period | Services Obtained S_a | Operating Outlays O_a | \multicolumn{7}{c}{Book Value by Formula:} |||||||
			1	2	3	4	5	6	7	8
0	0	$0	$100.00	$100.00	$100.00	$100.00	$100.00	$100.00	$100.00	$100.00
1	1	5	90.50	92.45	74.11	82.73	90.50	88.50	79.30	82.16
2	1	7	81.00	84.52	54.93	67.18	81.50	77.00	60.60	65.42
3	1	9	71.50	76.19	40.72	53.36	71.50	65.50	43.00	49.85
4	1	11	62.00	67.45	30.18	41.27	62.00	54.00	29.20	35.50
5	1	13	52.50	58.27	22.36	30.91	52.50	42.50	16.50	22.43
6	1	35	43.00	48.63	16.57	22.27	43.00	51.00	25.80	30.71
7	1	17	33.50	38.50	12.28	15.36	33.50	39.50	17.10	21.40
8	1	19	24.00	27.88	9.10	10.18	24.00	28.00	10.40	13.63
9	1	21	14.50	16.72	6.75	6.73	14.50	16.50	5.70	7.47
10	1	25	5.00	5.00	5.00	5.00	5.00	5.00	5.00	5.00

Schedule of Total Operating Costs per Unit of Service in Each Period as Found if Each of the Indicated Formulas Is Used

Period	1	2	3	4	5	6	7	8
1	$14.50	$12.55	$30.89	$22.27	$14.50	$16.50	$26.20	$27.843
2	16.50	14.93	26.18	22.55	16.50	18.50	26.20	27.843
3	18.50	17.33	23.21	22.82	18.50	20.50	26.20	27.843
4	20.50	19.74	21.54	23.09	20.50	22.50	26.20	27.843
5	22.50	22.18	20.82	23.36	22.50	24.50	26.20	27.843
6	44.50	44.64	30.79	33.64	44.50	26.50	26.20	27.843
7	26.50	27.13	21.29	23.91	26.50	28.50	26.20	27.843
8	28.50	29.62	22.18	24.18	28.50	30.50	26.20	27.843
9	30.50	32.16	23.35	24.45	30.50	32.50	26.20	27.843
10	34.50	36.72	26.75	26.73	34.50	36.50	26.20	27.843

With respect to range of error in unit costs, the first six formulas rank from best to worst as follows: 3, 4, 6, 1 and 5, and 2.

ASSET E

Schedule of Operating Outlays Made and of Services Obtained in Each Period and Book Value at the End of Each Period as Found by the Several Formulas

Period	Services Obtained S_a	Operating Outlays O_a	Book Value by Formula:							
			1	2	3	4	5	6	7	8
0	0	$0	$100.00	$100.00	$100.00	$100.00	$100.00	$100.00	$100.00	$100.00
1	1	1	90.50	92.45	74.11	82.73	90.50	90.50	90.50	92.45
2	1	1	81.00	84.52	54.93	67.18	81.00	81.00	81.00	84.52
3	1	1	71.50	76.19	40.72	53.36	71.50	71.50	71.50	76.19
4	1	1	62.00	67.45	30.18	41.27	62.00	62.00	62.00	67.45
5	1	1	52.50	58.27	22.36	30.91	52.50	52.50	52.50	58.27
6	1	1	43.00	48.63	16.57	22.7	43.00	43.00	43.00	48.63
7	1	1	33.50	38.50	12.28	15.36	33.50	33.50	33.50	38.50
8	1	1	24.00	27.88	9.10	10.18	24.00	24.00	24.00	27.88
9	1	1	14.50	16.72	6.75	6.73	14.50	14.50	14.50	16.72
10	1	1	5.00	5.00	5.00	5.00	5.00	5.00	5.00	5.00

Schedule of Total Operating Costs per Unit of Service in Each Period as Found if Each of the Indicated Formulas Is Used

Period	1	2	3	4	5	6	7	8
1	$10.50	$ 8.55	$26.89	$18.27	$10.50	$10.50	$10.50	$13.553
2	10.50	8.93	20.18	16.55	10.50	10.50	10.50	13.553
3	10.50	9.33	15.21	14.82	10.50	10.50	10.50	13.553
4	10.50	9.74	11.54	13.09	10.50	10.50	10.50	13.553
5	10.50	10.18	8.82	11.36	10.50	10.50	10.50	13.553
6	10.50	10.64	6.79	9.64	10.50	10.50	10.50	13.553
7	10.50	11.13	5.29	7.91	10.50	10.50	10.50	13.553
8	10.50	11.62	4.18	6.18	10.50	10.50	10.50	13.553
9	10.50	12.16	3.35	4.45	10.50	10.50	10.50	13.553
10	10.50	12.72	2.75	2.73	10.50	10.50	10.50	13.553

With respect to range of error in unit cost, the first six formulas rank from best to worst as follows: 1, 5, and 6, no error; 2, 4, and 3.

ASSET F

Schedule of Operating Outlays Made and of Services Obtained in Each Period and Book Value at the End of Each Period as Found by the Several Formulas

Period	Services Obtained S_n	Operating Outlays O_n	\multicolumn{8}{c}{Book Value by Formula:}								
			1	2	3	4	5	6	7	8
0........	0	$0	$100.00	$100.00	$100.00	$100.00	$100.00	$100.00	$100.00	$100.00
1........	1	15	90.50	92.45	74.11	82.73	90.50	88.50	96.40	97.65
2........	1	13	81.00	84.52	54.93	67.18	81.00	77.00	90.40	93.19
3........	1	11	71.50	76.19	40.72	53.36	71.50	65.50	82.60	86.51
4........	1	9	62.00	67.45	30.18	41.27	62.00	54.00	72.80	77.49
5........	1	7	52.50	58.27	22.36	30.91	52.50	42.50	61.00	66.01
6........	1	25	43.00	48.63	16.57	22.27	43.00	51.00	67.20	71.07
7........	1	5	33.50	38.50	12.28	15.36	33.50	39.50	51.40	56.22
8........	1	3	24.00	27.88	9.10	10.18	24.00	28.00	35.60	39.69
9........	1	1	14.50	16.72	6.75	6.73	14.50	16.50	17.80	20.33
10........	1	6	5.00	5.00	5.00	5.00	5.00	5.00	5.00	5.00

Schedule of Total Operating Costs per Unit of Service in Each Period as Found if Each of the Indicated Formulas Is Used

Period	1	2	3	4	5	6	7	8
1........	$24.50	$22.55	$40.89	$32.27	$24.50	$26.50	$18.80	$22.345
2........	22.50	20.93	32.18	28.55	22.50	24.50	18.80	22.345
3........	20.50	19.33	25.21	24.82	20.50	22.50	18.80	22.345
4........	18.50	17.74	19.54	21.09	18.50	20.50	18.80	22.345
5........	16.50	16.18	14.82	17.36	16.50	18.50	18.80	22.345
6........	34.50	34.64	39.79	33.64	34.50	16.50	18.80	22.345
7........	12.50	13.13	7.29	9.91	12.50	14.50	18.80	22.345
8........	12.50	13.62	6.18	8.18	12.50	12.50	18.80	22.345
9........	10.50	12.16	3.35	4.45	10.50	17.50	18.80	22.345
10........	15.50	17.72	7.75	7.73	15.50			22.345

With respect to range of error in unit costs, the first six formulas rank from best to worst as follows: 6, 2, 1 and 5, 4, and 3.

ASSET G

Schedule of Operating Outlays Made and of Services Obtained in Each Period and Book Value at the End of Each Period as Found by the Several Formulas

Period	Services Obtained S_a	Operating Outlays O_a	Book Value by Formula: 1	2	3	4	5	6	7	8
0	0	$0	$100.00	$100.00	$100.00	$100.00	$100.00	$100.00	$100.00	$100.00
1	50	5	90.50	92.45	74.11	82.73	85.16	88.50	64.84	68.92
2	50	7	81.50	84.52	54.93	67.18	70.31	77.00	31.69	38.28
3	45	9	71.50	76.19	40.72	53.36	56.95	65.50	4.54	12.23
4	40	11	62.50	67.45	30.18	41.27	54.00	54.00	−16.58	−9.03
5	35	13	52.50	58.27	22.36	30.91	34.69	42.50	−31.69	−25.24
6	30	15	43.00	48.63	16.57	22.27	25.78	51.00	−20.78	−16.15
7	25	17	33.50	38.50	12.28	15.36	18.36	39.50	−23.86	−20.50
8	20	19	24.00	27.88	9.10	10.18	12.42	28.00	−20.92	−18.95
9	15	21	14.50	16.72	6.75	6.73	7.97	16.50	−13.03	−11.22
10	10	25	5.00	5.00	5.00	5.00	5.00	5.00	5.00	5.00

Schedule of Total Operating Costs per Unit of Service in Each Period as Found if Each of the Indicated Formulas Is Used

Period	1	2	3	4	5	6	7	8
1	$0.290	$0.251	$0.618	$0.445	$0.397	$0.330	$0.803	$0.822
2	.330	.299	.524	.451	.437	.370	.803	.822
3	.411	.385	.516	.507	.497	.456	.803	.822
4	.513	.494	.538	.577	.572	.503	.803	.822
5	.643	.634	.595	.667	.668	.700	.803	.822
6	1.483	1.086	1.360	1.455	1.464	.883	.803	.822
7	1.060	1.488	.852	.956	.977	.950	.803	.822
8	1.425	1.481	1.109	1.209	1.247	1.525	.803	.822
9	2.033	2.144	1.557	1.630	1.697	2.167	.803	.822
10	3.450	3.672	2.675	2.673	2.797	3.650	.803	.822

With respect to range of error in unit costs, the first six formulas rank from best to worst as follows: 3, 4, 5, 1, 6, and 2. Note that formulas 7 and 8 find negative values for the 4th, 5th, 6th, 7th, 8th, and 9th periods. Unless there is some extraordinary reason for operating such an asset for a long time, the asset should have been abandoned before these negative valuations appeared. Note, too, that the other formulas serve no notice at all of the extraordinary rise of annual outlays in proportion to annual service yields.

APPENDIX

ASSET H

Schedule of Operating Outlays Made and of Services Obtained in Each Period and Book Value at the End of Each Period as Found by the Several Formulas

Period	Services Obtained S_a	Operating Outlays O_a	Book Value by Formula:							
			1	2	3	4	5	6	7	8
0	0	$ 0	$100.00	$100.00	$100.00	$100.00	$100.00	$100.00	$100.00	$100.00
1	50	1	90.50	92.45	74.11	82.73	85.16	88.50	81.47	83.15
2	50	1	81.00	84.52	54.93	67.18	70.31	77.00	62.94	65.46
3	45	1	71.50	76.19	40.72	53.36	56.95	65.50	46.36	49.17
4	40	1	62.00	67.45	30.18	41.27	45.08	54.00	31.74	34.35
5	35	1	52.50	58.27	22.36	30.91	34.69	42.50	19.06	21.07
6	30	21	43.00	48.63	16.57	22.27	25.78	51.00	28.34	29.42
7	25	1	33.50	38.50	12.28	15.36	18.36	39.50	19.58	20.46
8	20	1	24.00	27.88	9.10	10.18	12.42	28.00	12.77	13.35
9	15	1	14.50	16.72	6.75	6.73	7.97	16.50	7.91	8.16
10	10	1	5.00	5.00	5.00	5.00	5.00	5.00	5.00	5.00

Schedule of Total Operating Costs per Unit of Service in Each Period as Found if Each of the Indicated Formulas Is Used

Period	1	2	3	4	5	6	7	8
1	$0.210	$0.171	$0.539	$0.305	$0.317	$0.250	$0.391	$0.457
2	.210	.179	.404	.351	.317	.259	.391	.457
3	.233	.207	.338	.329	.319	.278	.391	.457
4	.263	.244	.289	.322	.322	.313	.391	.457
5	.300	.291	.252	.325	.325	.357	.391	.457
6	1.017	1.021	.893	.988	.997	.417	.391	.457
7	.420	.445	.215	.316	.337	.500	.391	.457
8	.525	.581	.209	.309	.347	.625	.391	.457
9	.700	.810	.223	.297	.363	.833	.391	.457
10	1.050	1.272	.275	.273	.397	1.250	.391	.457

With respect to range of error in unit costs, the first six formulas rank from best to worst as follows: 5, 3, 4, 1, 6, and 2.

ASSET I

Schedule of Operating Outlays Made and of Services Obtained in Each Period and Book Value at the End of Each Period as Found by the Several Formulas

Period	Services Obtained S_a	Operating Outlays O_a	Book Value by Formula:							
			1	2	3	4	5	6	7	8
0	0	$ 0	$100.00	$100.00	$100.00	$100.00	$100.00	$100.00	$100.00	$100.00
1	50	15	90.50	92.45	74.11	82.73	85.16	88.50	85.63	87.03
2	50	13	81.00	84.52	54.93	67.18	70.31	77.00	69.25	71.41
3	45	11	71.50	76.19	40.72	51.36	56.95	65.50	53.81	56.31
4	40	9	62.00	67.45	30.18	41.27	45.08	54.00	39.31	41.75
5	35	7	52.50	58.27	22.36	30.91	34.60	42.50	25.75	27.76
6	30	25	43.00	48.63	16.57	22.77	25.78	51.00	33.12	34.36
7	25	3	33.50	38.50	12.28	15.36	18.36	39.50	21.44	22.60
8	20	3	24.00	27.88	9.10	10.18	12.42	28.00	12.69	13.54
9	15	1	14.50	16.72	6.75	6.73	7.97	16.50	4.87	5.33
10	10	6	5.00	5.00	5.00	5.00	5.00	5.00	5.00	5.00

Schedule of Total Operating Costs per Unit of Service in Each Period as Found if Each of the Indicated Formulas Is Used

Period	1	2	3	4	5	6	7	8
1	$0.490	$0.451	$0.818	$0.645	$0.579	$0.530	$0.588	$0.659
2	.450	.419	.644	.531	.557	.490	.588	.659
3	.456	.430	.563	.507	.541	.500	.588	.659
4	.463	.444	.489	.527	.522	.513	.588	.659
5	.471	.462	.423	.496	.497	.520	.588	.659
6	1.150	1.155	1.026	1.121	1.130	.550	.588	.659
7	.500	.525	.292	.306	.417	.580	.588	.659
8	.625	.681	.309	.499	.447	.725	.588	.659
9	.700	.811	.223	.297	.363	.833	.588	.659
10	1.550	1.772	.775	.773	.897	1.750	.588	.659

With respect to range of error in unit costs, the first six formulas rank from best to worst as follows: 5, 3, 4, 1, 6, and 2.

APPENDIX

The rankings of the first six formulas, with respect to range of error in the unit cost figures for the nine types of asset may be arranged in a contingency table as follows:

FORMULA NUMBER

Rank	1	2	3	4	5	6
1	1	0	2	0	6	2
2	0	4	2	2	0	0
3	4	0	0	2	2	1
4	4	1	0	0	1	3
5	0	0	0	5	0	3
6	0	4	5	0	0	0

In the table any two formulas showing the same range of error for an asset are given the same rank. Thus on asset E, formulas 1, 5, and 6 give identical results without error. All three are given rank 1; and the next ranking formula, 2, is given rank 4, and so on.

APPENDIX B

CRITERIA OF SUPERIORITY: A METHOD OF TESTING THE RELATIVE MERITS OF TWO FORMULAS

In the writings on accounting a great deal of space is devoted to discussing the various modes of treating depreciation. The nature of depreciation is discussed at length, and certain of the objectives to be gained by a current statistical treatment of depreciation are much dwelt upon. There are endless descriptions of the various rules of procedure found in practice or projected by students of the theory of depreciation. The differences in numerical results in a given case that are contingent upon the formula selected are abundantly illustrated and commented upon.

Relatively little space, however, is given to relating the numerical results of the various rules to any expressed or implied theory of business enterprise. All who write on the subject say, for example, that the straight line rule apportions the expense of wearing-value, i.e., the difference between first cost and scrap value, in equal annual amounts over the years in which the asset is expected to remain in service. Very few, however, consider the *full statistical effect* of such a treatment. Very few show the conditions under which such a treatment produces numerical evidence of the most useful kind. Still fewer discuss the common significance of the element of expense represented by wearing-value and of those numerous other items of outlay to which the purchase of an asset commits the purchaser. That is to say, few have made clear the point that a series of outlays, dispersed in time, constitutes the outlay for a given set of services.

Still less attention has been given to showing the precise conditions under which one procedure will yield more significant results than those produced by another. This latter class of problem, in the writer's opinion, should become the chief preoccupation of the student of accounting theory. It is not limited, of course, to depreciation procedure; it includes every element of procedure if statistically different modes of operation present themselves for consideration.

While no attempt is made in this book to study accounting procedure by the method of statistical theory, it is not foreign to the purpose of this study to point out the nature of this much larger and more important problem, and to present an elementary illustration of the method of study contemplated.

If it be granted that under certain conditions (see Chapters XIII, XIV, and Appendix A) it is desirable that the figures representing cost per unit of service from a given source should fluctuate from year to year by a minimum, then one of the tests of excellence of a depreciation formula should be the extent to which it minimizes fluctuations in the figures for cost per unit of service. If, as between any two formulas, A and B, the conditions under which formula A does not introduce fluctuations in unit cost include (1) all cases in which formula B causes no fluctuation, and (2) some cases in which formula B does cause fluctuations, then formula A, *under those conditions* and *with respect to this one test of excellence,* is a better formula than formula B.[1]

Let this special test be made of the straight line formula and the service unit formula. From the straight line formula the total cost of the services of an asset in the ath period is

---

[1] Note that no *general test* of relative excellence of the two formulas is proposed in this paragraph. Not even a general statement of the conditions under which one formula is better than the other with respect to this one possible test is proposed. For this latter would require treatment of the cases, if any, in which *both* formulas introduce some fluctuations into unit cost figures. All that is proposed is a special trial, viz., the statement of the cases in which each of the formulas introduces no fluctuations at all.

CRITERIA OF SUPERIORITY

$$\frac{W}{n} + O_a = \frac{W + nO_a}{n} \tag{1a}$$

That is, it consists of the sum of the depreciation charge for the period and the operating outlays of the period upon the asset for maintenance, upkeep, repair, etc. The cost per unit of service is

$$\frac{W + nO_a}{nS_a} \tag{1b}$$

The total cost of all the services during the useful life of the asset is

$$W + \Sigma O \tag{2a}$$

and the cost per unit is

$$\frac{W + \Sigma O}{\Sigma S} \tag{2b}$$

(2a) and (2b) are true by definition no matter what formula is used. Since (2a) is a single, fixed quantity and there are n quantities (one for each operating period) like (1b), the straight line formula can avoid introducing fluctuations into cost per unit of service when, and only when, (1b) is a constant. That is, when

$$\frac{W + nO_a}{nS_a} = \frac{W + \Sigma O}{\Sigma S} \tag{2c}$$

Since W and n are both constants and $n > 1$, the condition can be fulfilled only when either:

(a) $W = $ zero and O/S is a constant; or when (3a)

(b) $W \neq $ zero and O and S are both constants (3b)

By the service unit formula (see page 279) the total cost of the services of an asset in the ath period is

$$\frac{S_a W}{\Sigma S} + O_a = \frac{S_a W + \Sigma S O_a}{\Sigma S} \tag{4a}$$

and the cost per unit of service is

$$\frac{S_a W + \Sigma SO_a}{S_a \Sigma S} \qquad (4b)$$

For the reasons given under (2a) and (2b) above, the service unit formula can avoid introducing fluctuations into cost per unit of service when, and only when,

$$\frac{S_a W + \Sigma SO_a}{S_a \Sigma S} = \frac{W + \Sigma O}{\Sigma S} \qquad (4c)$$

This condition is fulfilled when

$$O/S \text{ is a constant} = K \qquad (5)$$

for, upon substituting K for O/S, clearing of fractions, and transposing we obtain

$$S_a W \Sigma S + K S_a (\Sigma S)^2 - S_a W \Sigma S - K S_a (\Sigma S)^2 = 0 \qquad (6)$$

but it is evident by inspection that (5) will be true when either (3a) or (3b) is true, and that (5) can be true in indefinitely many cases when neither (3a) nor (3b) is true.

INDEX

Accountancy,
  early, an art only, 8
  early literature of, 8-9
  economists' study of, 330-331
  relation to economics, 4-5, 335-336
  subject matter different from that of economics, 310-311
Accountants,
  academic training of, 3, 328-330
  training in law, 329-330
  training in mathematics, 257, 308, 329
  training in statistics, 308, 329
Accountants' Certificates, 249-250
Accountants' Investigations, Scope of, 327-328
Accountants' Reports, (See also "Balance Sheet," "Balance Sheets," and "Income Statement")
  difficulties of interpretation, 24-46, 59-88, 311-314
  not prepared for economists, 322-324
Accounting,
  academic status of, 3, 328-330
  chief subject matter of, 314-316
  early teaching of, 3
  improving technique of, 328
  rising public interest in, 327
  terminology of, 8, 9-10, 313-314
Accounting Data,
  in working papers, 142
  prospective betterments of, 324-330
Accounting Practice,
  changing character of, 5
  more nearly uniform than accounting theory, 45-46
  uniformities in, 5, 45-46
Accounting Theory,
  chief problem of, 353-354
Accounts, Fund, 25-27
Accounts Receivable, Valuation of, 210-211
American Institute of Accountants, 66

American Society of Civil Engineers, Special Committee on Valuation, 293
Appreciation of Assets, 76-77
Assets,
  accountants' definitions of, 12-14
  acquired by stock issue, 248-249
  acquired in exchange for treasury stock, 248-249
  an economic concept, 19-20
  and sources of service, 15-16
  illustrated, 16-17
  appreciation of, 76-77
  attributes of, 14-23
  book value of, in excess profit earning concerns, 236-237, 241-242
  book value of, in losing concerns, 236-237, 239-241
  book values of, produced by certain formulas, 343-352
  convertible into money, 20-21
  cost of revaluing, 272-273
  defined, 22
  definition of, and working capital, 67-68
  definitions of, in writings, 12-13
  enterprise, 22-23
  illustrative scheme of, 343-352
  in relation to holder, 44-45
  interpretation of, 24-46
  legal title in, 14
  may have negative value, 256-257
  meaning of, 12-23
  not necessarily available to creditors, 21-22, 51-53
  personal, 22-23
  range of types, illustrated, 261-265
  redressible rights in, 17-18
  selection of, 290-292
  summation of, 45
  term excludes expectancies, 17-18, 20
  term excludes goodwill, 42-44
  term excludes valuation accounts, 27-46
  under executory contracts, 18-19

INDEX

Assets—(*Continued*)
　value of, identical with value of gross proprietorship, 48-50

Bad Debt Reserves, 28, 65, 211
Balance Sheet,
　and financial position, 178-182, 191-194
　"ideal," 194
　interpretation of, 24-46, 59-88
　limitations of, 194
Balance Sheets,
　comparative, 193-194
　Federal Reserve Board form, 87
　form of, often imposed by creditors, 86-88
　general purpose, 86-87
　　limitations of, 88
　special purpose, 86-87
　　limitations of, 88
Bell, W. H., 59-60, 137
Blichfeldt, H. F., 173
Bonds,
　discount on, 29, 36-37
　gross income from, 112-113
Book Value,
　as found by different formulas, illustrated, 337-352
　of assets, and rate of return, 258-259
　of assets in excess profit earning concerns, 236-237, 241-242
　of assets in losing concerns, 236-237, 239-241
　of shares of stock, 84-86
　of stock issues, 84-86
Business Ethics, 326-327

Capital Stock,
　defined, 71-72
　definitions of, 70-71
　discount on, 75-76
　distinguished from shares in a corporation's proprietorship, 75 note
　itemization of, 74-75
　measure of, 72-73
　preferred,
　　cumulative, 85-86
　　dividend arrearages on, 85-86
　　participating and non-participating, 85-86
　premiums on, 75-76
　shares with par value, 72-73
　shares without par value, 73
　sometimes called stated capital, 73

Capital Stock—(*Continued*)
　subscribers' liabilities on, 74, 248-250
　without par value, 73
Capital Surplus, 77
Capital Value,
　deficiencies of theory, 231-233
　economists' theory of, 229-231
　meaning of, 230-231
　of an enterprise, 187-189, 306-309
　　and going concern value, 189-191
　　and value of assets, 241-242
　　not reliably determinable, 246-247
　of assets, 258-259
　vs. prudent investor valuation, 229-236
Certificates, 249-250
Cole, W. M., 32
Comparative Balance Sheets, 193-194
Contingencies,
　indefinite meaning of, 81-84
　reserves for, 81-84
Contracts,
　executory, 18-19
　sinking fund, 79-80
　sinking fund reserve, 79-80
Cost,
　and original valuation, 248-250
　and valuation, 186
　and value, 186
　fallacy of minimum, 293
　meaning of, in inventory valuation, 215-217
　minimum, vs. maximum profits, 293
　most economical, vs. minimum cost, 293
　of a unit of product, 270-272
　of a unit of service, 267-272, 337-352, 353-356
　proper rôle of, in inventory valuations, 219-220
　rôle of, in valuation of fixed assets, 253-254
Cost Less Depreciation,
　not a rule of valuation, 254-255
Cost of Replacement,
　and damages, 255
　and going-concern value, 255
　and valuation, 243-246, 254-255
　of capital goods, 243-246
　of stocks of services, 243-246
"Cost or Market,"
　meaning of, 215-217

INDEX

Creditors,
  influence on form of balance sheets, 86-88
Criteria of Superiority,
  method of testing merits of formulas, 343-352, 353-356
Cyclopedia of Corporations, 70 note

Damages,
  and cost of replacement, 255
Deductions,
  distinguished from dispositions, 132-133
  from gross income, 127-136
    attributes of, 127-128
    not homogeneous with gross income, 133-135
    usually adverse to proprietary interest, 127-128, 131-132
Deferred Charges, 32-38, 311-312 note
Deficit,
  from discount on stock, 75-76
  initial, 75-76
  meaning of, 75
  valuation of a, 84
Depletion Fund Reserves, 66
Depletion Funds,
  varieties of, 26-27
Depreciation, (See also "Indirect Valuation" and "Valuation")
  of valuation account balances, 66-67
Depreciation Expense,
  independent of depreciation funds, 274-275
Depreciation Formulas (See "Valuation Formulas")
Depreciation Funds,
  independent of depreciation expense, 274-275
  varieties of, 27
Depreciation Reserves, 28, 65, 66
Differential Valuations, 238-239
Direct Valuation,
  advantages of, 209
  erratic procedure in, 212-214
  limits of, 209-210
  necessary conditions to, 206-208
  not always possible, 183-185
  of balance sheet items, 182-183
  preferable if reliable, 184-185
  proper rôle of, in inventory valuation, 219-220
Discount,
  on bonds, 29, 36-37
  on stock issues, 75-76

Disposition of Net Income, 132-133
Distribution,
  theory of, 318-319
Distribution of Enterprise Funds, 181, 194
Dividends,
  arrearages of, 84-86
  contractual restrictions upon declaration of, 78-81
Double Counting,
  avoidance of, 128-130

Earnings, 109-116
Economics,
  inductive, 6-7, 332-336
  originally a deductive philosophy, 6
  relation to accountancy, 4-5, 310-336
  shift of method in, 332-336
  subject matter different from accountancy, 310-311
  terminology of, 8
Economic Theory,
  inverted order of, 334-335
Economists,
  must make their own "translations," 322-324
Enterprise,
  capital value of, 187-189
  defined, 234
  erroneously personified, 55
  increasing stability of, 325-326
  nature of, 234
  valuations in a losing concern, 239-241
  valuations in an excess profit earning concern, 241-242
Enterprise Funds,
  distribution of, 181, 194
  sources of, 181
Enterprise Services,
  how selected, 235-236
  valuation of, 235
  when essential to an enterprise, 187-188
Equation of Accounts,
  an expression of an identity, 48-49
  nature of, 11-12, 47-49
Error,
  degree of, effect on valuations, 200
Ethics,
  accountants' code of, 249-250
  business, 326-327
Executory Contracts,
  assets arising under, 18-19
  liabilities under, 56-57

Expectancies,
  not assets, 17-18
  valuation of, 20

Federal Reserve Board,
  form of balance sheet, 87
Federal Trade Commission, 326
Finance,
  subject matter of, 180-181
Financial Items,
  valuation of, 210-214
Financial Position,
  and the balance sheet, 178-182, 191-194
  and the comparative balance sheet, 193-194
  betterments in determining, 191-193
  defined, 191
  four possible meanings, 181-182
  ideal meaning of, 191
  in successive balance sheets, 193-194
  nature of, 178-194
  not disclosed in income statement, 140-142
  vagueness of concept, 178-180
Finney, H. A., 66
Fish, J. C. L., 305
Fisher, Irving, 14, 90, 99, 135, 204-205, 207, 229, 333
  contributions to theory of income, 144-145
  theory of income appraised, 172-178
  theory of income contrasted with accountants', 158-172
  theory of income summarized, 144-158
    cancellation of couples, 151-154
    capital, defined, 146-147
    caution factor, 157-158
    disservices, defined, 148
    distribution of income, 147-148
    income defined, 146
    interactions defined, 148-149
    measures of income, 154-157
    method of couples, 149-150
    probability, 156
    property defined, 146
    social income, 151-153
    wealth defined, 146-147
Fixed Assets,
  valuation of, 248-309
Formulas for Depreciation (See "Valuation Formulas")

Formulas for Valuation (See "Valuation Formulas")
Fund Accounts, 25-27
Funds,
  depletion, 26-27
  depreciation, 27
  enterprise,
    distribution of, 181, 194
    sources of, 181
  monied, defined, 111

Gillette, H. P., 293, 305
Going-Concern Value,
  and capital value of enterprise, 189-191
  and cost of replacement, 255
  paradox of, 189-191
Goodwill,
  analysis of, 40-42
  a valuation account, 42-44
  definitions of, 38-40
  exhibit of, 43
  may be positive or negative, 188-189
  meaning of, 188 note
  not an asset, 42-44
  valuation of, 306-307
Gross Financial Income, 100-118, 121-123
  and earnings, 109-116
  compared with gross operating income, 116-118
  defined, 109
  determined by contract, 109-111
  from bonds, 112-113
  from corporate shares, 114-116
  physical analogue of, 121-123
  principal classes of, 112-116
Gross Income, 89-124 (See also "Gross Financial Income," "Gross Operating Income," and "Ultimate Total Income")
  alternative terms for, 92-93
  and fruition of operations, 109
  and inventory valuation, 105-108
  and subsequent cash receipts, 106-107
  conservatism, timeliness and reliability of measures of, 104-108
  criteria of, 101-104
  distinguished from assets, 101-102
  does not include all cash receipts, 109
  "most probable" estimate of, 105
  not homogeneous with deductions, 133-135
  of a period, 99-118

INDEX

Gross Income—(*Continued*)
  of a period, defined, 100
  taken up when "realized," 134
  under sales commitments, 107-108
Gross Income of a Period,
  deductions from, to find net income, 127-136
Gross Operating Income,
  a final conversion, 101
  a fruition of operations, 101
  compared with gross financial income, 116-118
  of a period, defined, 101
  physical analogue of, 118-121
Gross Proprietorship,
  nature of, 47-48
  value of, identical with value of assets, 48-50

Handley *v.* Stutz, 76
Hatfield, H. R., 32, 51
Holding Company Earnings, 114-116
Hotelling, H., 265, 273, 293, 298, 304
Hypotheses of Indirect Valuation, 187-188

Ideal Income,
  different from economists' concepts, 135-136
  not always determinable, 135-136
Income, (See also "Gross Income," "Net Income," "Ultimate Net Income," and "Ultimate Total Income")
  accountants' concept special and incomplete, 159-160
  accountants' measure of, a composite index, 168-170
  accountants' mode of analyzing, 160-161
  accountants' theory and Fisher's theory appraised, 172-178
  accountants' theory of, compared with Fisher's, 158-172
  chief subject matter of accounting, 314-316
  concept fundamental to other economic ideas, 175-176
  deficiencies of accountants' consideration of, 93
  distribution of, 91-92
  economists' concepts, 143-144
  elementary nature of concept, 174-176
  elements of, do not preserve their identity, 170-171

Income—(*Continued*)
  final objective, accountants' measure of, 163-168
  Fisher's theory and accountants' theory appraised, 172-178
  Fisher's theory of, compared with accountants', 158-172
  Fisher's theory of, summarized, 144-158
  importance of concept, 90, 175, 334-336
  measurement of, 143-178
  never consists of money, 95
  not traceable through successive operations, 171
  of a specified period, 94, 97-99
  position in economic theory, 174-176, 334-336
  problems of the accountant, 91-92
  problems of the economist, 91-92
  theory lags behind practice, 160-161
  theory of, contributions to, by Irving Fisher, 144-145
Income of a Specified Period,
  contrasted with ultimate income, 97-99
Income Statement,
  an expository exhibit, 137
  bases of classification in, 138-140
  classification and content, 136-142
  data in, 140-142
  defects of, from economists' point of view, 140-142
  diversity of forms, 138-140
  does not disclose financial position, 140-142
  limitations of, 138-142
  not a means of determining net income, 136-138
Indirect Valuation,
  and opportunity differences, 238-239
  certain postulates of, 290-292
  deficiencies in procedure, 246-247
  hypotheses of, 187-188
  of balance sheet items, 183-184
  theory of, 229-247
Insurance Prepaid,
  not an asset, 37-38
Intangibles, 38-44
  not assets, 40
Interest,
  prepaid, a misnomer, 32-35
  rate of, and rate of depreciation, 274

Interest on Investment,
  and book values, 297-298
  limitations upon charging, 297-298
  theoretical propriety of, 296-298
Interest Receivable Accrued, 211-212
Intra-firm Debts, 61, 63
Inventories,
  choice of rule in valuing, 218
  going-concern value of, 218-219
  multiple valuations of, 223-227
  proper rôles of direct valuation, of cost and of market, 219-220
  spurious conservatism in valuing, 225
  valuation at selling price minus, 220-223, 225-226
  valuation of, 214-227
Inventory Losses, Reserves for, 65-66
Investigations, 327-328
Investments, Valuation of, 212

Jackson, J. H., 66, 137

Kester, R. B., 21-22
Kleinwachter, F., 144

Law,
  accountants' training in, 329-330
Liabilities,
  and working capital, 67-68
  claims against the proprietor, 53
  concept of, changing, 57
  defined, 55-56
  interpretation of, 59-88
  nature of, 47-63
  not always claims against assets, 52
  not interchangeable with "debts," 63
  reclassification of, 68
  under executory contracts, 56-57
  under purchase commitments, 57
  under sales commitments, 57
Liabilities and Net Proprietorship,
  distinctions between, 59-64
  interpretation of, 59-88
  priority of claims not conclusive, 63-64
Losses,
  taken up as soon as foreseen, 134-135

McKinsey, J. O., 66
Machine Design, 282, 308
Major Repairs, 262, 284-287

Market,
  meaning of, in inventory valuation, 217
  proper rôle of, in inventory valuation, 219-220
Marshall, Alfred, 332
Mathematics,
  in valuation, 308
  training of accountants in, 257, 308, 329
Measurement,
  theory of, in valuation, 279-281
Methods of Valuation,
  incompletely discussed in the literature, 202-205
Minimum Cost,
  fallacy of, 293
Mitchell, W. C., 332-333, 334
Montgomery, R. H., 57, 60-61, 66, 87, 214

Net Income, (See also "Ultimate Net Income")
  and reconcilement of surplus, 132-133
  a quantity only, 126-127, 133-135
  betterments of measuring, 135-136
  defined, 127
  determination of, 127-140
  dispositions of, distinguished from deductions, 132-133
  found in working papers, 136-138
  has no qualitative nature, 126-127, 133-135
  meaning of, 125-142
  not determined by income statement, 136-138
  other terms for, 93, 125
Net Profits (See "Net Income")
Net Proprietorship,
  bases of analysis, 69-70
  defined, 56
  difficulties of analysis, 68-69
  figure for, not precisely significant, 58
  interpretation of, 59-88
  itemization of, the result of analysis, 64-65
  nature of, 47-63
  of a corporation, 68-88
  other terms for, 53-55
  term has no substantive meaning, 58
Notes Receivable,
  valuation of, 211-212

INDEX

Obsolescence,
  not a surprise factor, 265
  reserves for, 65
Opportunity Differences,
  and fixed tangible assets, 241
  and indirect valuation, 238-239
  nature of, 237-239
Organization Expense, 28, 30-32
Original Valuations,
  and cost, 248-250
  and good faith of purchaser, 248-250

Palmer, L. E., 137
Paradox of Going-Concern Value, 189-191
Paton, W. A., 32, 39-40, 102
Plehn, Carl, 145
Postulates,
  certain, underlying valuation, 290-292
Powelson, J. A., 59-60
Prepaid Expense, 32-38, 311-312 note
Prepaid Insurance,
  not an asset, 37-38
Prepaid Taxes,
  not an asset, 37-38
Production,
  theory of, 316-317
Professional Ethics,
  and valuation, 249-250
Profit and Loss Statement (See "Income Statement")
Profits (See "Income")
Profits, Rate of (See "Rate of Return")
Proprietorship, (See also "Gross Proprietorship" and "Net Proprietorship")
  defined, 55
Proprietorship and Liabilities,
  distinction between, 50-53
  not homogeneous, 50-53
  other terms for,
    Cole's "ownership claims," 51-53
    Paton's "equities," 51-53
Provision for Taxes, 66
Public Accountants,
  training of, 328-330

Rate of Depreciation,
  and rate of interest, 274
Rate of Interest,
  and rate of depreciation, 274

Rate of Profits (See "Rate of Return")
Rate of Return,
  and book value of assets, 258-259
  and modified service unit formulas, 291, 301-303
Realized Income, 155
Realized Money Income, 99
Replacement Funds,
  varieties of, 27
Replacement Reserves, 66
Reserves,
  bad debts, 28, 65, 211
  confusion of meanings of, 65-67
  contingency, 81-84
    diverse meanings of, 82-83
  depletion funds, 66
  depreciation, 28, 65, 66
  inventory losses, 65-66
  obsolescence, 65
  replacement, 66, 80-81
  sinking fund, 66, 79-80
  taxes, 66
Revaluation (See "Valuation")
Revaluation Technique, (See also "Valuation")
  adjusted measures, 284-309
  simple measures, 248-283
Ripley, W. Z., 123, 327
Robbins, C. B., 73

Sales Commitments,
  and income, 107, 108
Scovell, C. H., 272
Scrap Value,
  defined, 255-257
  may be greater than initial, 256-257
Service Unit,
  meaning of, 280-281
Service Unit Costs, (See also under "Valuation Formulas")
  and valuation, illustrated, 337-352
  produced by certain formulas, 343-352
  systematically compared, 353-356
Services,
  as income, 14
  constitute essence of assets, 188
  essential to an enterprise, 187-188
  measurement of, 280-281
  "natural," 208
Shares of Stock,
  book value of, 84-86
  not a portion of a corporation's "capital stock," 75 note

Short-term Debts,
  valuation of, 212
Sinking Fund Reserves, 66
Sinking Funds,
  contracts underlying, 79-80
  not always assets of debtor, 25-27
  relation to sinking fund reserves, 79-80
  varieties of, 25-27
Social Income, 92
Specific Productivity,
  not measurable, 170-172, 185-186
Speculative buying, 233
Sprague, C. E., 22, 51
Standard Cost,
  a misnomer, 271
Standard Income, 99 note
Stated Capital,
  interchangeable with capital stock, 73
Statistical Populations,
  classes of, 200-202
  nature of, 199
  samples from, 201-202
  when to classify, 200-201
  when to employ samples of, 201-202
Statistical Theory,
  in accounts, 319-322
Statistics,
  accountants' training in, 308, 329
  in valuation, 308
Stevenson, R. A., 32
Stock Issues,
  book value of, 84-86
  in exchange for assets, 248-249
  unlimited variety of, 69
Structural Design, 308
Subordinated Debts, 60-63
Subscribers' Liabilities,
  only incidentally related to amount of capital stock, 74
Substitutes,
  availability of, 253-254
Surplus, 75-86
  appropriated, 77
  capital, 77
  contractual limitations upon dividends from, 78-81
  from appreciation, 76-77
  meaning of, 75
  paid-in, 75-76
  reservations of, 78-84
Suspense Accounts,
  purpose of, 29-30

Taxes Prepaid,
  not an asset, 37-38
Taxes, Reserves for, 66
Taylor, J. S., 292-293, 298, 304, 305
Technological Services, 208
Theory of Measurement,
  in valuation, 290-292
Terminology,
  confusion of, 9-10
  obstacle to understanding, 313-314
  of accounting, need for interpretation, 9-10
  of early accounting, 9
  of economics, 8

Ultimate Net Income,
  defined, 126-127
  in an enterprise, 127
  to a proprietor, 127
Ultimate Total Income,
  a matter of observed fact, 95-99
  contrasted with annual income, 97-99
  defined, 95
  illustrated, 96-97
  in an enterprise, 98-99
  to a proprietor, 98-99
Unit Cost, (See also under "Valuation Formulas")
  and valuation, 259-260
  of product, 270-272
  of service, 267-272
Unit of Measure, 199, 280-281
Utility,
  accountant not concerned with elements of, 108
  elementary classes of, 108

Valuation (See also "Valuations" and "Value")
  a branch of the theory of measurement, 198
  accountants' hypotheses of, 187-189
  accountant's problem of, 195-205
  accountant values service, not agent, 235
  adjusted measures, 284-309
  a function of what profession, 307-309
  and alternative source of service, 252-253
  and cost, 186
  and cost of replacement, 243-246, 254-255
  and future outlay costs, 252
  and machine design, 282, 308

INDEX

Valuation—(*Continued*)
  and operating policy, 307, 308
  and service still available, 251
  and service unit costs, illustrated, 337-352
  and structural design, 308
  and theory of measurement, 198-205
  and time-distribution of future outlays, 252
  and time-distribution of services, 251-252
  and unit costs, 259-260
  and value, 186, 197-199
  certain hypotheses of, 187-188
  cost of, 272-273
  differential, 238-239
  effect of errors in, 259-260
  errors in original, 248-250
  interdependence of variables affecting, 257-259, 272-273
  mathematics of, 308
  of an asset may be negative, 256-257
  of assets of excess-profit earning concerns, 236-237, 241-242
  of assets of losing concerns, 236-237, 239-241
  of financial items, 210-214
  of fixed tangible assets, 241
    rôle of cost in, 253-254
  of objects vs. valuation of services, 187
  of services, 187
  of services, not derivable from cost, 233
  original, and cost, 248-250
  original, and good faith of purchaser, 248-250
  postulates underlying, 290-292
  simple measures, 248-283
  theory of, 317-318
    and theory of measurement, 198-205
  theory of measurement in, 279-281
  theory of, vs. theory of value, 197-199
  variables affecting, 250-260
  vs. value, 317-318
Valuation Accounts,
  and net proprietorship, 31-32
  depreciation of, 66-67
  how exhibited in balance sheets, 28-29
  nature of, 27-46
  not assets, 29-46

Valuation Accounts—(*Continued*)
  purposes of, 27-31
  varieties of, 28-43
Valuation Formulas,
  effect of erratic, 260
  equal profit ratios, 305-306
  fixed percentage on declining balance, 276-277
    calculation of, 276
    deficiencies of, 276-277
    emphasis given to scrap value, 276
    general forms, 276
    when appropriate, 277
  illustrative comparison of results, 337-352
  modified fixed percentage and sum-of-the-year-digits rules, 289-290
  modified service unit, interest included, 296-305
    and rate of return, 291, 301-303
    compared with form neglecting interest, 303-305
    effect of error in estimates, 301-302, 303-305
    excessive claims for method, 298-299
    general forms, 300
    in corporate consolidations, 299-300
    in public utility rate determinations, 299-300
    limitations on use, 299, 301, 303-305
    limitations upon charging interest, 297-298
    properties of formula, 301-303
    when appropriate, 299-300
  modified service unit, neglecting interest, 290-300
    and book values, 294-295
    and cost accounts, 294-295
    and length of service life, 291, 294
    and minimum cost of service, 293-294
    and most economical cost of service, 293-294
    and rate of return, 291
    compared with other formulas, 295-296
    effect of errors in estimates, 295-296
    general forms, 292
    merits of formula, 294-295
    postulates underlying, 290-292

366 INDEX

Valuation Formulas—*(Continued)*
  postulates underlying—*(Con.)*
    theory of measurement in, 290-292
  modified sinking fund, 289
  modified straight line, 284-288
    and cost of unit of service, 287-288
    and extraordinary outlays, 285-287
    deficiencies of, 287, 288
    general forms, 285
    possible further modifications, 287
    when appropriate, 286-288
  relative merits illustrated, 337-352
  service unit, 279-283
    and cost of unit of service, 279, 283, 354, 356
    and length of service life, 282-283
    compared with straight line, 281-282, 353-356
    effect of errors in estimates, 281-283
    general forms, 279-280
    general theory of, 279-281
    meaning of unit of service, 280-281
    primary estimates for, 281-283
    special merits of, 281-283
    when appropriate, 281-283
  sinking fund, 273-276
    and cost of a unit of service, 275-276
    and interest on investment, 275
    compared with straight line, 275-276
    deficiencies of, 275-276
    depreciation expense and depreciation funds, 274-275
    general forms, 273
    rate of depreciation and rate of interest, 274
    when appropriate, 275-276
  straight line, 265-273
    and book values, 267
    and burden distribution, 271-272
    and cost of a unit of service, 267-268, 270-272, 354-355
    and operating policy, 271-272
    and unit product cost, 270-272
    compared with service unit, 281-282, 353-356
    compared with sinking fund, 275-276

Valuation Formulas—*(Continued)*
  straight line—*(Continued)*
    effect of error in estimates, 268-272
    general forms, 265
    primary estimates for, 265-266
    simplicity of, 272-273
    spurious book valuations, 271-272
    when appropriate, 268
  sum-of-the-year-digits, 277-279
    deficiencies of, 277-278, 279
    general forms, 277
    when appropriate, 278-279
  unit cost, 305
  variants of, 284
Valuation Methods,
  "best" measure vs. many measures, 203-204
  criteria of superiority, 202-203
Valuation of Assets (See "Valuation Formulas," "Valuation of Inventories," etc.)
Valuation of Inventories, 214-227
  and going-concern value, 218-219
  at cost or market, 215-217
  at selling price minus, 220-223
  choice of rule, 218
  cost or market rule, 215-217
  diversity of rules, 214
  meaning of cost, 215-217
  meaning of "cost or market," 215-217
  meaning of market, 217
  multiple valuations, 223-227
  proper rôles of direct valuation, of cost and of market, 219-220
  spurious conservatism of cost or market rule, 225
Valuation Procedure, 206-228
Valuation Technique (See also "Valuation Formulas")
  adjusted measures, 284-309
  simple measures, 248-283
Valuation Theory,
  in modified service unit formula, 290-292
Valuations,
  and character of data, 196-197
  and character of engagement, 196
  degree of error in, 200
  differential, 238-239
  restraints upon accountants in, 195-197

Value,
    accountants profess no theory of, 198-199
    and cost, 186
    theory of, 317-318
    theory of, vs. theory of valuation, 197-199
    vs. valuation, 317-318

Working Capital,
    and definition of assets, 67-68
Working Capital Ratios, 67-68
Working Papers, 137, 142
    as sources of economic data, 142

Yang, J. M., 39-40

THE DEVELOPMENT OF
CONTEMPORARY ACCOUNTING THOUGHT

An Arno Press Collection

Baldwin, H[arry] G[len]. **Accounting for Value As Well as Original Cost** *and* Castenholz, William B. **A Solution to the Appreciation Problem.** 2 Vols. in 1. 1927/1931

Baxter, William. **Collected Papers on Accounting.** 1978

Brief, Richard P., Ed. **Selections from Encyclopaedia of Accounting, 1903.** 1978

Broaker, Frank and Richard M. Chapman. **The American Accountants' Manual.** 1897

Canning, John B. **The Economics of Accountancy.** 1929

Chatfield, Michael, Ed. **The English View of Accountant's Duties and Responsibilities.** 1978

Cole, William Morse. **The Fundamentals of Accounting.** 1921

Congress of Accountants. **Official Record of the Proceedings of the Congress of Accountants.** 1904

Cronhelm, F[rederick] W[illiam]. **Double Entry by Single.** 1818

Davidson, Sidney. **The Plant Accounting Regulations of the Federal Power Commission.** 1952

De Paula, F[rederic] R[udolf] M[ackley]. **Developments in Accounting.** 1948

Epstein, Marc Jay. **The Effect of Scientific Management on the Development of the Standard Cost System** (Doctoral Dissertation, University of Oregon, 1973). 1978

Esquerré, Paul-Joseph. **The Applied Theory of Accounts.** 1914

Fitzgerald, A[dolf] A[lexander]. **Current Accounting Trends.** 1952

Garner, S. Paul and Marilynn Hughes, Eds. **Readings on Accounting Development.** 1978

Haskins, Charles Waldo. **Business Education and Accountancy.** 1904

Hein, Leonard William. **The British Companies Acts and the Practice of Accountancy 1844-1962** (Doctoral Dissertation, University of California, Los Angeles, 1962). 1978

Hendriksen, Eldon S. **Capital Expenditures in the Steel Industry, 1900 to 1953** (Doctoral Dissertation, University of California, Berkeley, 1956). 1978

Holmes, William, Linda H. Kistler and Louis S. Corsini. **Three Centuries of Accounting in Massachusetts.** 1978

Horngren, Charles T. **Implications for Accountants of the Uses of Financial Statements by Security Analysts** (Doctoral Dissertation, University of Chicago, 1955). 1978

Horrigan, James O., Ed. **Financial Ratio Analysis—An Historical Perspective.** 1978

Jones, [Edward Thomas]. **Jones's English System of Book-keeping.** 1796

Lamden, Charles William. **The Securities and Exchange Commission** (Doctoral Dissertation, University of California, Berkeley, 1949). 1978

Langer, Russell Davis. **Accounting As A Variable in Mergers** (Doctoral Dissertation, University of California, Berkeley, 1976). 1978

Lewis, J. Slater. **The Commercial Organisation of Factories.** 1896

Littleton, A[nanias] C[harles] and B[asil] S. Yamey. Eds. **Studies in the History of Accounting.** 1956

Mair, John. **Book-keeping Moderniz'd.** 1793

Mann, Helen Scott. **Charles Ezra Sprague.** 1931

Marsh, C[hristopher] C[olumbus]. **The Theory and Practice of Bank Book-keeping.** 1856

Mitchell, William. **A New and Complete System of Book-keeping by an Improved Method of Double Entry.** 1796

Montgomery, Robert H. **Fifty Years of Accountancy.** 1939

Moonitz, Maurice. **The Entity Theory of Consolidated Statements.** 1951

Moonitz, Maurice, Ed. **Three Contributions to the Development of Accounting Thought.** 1978

Murray, David. **Chapters in the History of Bookkeeping, Accountancy & Commercial Arithmetic.** 1930

Nicholson, J[erome] Lee. **Cost Accounting.** 1913

Paton, William Andrew and Russell Alger Stevenson. **Principles of Accounting.** 1918

Pixley, Francis W[illiam]. **The Profession of a Chartered Accountant and Other Lectures.** 1897

Preinreich, Gabriel A. D. **The Nature of Dividends.** 1935

Previts, Gary John. Ed. **Early 20th Century Developments in American Accounting Thought.** 1978

Ronen, Joshua and George H. Sorter. **Relevant Financial Statements.** 1978

Shenkir, William G., Ed. **Carman G. Blough: His Professional Career and Accounting Thought.** 1978

Simpson, Kemper. **Economics for the Accountant.** 1921

Sneed, Florence R. **Parallelism in Two Disciplines.** (M.A. Thesis, University of Texas, Arlington, 1974). 1978

Sorter, George H. **The Boundaries of the Accounting Universe** (Doctoral Dissertation, University of Chicago, 1963). 1978

Storey, Reed K[arl]. **Matching Revenues with Costs** (Doctoral Dissertation, University of California, Berkeley, 1958). 1978

Sweeney, Henry W[hitcomb]. **Stabilized Accounting.** 1936

Van de Linde, Gerard. **Reminiscences.** 1917

Vatter, William J[oseph]. **The Fund Theory of Accounting and Its Implications for Financial Reports.** 1947

Walker, R. G. **Consolidated Statements.** 1978

Webster, Norman E., Comp. **The American Association of Public Accountants.** 1954

Wells, M. C., Ed. **American Engineers' Contributions to Cost Accounting.** 1978

Worthington, Beresford. **Professional Accountants.** 1895

Yamey, Basil S. **Essays on the History of Accounting.** 1978

Yamey, Basil S., Ed. **The Historical Development of Accounting.** 1978

Yang, J[u] M[ei]. **Goodwill and Other Intangibles.** 1927

Zeff, Stephen Addam. **A Critical Examination of the Orientation Postulate in Accounting, with Particular Attention to its Historical Development** (Doctoral Dissertation, University of Michigan, 1961). 1978

Zeff, Stephen A., Ed. **Selected Dickinson Lectures in Accounting.** 1978